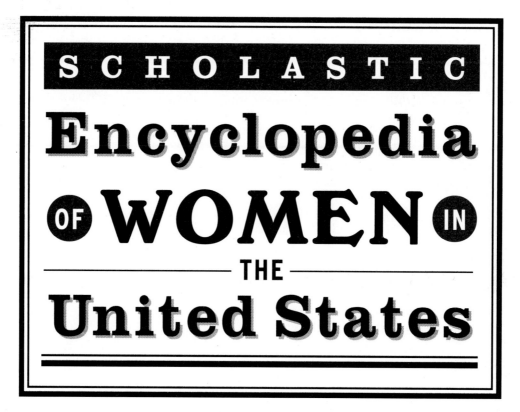

SCHOLASTIC Encyclopedia OF WOMEN IN THE United States

SHEILA KEENAN

Scholastic
Reference

NEW YORK TORONTO LONDON AUCKLAND SYDNEY

For Kevin, and for all the wonderful women in my life.
Special thanks to Barbara Glauber. – SMK

Produced by Sheila Keenan
Designed by Barbara Glauber/Heavy Meta

Grateful acknowledgment is to Gail Wood, Director of Libraries and Instructional Technologies,
SUNY College of Technology at Alfred, New York

Photo credits:
Every effort has been made to determine and credit the rightful copyright owner of all photos and illustrations contained herein.

Berenice Abbott/Commerce Graphics Ltd., Inc.: 100; Albany Institute of History & Art: 10; AP/Wide World Photos: cover (top, right; bottom, middle), 104 (bottom), 131-132, 133 (bottom), 134-136, 142, 151, 154, 160, 173, 195; Bettman Archive: cover (bottom, middle), 53, 54, 57, 59 (top), 64 (top), 96 (top), 98, 99 (bottom); Brown Brothers: 66, 106 (top), 118, 133 (top), 148, 196 (top); Children's Defense Fund/Katherine Lambert: 167; Culver Pictures: 50; General Electric: 156; Harcourt, Brace, Jovanovich/Jim Marshall: 197; Harpo Entertainment Group: 198; Henry Street Settlement: 64; Martin Luther King Memorial Library: 158; Knopf/Rubén Guzmán: 163, Knopf/Franco Salmoiraghi: 178; R. Kravette, Jericho, NY: 145; Library of Congress: back cover, 6-8, 12 (bottom), 15-16, 19 (top), 20, 24-26, 28, 29, 30 (bottom), 32 (top), 33, 35 (bottom), 38, 41, 42, 45, 49 (bottom), 51, 55 (bottom), 56, 58, 59 (bottom), 61 (bottom), 62-63, 67, 68 (top), 69, 71-72, 74-77, 79-80, 82-85, 87, 89 (top), 97, 101-103, 105, 111-112, 114 (bottom), 116 (bottom), 117, 119-123, 126-127, 130, 138 (top), 139, 146 (top), 149, 150 (bottom), 153, (top), 157, 164, 172, 187, 189, 191; Longyear Museum and Historical Society: 39; Lordly & Dame Associates: 160; C. Love: 193; Lowell National Historic Park: (cover, middle), 27, Massachusetts Historical Society: 21 (top); Medical College of Pennsylvania: 86; Metropolitan Museum of Art, George A. Hearn Fund, 1909: 89; Museum of American Textile History: 30 (top); NASA: cover (top left), 176, 192; National Archives: 78; National Baseball Library & Archive, Cooperstown, NY: cover (bottom, right), 127 (bottom); National Historic Preservation Center, Girl Scouts of the USA, 81; NBC: 162; Nevada State Historical Society: 60; New York Public Library Picture Collection: 9, 12 (top), 13, 18, 19 (bottom), 21 (bottom), 22-23, 35 (top), 40, 43, 44 (bottom), 46, 49 (top), 52, 65, 99, 109; Oberlin College Archives: cover (top, middle); Retna Ltd., NYC/Freeberg: 165; Reuters/Bettman: 159 (bottom), 171, 181 (bottom); The Sargent House Museum: 17; Schomburg Center for Research in Black Culture: 34, 46 (top), 68 (bottom), 95, 110, 124 (top), 152, 153 (bottom); Sire Records/Just Loomis: 182; Smithsonian Institution: 48; Sony Music: 169; Sophia Smith Collection/Smith College: cover (right, middle); Tribune Media Services: 104 (top); United Airlines: 106; UPI/Bettman Newsphotos: cover (bottom, left), 73, 96 (bottom), 108, 113, 115, 124 (bottom), 128-129, 140-141, 143 (bottom), 144, 146 (bottom), 149 (bottom), 150 (top), 155, 159 (top), 166, 168, 170, 174-175, 179-180, 181 (top), 183-186, 188, 194, 196 (bottom), 199; U.S. Army: 114 (top); Estate of Carl Van Vechten: Joseph Solomon, Executor, cover (right, middle), 116 (top); Werner Wolfe, Black Star: cover (middle, left)

ISBN 0-590-22793-9

12 11 10 9 8 7 6 5 4 3   3   8 9/9 0 1 2 3/0

Printed in the U.S.A.   09

Introduction

Pocahontas

A woman helped save the first English colony in America.

Harriet Tubman

A woman led more than 300 slaves north to freedom.

Nellie Bly

A woman set an 1890 world travel record.

Martha Graham

A woman revolutionized modern dance.

Grace Hopper

A woman invented one of the first easy-to-use computer languages.

Maya Lin

A woman designed the national Vietnam Veteran's memorial.

History... and Herstory

Women have always made history in the United States, but they haven't always made it into history books. This book addresses that omission. It tells the story of women's many contributions to the shaping of our nation. Some women became famous for their work, their ideas, or their leadership. Other women – just by surviving on the frontier, in factories, or on the frontlines of reform movements – proved they were hardly the "weaker sex." Many endured poverty, racism, and sexism to accomplish their goals. In this book, you may find women you have never heard about, and you may learn new things about women you already know.

Making Choices

This book includes brief biographies of 217 women. You can also read about the significant contributions of more than 43 others. They represent the broad range of women's lives from before the 1500s to today. Naturally, there's not room in this book to include everyone, but we have attempted to find representatives from many fields and walks of life. The entries balance the famous, such as suffragist Susan B. Anthony, with the should-be-famous, such as radical women's rights activist Alice Paul. It includes women who represent the spirit of their times, such as historian Mercy Otis Warren or writer Toni Morrison, and women who stand for the many others in their field. For example, there are thousands of women poets, but Anne Bradstreet and Gwendolyn Brooks are included not only for their fine poetry, but because Bradstreet was the first published poet in America and Brooks the first African-American poet to win the Pulitzer Prize. Other women, such as soldier Deborah Sampson, lawyer Charlotte E. Ray, politician Jeannette Rankin, labor leader Dolores Huerta, scientist Dr. Chien-Shiung Wu, and Cherokee Chief Wilma Mankiller, are included for their important contributions, especially because they filled roles that were traditionally off-limits to women and to people of color.

This story of American women begins more than 100 years before Martha Washington became First Lady and continues to the time when Hillary Rodham Clinton took on the same job. It's a story that has no ending, because women's roles in the United States are ever-changing. Right this minute, women are making history and future female history-makers are being born!

Table of Contents

How To Use This Book

There are several types of entries about women in United States history in this book: biographies and Cameos which are arranged alphabetically within six different time periods, plus Women's Words and Women's Sphere sidebars, which appear throughout each chapter.

There are several different ways you can find all this information. Check the Table of Contents to locate the time periods, biographies, and Cameos. You can also use the Alphabetical Index to find particular women, places, events, and topics. If you are interested in women in a special field – aviation, for example – you will find them in the Topical Index.

Here are some other aids to finding the information you need:

Chapters

This book is divided into six chronological chapters, each with its own introduction. The chapters correspond to important periods in United States history. Some women's lives spanned more than one chapter, but you will find them in the chapter that covers the period when they had the most impact. When a woman's name appears in **bold face**, look in the Alphabetical Index for a cross reference to more information.

Biographies

The icon to the left of each name makes it easy to find women in any one of the 10 subject areas shown at left. You can look up everyone from authors to actors in Arts/Entertainment; entrepreneurs to labor leaders in Business/Labor; teachers to college presidents in Education; print to television journalists in Media; soldiers to spies in Military; historians to suffragists to senators in Politics/Law; temperance leaders to social workers in Reform/Social Service; spiritual leaders in Religion; biologists to physicians in Sciences/Math; and all types of athletes in Sports.

 Arts/Entertainment

 Business/Labor

 Education

 Media

 Military

 Politics/Law

 Reform/Social Service

 Religion

 Sciences/Math

 Sports

Molly Pitcher MARY LUDWIG HAYS MCCAULEY

Women are listed by the names by which they are most commonly known, so you'll find Molly Pitcher under "P," rather than under her real name, Mary Ludwig Hays McCauley. Real names appear in smaller print to the right.

Many, but not all, women's last names change when they marry. In that case, married names are used in the biographical entry unless the woman's childhood or family is being discussed. Then the "maiden" name is used.

born c. 1865 – died 1922

This boxed copy gives a woman's date of birth and date of death. A "c." stands for circa, or around, and indicates that the exact date is not known.

ASTRONOMER There is also a label telling what each woman was most noted for. However some women worked in many fields, so you may find them listed under more than one heading in the Topical Index.

Sidebars

There are three different types of sidebars which appear in red in the side columns throughout this book. The Cameos are arranged alphabetically, and the Women's Words and Women's Sphere sidebars provide further insights into some of the issues raised in the biographical entries.

Topical Index

Check this index if you are looking for women in a particular field, such as painting or the military. You will also find women in this book listed in noteworthy categories, such as Olympic-medal or Nobel-Prize winners.

Alphabetical Index

Here you will find a list of all of the women included in this book and the pages on which information about them appears. You'll also find references to major historical points such the 19th Amendment or World War II, and key ideas important to women's history such as suffrage, labor, or equal rights issues.

Cameos

These entries are also arranged alphabetically within a chapter. Cameos highlight women who may be famous for a very important single achievement, or other notable women whose broader lives could not be detailed here.

Women's Words

Here you'll find quotes by and about women. You'll also find the definitions of words such as "alewife," "flapper," and "bra-burners" that appeared during a particular period in women's history.

Women's Sphere

In the 1800s, there was a big discussion about "women's sphere" or where women should be allowed to live their lives. The answer then was at home and at church. This sidebar provides information about what women's lives were really like or what women were really doing in their "sphere."

The First American Women

Colonial women arrive

Nearly all of the first Europeans to arrive in North America were male explorers or adventurers. But by the late 1500s, men wanted to establish colonies, so they started bringing European women to marry, have children, and help build the colony. By 1700, roughly 360,000 European immigrants and their descendents lived in America.

Most women, like men, left Europe to escape poverty, war, or religious persecution. Colonial women had far fewer rights than men, but they were partners in the struggle to survive. Women became influential because the success of a colony heavily depended upon the good health and hard work of all its members.

Colonial women worked hard at home. However, many worked in the fields with men, too. They tended the cows, pigs, goats, or chickens, and hauled water for the household. Inside, they had to keep the smoky fireplace lit at all times. They lugged 40-pound pots and 15-gallon kettles for boiling the fish, cornmeal, and root vegetables that they served. They washed on Monday and baked on Saturday. Any day might find women spinning, sewing, knitting, gathering herbs for medicines, preserving meat, brewing beer, or making butter, cheese, soap, or candles. Since they gave birth an average of eight to 10 times, women often did all these chores while they were pregnant.

Life was even harder for indentured women. They were given passage to America in return for four, five, even seven years of work without pay. Indentured servants were often beaten, starved, and not properly clothed. Women who survived might get a new set of clothes and a year's supply of corn. Then they could marry – and keep working.

Enslaved Women

In 1619, a Dutch ship brought 20 Africans, three of them women. The brutal system of African slavery had begun. Women, men, and children were kidnapped from West Africa and sold to colonists, mainly in the South. Most labored to plant and harvest rice, indigo, tobacco, and eventually

Nearly 20,000 years ago, the first women settled in North America. Within the 500 tribal nations that scattered across the continent over time, women had important, respected roles. They were usually in charge of food, clothing, and shelter. They gathered seeds, roots, and berries, or planted crops such as maize, beans, pumpkins, and squash. They tanned deerskin and other animal hides to make clothes and moccasins. Many women built their tribes' bark lodges or tipis. These jobs gave women authority. In some tribes, such as the Hopi and Navajo, women owned all the homes and crops. In matrilineal tribes, such as the Iroquois, family members traced their ancestors through the mother. Older Iroquois women could nominate or dismiss tribal chiefs. The Cherokee had a similar council of women.

◀ In 1619, the Virginia Company sent "tobacco brides" from England to Jamestown, Virginia. There, male colonists purchased a wife for 120 pounds of tobacco. Each young woman had the right to accept or refuse a husband. Only 35 of the 144 "brides" survived the hardships of their first six years in America.

cotton. A few worked under better conditions in the plantation house. Colonists' wives oversaw the household and slaves, and often did the bookkeeping.

Revolution!

By the 1760s, English colonists had to decide whether to stay loyal to the British government or join the Patriots' fight for independence. Women didn't have a say in the final decision – but they made their wishes known!

While the all-male Continental Congress debated the colonies' future in Philadelphia in 1774, Patriot women formed the Daughters of Liberty and used their household economic power. They refused to buy British goods and boycotted tea, sugar, and wine. They held spinning bees and made their families' clothes from rough homespun cloth instead of fine materials from Europe. When war broke out, both Patriot and Loyalist women managed homes, businesses, and farms while their sons and husbands went off to Congress or to fight. Several women fought in battles; many more were spies. Nearly 20,000 women marched with troops on both sides. These "camp-followers" provided food, laundry, nursing care, and other services for family members or in exchange for money.

Liberty...for some

Who would govern the new republic? Who would elect its leaders? Who was to be protected by the newly written Constitution? Not women, slaves, or Native Americans it was decided.

The Constitution (1789) and the Bill of Rights (1791) guaranteed rights and liberties for white male property owners. Only they were allowed to vote. Despite their sacrifices during the Revolution, white women and all free African-Americans were not protected by most laws. Slavery remained legal, although the Constitution called for a ban on importing slaves after 1808. And the new nation spread onto native lands with little concern for those already living there.

Republican Mothers

After the Revolutionary War, some people supported education for white women. This was not an equal rights issue. People believed a successful democracy needed educated citizens, which meant mothers needed to be better prepared to teach their children. Women were hailed as the "mothers of the Republic." This gave women a role, but neatly skirted the issue of giving them any rights, as citizens of the United States.

▲ Betsy Ross owned a successful upholstery business in Philadelphia, Pennsylvania. According to legend, at George Washington's request, she sewed the first U.S. flag in 1776. However, there are no accurate records of this event.

⚖ Abigail Adams

born 1744 – died 1818

FIRST LADY, WRITER

Even the thunder of nearby British cannons did not keep patriot Abigail Adams from writing one of her famous letters to her dearest friend and husband, statesman John Adams.

Abigail Smith was a self-educated girl from a leading Weymouth, Massachusetts, family. She spent much of her sickly youth reading Shakespeare and classical literature and teaching herself French. On October 25, 1764, Abigail married a young lawyer, John Adams. Their extraordinary marriage lasted 54 years, until Abigail's death in 1818.

In 1774, John Adams traveled to Philadelphia to attend the Continental Congress. Politics would keep the Adamses apart for nearly a decade. While John served the country, Abigail preserved the family. She managed the farm, paid the bills, hired the help, and educated their four children. She managed to survive the hardships of the Revolutionary War, a period when everything from sewing pins to sugar was scarce.

Abigail wrote to John at least once a day from 1774 to 1784. Her letters were full of family tidbits, financial reports, news of the war, and political wisdom. She cautioned John and others at Congress to "Remember the Ladies…we are determined to foment a Rebelion, and will not hold ourselves bound by any Laws in which we have no voice or Representation." Abigail Adams also exchanged letters with other revolutionary figures such as Thomas Jefferson and **Mercy Otis Warren**.

After the Revolutionary War, John Adams became U.S. commissioner in Paris in 1777 and the first U.S. minister to Great Britain in 1785. Abigail spent five years in Europe with her husband and some of her children. She continued writing letters home, telling all about life in the European capitals. When the Adamses returned to the United States, John was elected vice-president in 1789, then president in 1797. During the

In 1785 **SARAH TODD ASTOR** (b.?–1834) was newly married to John Astor. She opened a musical instruments store in New York. He used his wife's $300 dowry to open a fur business. Sarah cleaned the smelly furs and sold them to her music customers. She became an excellent judge of fur quality. The Astors branched out into the real estate business and shipping. They became one of America's richest families. At John's request, Sarah still inspected the Astor fur shipments. She charged her husband $500 an hour for this service, then donated the money to charity.

▶ Abigail Adams supported the colonial revolt against the British. "Let us separate; they are unworthy to be our brethren," she wrote to John Adams several months before the Declaration of Independence was signed on July 4, 1776.

last three months of John's term, the Adamses moved to the new presidential home in Washington, D.C. In her letters, Abigail noted that "not one room or chamber is finished…. It is habitable by fires in every part, thirteen of which we are obliged to keep daily, or sleep in wet and damp places." She hung the laundry in what is now the East Room of the White House.

Abigail Adams's hundreds of letters describe life during the American Revolution and in the early days of our nation. Her love, ideas, and opinions had an important influence on her husband and on her son, John Quincy Adams, the nation's sixth President.

Anne Bradstreet

born c. 1612 – died 1672

POET

"I am obnoxious to each carping tongue,/Who says my hand a needle better fits," Anne Bradstreet wrote in one of her early poems. That poem and others were printed in London in 1650 as *The Tenth Muse Lately Sprung Up In America*. The Puritan woman had become the first published poet in America.

Anne had left an elegant home in Lincolnshire, England, in 1630 with her father and her husband, Simon Bradstreet, to settle in the wilderness of North Andover, Massachusetts. Anne's early writing tells little about her difficult new life. In her first poems, she copied the style of European writers. Later, she used her personal and spiritual life as inspiration. Her loving poems to her husband – "If ever two were one, then surely we/If ever man were lov'd by wife" – and to her children – "Long did I keep you soft and warm/And with my wings kept off all harm" – are famous for their simple beauty. Bradstreet's poems about home, nature, and religion are thoughtful, detailed records of 17th-century Puritan life.

++++++++++++++++++

Cape Cod, Massachusetts, 1620. Puritan women were not asked to sign the Mayflower Compact, which organized the ship's male passengers into a "civil Body Politick" to pass "just and equall Lawes."

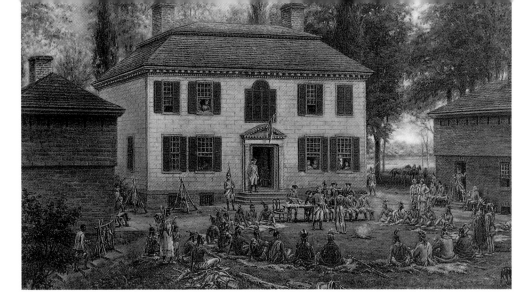

► Iroquois councils were held at Johnson Hall, also home to Molly Brant. Women did not sit in the councils, but they controlled distribution of the tribe's food, which affected any decision about men's war parties or hunting parties.

⊛ Molly Brant MARY BRANT/DEGONWADONTI/GONWATSIJAYENNI

born c. 1736 – died 1796
MOHAWK LEADER

Daughter of a Mohawk chief and the common-law wife of the British Superintendent of Indian Affairs, Molly Brant was a powerful woman.

Molly was probably born and raised in the Mohawk Valley of New York. She lived with Sir William Johnson, the Superintendent of Indian Affairs, from around 1759 to his death in 1774. William and Molly had nine children together. She ran Johnson's household and entertained distinguished guests at his New York mansion. Still, in his will, Johnson referred to Brant as his "prudent & Faithfull Housekeeper."

Through Brant's influence, the Iroquois nation sided with the British during the Revolutionary War. So did her family. Her brother, Joseph Brant, was the war's most famous Native American warrior. Her son Peter captured the Patriot soldier Ethan Allen. Molly herself spied on the Patriots for the British, sent ammunition to Loyalist troops, and hid Loyalist soldiers. After the peace treaties of 1783, Molly Brant moved to Kingston, Ontario. She received a lifetime annual pension of £100 (pounds) from the British for her efforts.

+ + + + + + + + + + + + + + + + +

New Jersey was the only place where women could vote in 1776. They were required to own property worth £50 (pounds). In the 1790s, the new political parties, the Republicans and the Federalists, tried to win over these female voters. Men who lost elections blamed women. They lobbied for "election reform," which led the state legislature to cancel New Jersey women's right to vote in 1807.

Ⓢ Margaret Brent

born c. 1601 – died c. 1671
LANDOWNER

Maryland was only a four-year-old-colony when Margaret Brent, a wealthy Catholic, arrived from her home in Gloucestershire, England. Brent and her sister, Mary, were the first women to own land in Maryland. Colonial officials granted them the rights to 70½ acres. Margaret forced her brother to give her another 1,000 acres to settle a debt. She raised livestock,

ran a mill, bought more land, and lent money to make money. If people fell into debt with Margaret Brent, she went to court to collect. Brent represented herself in court more than 130 times between 1642 and 1650. She usually won.

Maryland's Governor, Leonard Calvert, was a close friend of the Brents. On his deathbed in 1647, he told Margaret to "take all and pay all." Calvert's dying words made Brent responsible for the governor's estate. She also became the legal representative of the governor's brother, Lord Baltimore of England.

Maryland was in chaos. The colony's hungry, unpaid army was ready to mutiny. Brent took charge. She sold Lord Baltimore's cattle and paid the soldiers. She helped the new Maryland assembly gain control of the colony. On January 21, 1647, Margaret Brent demanded two votes in this assembly, one because she owned land and one because she was Lord Baltimore's attorney. The shocked assemblymen refused to give a woman any votes. Margaret Brent left Maryland around 1651 and moved to Westmoreland, Virginia. For the next two decades until her death, Brent ran her large plantation called "Peace."

⊛ Margaret Corbin CAPTAIN MOLLY

born 1751 – died c. 1800

CANNONEER

When Margaret Corbin's husband fell dead in the 1776 battle at Fort Washington, New York, she immediately took his place. "Captain Molly" kept the cannon booming until she was torn up by grapeshot, the small iron balls fired from enemy cannons. She lost all use of her left arm because of her wounds. On July 6, 1779, the Continental Congress voted to reward Corbin for her heroism and sacrifice. It gave her a lifetime pension: one-half of a soldier's pay and a clothing allowance. She petitioned for – and won – the rest of every soldier's pension: an annual ration of rum or whiskey. Captain Molly is the only Revolutionary War veteran to be buried at West Point.

+ + + + + + + + + + + + + + + + +

 During the Revolutionary War, women gave up their pewter cups, dishes, and household items to make cannonballs and other ammunition.

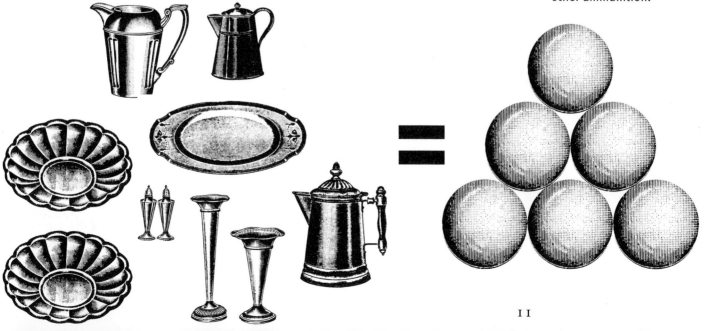

⦿ Mary Dyer

born (unknown) – died 1660
QUAKER MARTYR

Little is known about English-born Mary Barrett before she married William Dyer in London in 1633 and sailed with him to Boston around 1635. Mary joined two of the outlawed religions of her time. First she became a public follower of **Anne Hutchinson**'s Puritanism. Then, during a visit to England from 1652 to 1657, Dyer joined the Society of Friends, also known as Quakers. Quakers believed people were directly responsible to God, not to church officials. They supported women's rights and were against war. The leaders of the Massachusetts Bay Colony forbade the practice of Quakerism because it was a challenge to their Puritan authority. When Dyer returned to Boston in 1657 as a Quaker missionary, she was thrown in prison.

William Dyer won his wife's release by promising to keep her out of the Bay colony. Two years later, Mary Dyer went to visit two imprisoned Quakers in Boston and was jailed herself. In September 1659, Mary was banished, which meant if she set foot in Massachusetts again, she would be executed.

Yet, the devout Quaker returned in less than a month to care for other prisoners and was condemned to be hanged. Drums were loudly beaten to drown out Mary's preaching as she was led to the gallows. The noose was on her neck when, thanks to her son and others, a reprieve came. She was released and her family took her first to Rhode Island, and then to Long Island, New York. But Dyer was determined to fight the unjust laws against her religious beliefs. She traveled to Boston one last time with her Quaker message, but was caught and publicly hanged on June 1, 1660.

• • • • • • • • • • • • • • • • • •

🌎 In 1777 during the Revolutionary War, British troops controlled Philadelphia. British General William Howe and his officers held a secret meeting in the home of **LYDIA DARRAGH** (1729–1789). Lydia eavesdropped on their plan for a surprise attack on General Washington's army at Whitemarsh, Pennsylvania.

The next morning, Lydia crossed British lines carrying an empty sack. She told the soldiers she was going to buy flour. Once past them, Darragh walked several miles through snow toward Whitemarsh. On the way, she met a fellow patriot, Colonel Thomas Craig. She gave him the warning for Washington, and when General Howe's army attacked, Washington's men were ready. No records of Darragh's deed exist from her lifetime. The first account of this popular story was printed in 1827.

⦿ Rebecca Gratz

born 1781 – died 1869
PHILANTHROPIST

She was educated, rich, and beautiful. Rebecca Gratz spent her entire life helping others. The daughter of a successful fur trader, Rebecca was a prominent member of Philadelphia society. By the time she was in her early 20s, she had already helped start the Female Association for the Relief of Women and Children in Reduced Circumstances. Inspired by schools in other religious communities, Gratz founded the Hebrew Sunday School Society in 1838. She served as both teacher and president at the Society's first school, which became a model for all other Jewish Sunday schools to come. Gratz was famous for her generosity.

◄ The English writer Sir Walter Scott used Rebecca Gratz as the model for the heroine of his popular 1819 novel *Ivanhoe*.

∞ Barbara Heck

born 1734 – died 1804
METHODIST LEADER

Barbara Ruckle was born in Ireland, but her parents were German refugees. When she was 18, she was inspired by the evangelist preacher John Wesley and converted to Methodism. In 1760, Barbara and her new husband, Paul Heck, sailed for America. Within eight years, she helped establish a Methodist Society and opened the Wesley Chapel on John Street in New York City. Because the Hecks supported the British cause, they left for Canada during the Revolutionary War. Barbara Ruckle Heck, "the mother of American Methodism," organized churches throughout New York state and Canada.

∞ Anne Hutchinson

born c. 1591 – died 1643
PURITAN LEADER

Anne and William Hutchinson left Lincolnshire, England, and arrived in the Massachusetts Bay Colony in 1634. The Puritan settlement in Boston was not ready for an independent woman like Anne who publicly spoke her own mind on religious issues. Within three years, she was tried by the General Court and banished from the colony as "a woman not fit for our society."

The colony's government was based on Puritan religious ideas. Officials such as Governor John Winthrop believed people would be saved only through hard work, good deeds, and righteousness. Anne Hutchinson believed salvation lay in a direct, personal relationship with God. She encouraged people to make their own moral choices, and thought women had the same right to preach as men. Anne claimed she had divine messages from God.

Hutchinson expressed her ideas publicly. In addition to being a healer, midwife, housewife, and mother of 15 children, Anne was a Bible scholar. She held weekly meetings at her house to discuss scriptures and church sermons. At first, the meetings were limited to women. Since Puritan women could not preach or speak in church, many were eager to attend Anne's meetings where they could participate. She soon

◄ Anne Hutchinson was 47 years old, pregnant, and sick when she was accused by the Massachusetts Bay Colony General Court of breaking religious laws. She defended herself with examples from the Bible and outraged the court by asking that its witnesses testify under oath.

MARY KATHERINE GODDARD (1738–1816) was an excellent businessperson who often cleaned up her brother William's financial messes. She took over his Rhode Island print shop and published the *Providence Gazette*, a weekly newspaper, in 1765. In 1768, she took charge of the *Pennsylvania Chronicle*. When William brought Mary in to run the *Maryland Journal* in 1774, her name finally appeared on a masthead the next year. From 1775 to 1789, Mary Goddard also was the Baltimore postmistress and ran the only print shop in the city, operating the presses herself. In 1777 she got an important order: print the first official version of the Declaration of Independence, including all 56 signers' names. Not only did Mary print the historic document, she paid post riders to deliver it all through the colonies.

added a second meeting and admitted men, although they had to sit on their own side of the Hutchinson parlor.

Sometimes more than 80 people would crowd into Anne's house. She preached her unique ideas about grace and salvation. She criticized the teachings of traditional Puritan leaders. Her enthusiastic audience included some of Boston's leading families, merchants, intellectuals, and even some government officials. The Colony's Puritan leaders considered Anne a threat to their authority. Led by Governor Winthrop, they banned her meetings for being "disorderly and without rule." As a warning, they fired her husband and her friends from government jobs, but Anne kept preaching.

In November 1637 and again in March 1638, Anne Hutchinson was brought to a court made up of Puritan leaders. There was no jury. Her enemy, Governor Winthrop, was the prosecutor and judge. Unable to find any unlawful charges against Anne, the court claimed she had broken the Bible's Fifth Commandment to obey one's father and mother. Winthrop claimed he and the court were "father and mother" to the colony. Anne had disobeyed by preaching. For her "crimes," Anne Hutchinson was thrown out of the Boston Anglican Church and banished from Massachusetts. She walked out of the courtroom with her head high; **Mary Dyer** walked beside her. The Hutchinsons and 35 other families moved to Rhode Island, where they established a community. After her husband's death in 1642, Anne moved her family to Pelham Bay, New York. She and most of her children were killed in a Mohegan Indian attack in 1643. The nearby Hutchinson River is named in her honor.

> *Alewife:* a woman who makes ale or beer. Beer was an important part of 17th-century European diets. Water and milk were sometimes not fit to drink. Tea and coffee were expensive. Beer was cheap and easy to make. The Puritans brought it to New England on the *Mayflower*. In the colonial settlements, alewives used corn, oats, even pumpkins in brewing.

Mary Jemison DEH-GE-WA-NUS

born 1743 – died 1833

WRITER

"The White Woman of the Genesee" was just a 14-year-old girl when she was captured in a raid on her Irish family's Pennsylvania farm during the French and Indian War. Mary married a Delaware warrior in 1760 and had two children. After her first husband's death, she married a Seneca warrior in 1765 and moved to the Genesee Valley in western New York. Mary Jemison raised a family, lived by tribal customs, and became a large cattle and land owner. Mary later dictated her autobiography, *A Narrative of the Life of Mrs. Mary Jemison*, to a schoolteacher. She explained the Native American view of the Revolutionary War and how the League of Six Nations (Cayuga, Seneca, Onondaga, Oneida, Mohawk, and Tuscarora tribes) tried unsuccessfully to "live on neutral ground, surrounded by the din of war, without being engaged in it." When Jemison's book was published in 1824, it outsold the works of the popular novelist James Fenimore Cooper, who later wrote *The Last of the Mohicans*.

◄ A Shaker meeting. Shaker men and women lived in separate houses. They did not have children. Their communities grew when new members joined or when orphans were adopted.

∞ Mother Ann Lee

born 1736 – died 1784
SHAKER LEADER

In 1758, Ann Lee, a young English millworker, joined a religious group called the United Society of Believers in Christ's Second Appearing. The group was also called the Shakers because of the shaking and fevered dancing that went on at their meetings. Ann married in 1762 and had four children. They all died as babies and Lee blamed herself. Shortly afterward, she had a vision. She began to preach that God was both male and female; that men and women were equal, but that sexual relations were wrong. The English Shakers accepted Ann Lee as their spiritual leader and gave her the title of Mother. They believed Ann was the spirit of Jesus.

Mother Lee had a vision about America, so she and a few Shakers left for the colonies. Lee started a Shaker community in Watervliet, New York, in 1776. The Shakers raised their own food and livestock, made their own cloth, and invented tools, such as a clothespin, a washing machine, and a circular saw. They built the houses, barns, and furniture that are famous today for their elegant designs. The Shakers' simple lifestyle and ideals of gender and racial equality appealed to many people. By the time Ann Lee died, 11 Shaker communities had started.

⚖ Lady Deborah Moody

born c. 1580 – died c. 1659
LANDOWNER, MAYOR

Even though she had an aristocratic title, Lady Deborah Moody, like other English Puritans, felt persecuted in her own country. After she became a widow, Lady Moody sold her large house and property. She left for Boston in 1639 with a young son and a good amount of gold.

When she arrived, Moody found the New England Puritans too strict. She did not like the harsh ways they treated non-Puritans and Native Americans. Moody filled a ship with supplies and sailed with several friends until they came to the Dutch colony of New Amsterdam, present-day New

+++++++++++++++++++

The Great Awakening was a wave of gospel preaching that swept through the colonies in the 1730s and 1740s. Just as **Anne Hutchinson** had done 100 years earlier, women and men challenged traditional church authority. They were looking for a more direct and emotional relationship with God. During religious meetings, preachers shouted fiery sermons. Listeners wailed and moaned in response. The Great Awakening also stressed moral values. This religious movement was partly a response to social change. Colonial life, especially for men, was centered increasingly around politics and business, rather than religion. Colonial women, looking for comfort from the pain of the early deaths of children, female friends, and relatives, or the fear of their own early deaths, were drawn into the revival.

+ + + + + + + + + + + + + + + +

The Massachusetts Bay Colony had many problems in 1692: angry Native Americans, smallpox, pirates, taxes, land fights. People were looking for a reason for these troubles. Many people believed in witchcraft and the devil. In Salem, Massachusetts, the result was a terrible witchhunt. It started with a few young girls who became hysterical after listening to voodoo stories told by a West Indian slave, Tituba. The girls said witches were pinching and biting them. They named many of their Puritan neighbors, mostly women, as the witches. The accused were jailed, often tortured, and brought to court. The Salem witch trials lasted four months. Fourteen women and six men were executed.

York. The Dutch gave her a land grant in 1645, making Deborah the first woman to head her own colonial settlement. Called Gravesend, Moody's land extended over several large sections of modern Brooklyn. She even wrote the laws and designed the town. Gravesend was laid out with a town green or park in the center. The streets followed a neat grid pattern that can still be seen today. Moody allowed freedom of religion and banned slavery.

📖 Judith Sargent Murray

born 1751 – died 1820
FEMINIST ESSAYIST

Judith Sargent Murray wrote poems and plays, but was most famous for her essays on equality and education. Her first essays were published in *Gentleman and Lady's Town and Country Magazine*. From 1792 to 1794, Murray was a regular contributor to *Massachusetts Magazine*. Adopting the fictional role of a man so her ideas would be taken seriously, Judith wrote a series of essays called "The Gleaner," in which she commented on public affairs and promoted her ideas about female equality.

Murray thought women had an intellectual and moral right to an education. In her 1790 essay *On The Equality of the Sexes*, she argued that any advantage men had intellectually was due to their superior education, not to women's inferior minds. She added that an uneducated woman "is most unhappy; she feels the want of a cultivated mind."

Judith Sargent Murray pointed out that female education was practical. She recognized that colonial women were responsible for the teaching of their

young children. A mother educated in history, language, and the sciences would be able to share all this with her children. Murray also believed educated women would contribute more to family businesses and, if widowed, handle their affairs better.

In 1798, Murray's popular columns were collected and published in three volumes also called "The Gleaner." President George Washington was among those who bought the collection.

◀ Judith Sargent Murray came from a wealthy Gloucester, Massachusetts, family. Like **Abigail Adams**, **Mercy Otis Warren**, and other women of the time, she had a keen mind, but did not have a formal education. Like Adams and Warren, Murray was a firm advocate of women's right to education.

⑤ Eliza Lucas Pinckney

| born 1722 – died 1793 |
| **AGRICULTURIST, LANDOWNER** |

When Eliza Lucas was only 16, her father, a British colonel, went off to the West Indies. He left Eliza in charge of Wappoo, his South Carolina plantation. And Eliza took charge. She rose at five each morning to oversee the planting, business accounts, and crop shipments from the 600-acre rice plantation. She took care of her ailing mother, her young sister, and the plantation's 20 slaves. She taught two slave girls to read so that they could teach the other slave children.

Eliza Lucas's most extraordinary accomplishment changed life at Wappoo and plantations throughout South Carolina. After several years of plant experiments, in 1744 she successfully grew a crop of indigo. Indigo was prized for the blue dye the plant produced. England, a great cloth manufacturing country, needed the dye. Eliza sent several pounds of her crop's dye to London. She shared the seeds from her crop with any South Carolina plantation owner who wanted them. In three short years, the colony exported nearly 100,000 pounds of indigo and Parliament voted a cash bonus for indigo grown in the British colonies. By the 1760s, South Carolina produced more than a million pounds a year. The boom lasted until the Revolutionary War blocked trade with England.

In 1744, Eliza Lucas married Charles Pinckney. She continued her work with indigo and also grew silkworms. The couple had four children. Charles Pinckney died in 1758, and Eliza became manager of his seven plantations. When Eliza Pinckney died in 1793, President George Washington was among her pallbearers.

🔍 *Femme covert:* a married woman whose legal rights were "covered" by her husband. *Femme sole:* a woman "solo," a single woman or widow, who could act on her own behalf in business or law. The American colonies adopted English Common Law in the 1600s, which defined women as either covert or sole. Married women usually could not own property, keep their own money, or have legal custody of their children. Husbands had complete legal control over their wives. A wife had a legal right to share her husband's home, to be supported by him, and not be abused by him. However, she could not sue in court if her husband broke these laws. A *femme sole* had to take care of herself, so her legal rights were similar to a man's.

⊛ Molly Pitcher MARY LUDWIG HAYS MCCAULEY

born 1754 – died 1832

CANNONEER

When her first husband, John Hays, left Pennsylvania with the Continental Army, Mary Hays did what many Patriot wives did – she went with him. The former dairy maid traveled with the Pennsylvania 7th Regiment and did laundry, cooking, and nursing. Then at the Battle of Monmouth, New Jersey, Mary Hays became better known as Molly Pitcher, one of the most popular female images of the Revolutionary War.

The battle took place on a sweltering June 28, 1778, in Freehold, New Jersey. Mary trudged back and forth from a nearby spring, bringing water to the soldiers on the hot and smoky battlefield. The thirsty men called her "Molly Pitcher." When John Hays collapsed, an officer ordered his cannon pulled back, because there was no one left to fire it. According to some accounts, Molly dropped her pitcher and started loading the cannon. She fired that cannon throughout the bloody battle. Other accounts of the battle say Molly was made a sergeant right on the battlefield, some say by George Washington himself.

After the war, Molly returned to Pennsylvania, where John Hays died. Molly married another war veteran and worked odd jobs. In 1822, 30 years after the Battle of Monmouth, the Pennsylvania Legislature honored Molly Pitcher for her "services during the Revolutionary War." It gave her a $40-a-year pension.

🌐 In support of the American Revolution, Esther Reed wrote a broadside called "The Sentiments of an American Woman." She and Sarah Franklin Bache organized the Philadelphia Ladies Association, America's first women's organization, in the summer of 1780. Its goal was to raise money for General George Washington's troops. They collected around $7,500, a great sum at the time. Esther wanted to give the money to the soldiers, but Washington asked that the women make shirts for the men instead. By December 1780, the group had stitched over 2,200 linen shirts. Each shirt was embroidered with the name of its maker.

▶ Even when enemy fire ripped through Molly Pitcher's petticoat, she did not leave her post at the cannon.

Pocahontas MATOAKA/REBECCA ROLFE

born c. 1595 – died 1617

NATIVE AMERICAN HEROINE

Pocahontas was the daughter of Powhatan, chief of 30 tribes in the Chesapeake Bay area. Though there is no accurate record of the event, she is credited with saving the life of Captain John Smith, the leader of the English colony at Jamestown. Just how she did it is not clear. According to popular legend, Pocahontas threw herself across Smith to stop her father's warriors from beating their captive to death in 1607. She may have been only 12 years old at the time.

Pocahontas often visited Jamestown, sometimes representing her powerful father, sometimes bringing food to the struggling colonists. She helped keep the peace between colonists and tribe members and taught Captain Smith her language. Smith wrote she "presurve(d) this colonie from death, famine and utter confusion." He admired the wit and spirit of the young Native American woman whose real name, Matoaka, meant "playful."

When Captain Smith returned to England in 1609, Pocahontas stopped visiting the colony. Four years later, another captain, Samuel Argall, lured Pocahontas aboard his ship. He held her hostage, although in comfortable style, in Jamestown. Argall planned to exchange the chief's daughter for some English prisoners. During the several months Pocahontas was held hostage, she learned English and became a Christian. In 1614, with her father's approval, she married John Rolfe, the planter who introduced tobacco to Virginia. The Rolfes, with their son, traveled to England in 1616. Pocahontas was hailed as an Indian princess and presented to the king and queen in 1617. She saw Captain Smith, who remarked how formal and civil she was "after our English manner." Pocahontas, now called Rebecca Rolfe, was not eager to leave England when her husband needed to return to Jamestown. And, in fact, Pocahontas never left. She became ill in London and died before the ship sailed.

◀ A portrait of Pocahontas in English court dress.

" " " " " " " " " " " "

Spinster: Spinning was work associated with women. A spinster was what society and the law called unmarried women in the 17th century. It was considered desirable to marry, so spinsters were often pitied or mocked.

▲ An 1873 reprint of Susanna Haswell Rowson's story, *Charlotte Temple.*

• • • • • • • • • • • • • • • •

From 1730 to her death in 1774, **DEBORAH READ** (c. 1707) was the common-law wife of Benjamin Franklin. In his autobiography, the great statesman and scientist wrote, "It was lucky for me that I had one as much disposed to industry and frugality as myself." She helped run the Franklins' Philadelphia store, which sold everything from pencils to codfish. By 1735, Ben was the public printer for Delaware, New Jersey, and Pennsylvania, as well as the publisher of *Poor Richard's Almanac*. Deborah kept the business accounts and was Philadelphia's postmistress in Ben's absence.

Susanna Haswell Rowson

born c. 1762 – died 1824
AUTHOR, EDUCATOR

Susanna Rowson was the author of *Charlotte Temple*, the first bestseller in America. Born in England, Susanna Haswell moved with her father to Massachusetts in 1768. They were loyal to the British crown, and Massachusetts became a difficult place for a Loyalist family to be. The Haswells were sent to prison during the Revolutionary War. They were left penniless and decided to go back to England in 1778. There, Susanna worked as a governess, wrote poems and essays, and became an actress. *Charlotte Temple* was published in England in 1791 and reprinted in Philadelphia in 1794. Rowson's novel was about a young schoolgirl seduced and abandoned by a soldier. The story showed how powerful physical love was for both sexes, but warned about the "double standard" that treated women more harshly than their male lovers. It was a sensation for decades and went through more than 200 editions.

Susanna returned to the United States in 1793 with her husband, William Rowson. Both of them performed in Susanna's operas, musicals, and comedies. Her work often included plots about American patriotism.

When Rowson retired from the stage, she opened the Young Ladies Academy in Boston in 1797. The Academy was one of the first schools in the United States to offer girls a full education. Rowson was the school's director and wrote its geography, history, and spelling textbooks. She also contributed to *Boston Weekly Magazine*, among others, and wrote four more novels.

Deborah Sampson GANNETT

born 1760 – died 1827
REVOLUTIONARY WAR SOLDIER

At 18, Deborah Sampson dressed up as a man and drank in taverns. At 21, she enlisted in the Continental Army, wearing men's clothes she had woven and sewn herself. She added a musket to her disguise and fought in several battles against the British.

The Revolutionary War gave Sampson a chance at adventures usually only open to a man. The Continental Army desperately needed recruits in 1781 to continue the war against the British. The Army was even willing to pay cash to new enlistees. Deborah, at five feet seven inches, was already above average in height for a woman. When she bound her breasts with a cotton strip, combed her hair back, and pulled on a pair of breeches, she made

a very convincing man. On May 20, 1782, Deborah walked nearly 50 miles in this disguise to Bellingham, Massachusetts. The young woman had no trouble enlisting as Private Robert Shurtleff, 4th Massachusetts Regiment.

Sampson cleverly maintained her disguise among the other soldiers. She changed clothes in the dark, avoided the latrine, and bathed alone in the early morning. Even when she was shot in a skirmish with the British near Tarrytown, New York, Deborah was more worried about her secret identity than her injury. So she stole a needle and bandage, pried a musketball out of her thigh, and sewed up the wound herself.

Private Shurtleff was sent to Philadelphia in 1783 and caught a fever. The private became so weak, she appeared to be dead. The undertakers came to take her away. Luckily, a doctor discovered that Deborah's heart was still beating. But he also discovered that heart beat in a female body!

The news about Deborah was a shock to her commanders. Still, she *had* been a brave soldier. So on October 25, 1783, "Private Robert Shurtleff" was honorably discharged at West Point.

After the war, Deborah Sampson went to her uncle's home in Sharon, Massachusetts. She married Benjamin Gannett, a local farmer, and had three children. In 1792, Deborah asked the Massachusetts State Legislature for back pay from her army days. She got £34 (pounds) for her "extraordinary instance of female heroism." Thirteen years later, Paul Revere helped Deborah get the same Congressional pension – $4 per month – that male veterans got.

Deborah Sampson's autobiography, *The Female Review, Memoirs of an American Young Lady*, was published in 1797. In 1802, she became one of the nation's first women lecturers. Deborah was paid to appear in her military uniform and do musket maneuvers on stage while she thrilled audiences with her strange soldier's story.

◄ Deborah Sampson was born in Plympton, Massachusetts. She learned to read at a local school and later borrowed newspapers to keep up with the colonial revolt against British rule.

THE GOOD WOMAN

+ + + + + + + + + + + + + + + + +

In the early 1700s, women ran 12 out of Boston's 34 tavern-inns. During the Revolutionary War, six out of 40 colonial newspapers were owned by women; many other women ran print shops.

✪ Nancy Ward NANYE'HI

born c. 1738 – died 1824

CHEROKEE LEADER

Nancy Ward was called the "**Pocahontas** of the West." Like Pocahontas, she was an important link between Native Americans and colonists. She was born Nanye'hi in Chota, a Cherokee village in Tennessee. Nanye'hi earned the title Beloved Woman when she took her fallen husband's place in a Cherokee battle with the Creeks. Because of her bravery, Nanye'hi also became part of the influential Cherokee Women's Council and the General Council.

Her name changed to Ward when she married a white trader. Nancy Ward was well-known among the settlers who were moving into eastern Tennessee, then the western frontier. She believed that harmony between the Cherokee and colonists was better than war.

In July 1776, Ward forewarned colonist John Sevier and the Watauga settlement of a secret pro-British Cherokee attack. She also saved the life of a white woman captive. When the colonial militia destroyed Cherokee villages in October, they spared Ward's village.

Nancy learned how to make butter and cheese from the woman she rescued. Convinced that it would help her tribe, Ward bought cattle and introduced dairy farming to the Cherokee. She continued her efforts as peacemaker, representing the defeated Cherokee at talks with the colonists in the 1780s. Nancy Ward was an eloquent speaker, calling for a "chain of friendship." Settlers broke the chain by ignoring the 1785 treaty that protected Cherokee land.

The Cherokee's Beloved Woman tried to keep the Council from giving up too much tribal land to the white people flooding the area. When Cherokee lands north of the Hiwassee River were sold in 1819, Ward left Chota. She moved to southeastern Tennessee and opened an inn. She later returned to Chota and died there. Thirteen years later, all the Cherokee lost their homes and were forced to march the famous "Trail of Tears" into exile in the Southwest.

+ + + + + + + + + + + + + + + + +

 During the Revolutionary War, many people burned their fields so the British Army could not harvest the food crops. In 1777, Patriot Catherine Schuyler sneaked through enemy lines to burn her wheatfields.

⚖ Mercy Otis Warren

Mercy Otis Warren was the first woman historian in the United States.

born 1728 – died 1814

WRITER, HISTORIAN

Mercy Otis Warren knew the major figures of the American Revolution personally – she had been entertaining them for years in her Plymouth, Massachusetts, home. Her Patriot brother, James Otis, coined the Revolution's war cry: "Taxation without representation is tyranny." Among her acquaintances were **Abigail Adams** and her husband John, George and **Martha Washington**, Thomas Jefferson, and John Hancock. Mercy used her firsthand experiences of the people and the times to write an important three-volume history, *A History of the Rise, Progress, and Termination of the American Revolution* (1805).

Mercy grew up on Cape Cod in a leading Massachusetts family. She did not go to school, but educated herself, sometimes when her brother was tutored, sometimes by browsing through her uncle's library. When she was 26, Mercy married James Warren, a Plymouth merchant and Patriot. They had five sons together. The Warrens formed an interesting union. He urged the country on to war through political planning; she championed independence through her writing.

Since plays were banned in Puritan Massachusetts, Mercy Otis Warren had probably never seen one. Yet she published several popular plays with patriotic messages. *The Adulateur* (1772) made fun of the colony's royal governor. *The Group* (1775) satirized Boston's Loyalists. During the Revolutionary War, Mercy Warren thought too many Bostonians spent too much money on idle pleasures, while brave Patriot soldiers were at war. She mocked the city people in *The Motley Assemblage* (1779). It was the first play written in America to have all American characters.

In the late 1770s, Warren began work on her three-volume history of the Revolution. It took nearly 30 years to finish. She did not support the Constitution in 1787 and opposed it in her controversial *Observations on the New Constitution* (1788). Warren and other Patriots thought the Constitution should say more about individual liberties and freedom of the press. The Bill of Rights, which did spell out basic rights and freedoms of United States citizens, became the first Ten Amendments to the Constitution in 1791. Mercy Otis Warren's *Observations* helped convince the Constitution's supporters of the Amendments' importance.

++++++++++++++++++

The nation's first public schools opened in New England in 1635. Most Puritan girls learned reading and writing in "dame" schools, when they were between five and seven years old. The schools were run by dames, a term used at the time for woman or schoolteacher. In the Middle Colonies of Pennsylvania, New York, New Jersey, and Delaware, Quakers and other religious groups had church schools. But most children were taught at home. Young girls in the South might be instructed by tutors, along with their brothers. Few colonial women had more than a few years of formal education.

⚖ Martha Washington

born 1731 – died 1802

FIRST LADY

Born Martha Dandridge, the country's first First Lady grew up in Virginia plantation society. She learned all the domestic arts from embroidery to household management. After her first husband's death in 1757, Martha became very wealthy. She owned two mansions, 18,000 acres of land, more than $30,000, and a number of slaves.

In 1759, Martha married George Washington, a Virginia gentleman farmer. She and her two children moved to Washington's plantation, Mount Vernon. There Martha looked after the household, the servants, and the plantation's several small businesses. It had a dairy, a smokehouse, and a very productive spinning and weaving center.

Throughout the Revolutionary War, while her husband commanded the army, Martha traveled from home to share winter quarters with him. Her calm, steady, cheerful spirit was a comfort to the soldiers. So were the socks and shirts she made for them.

By war's end, George Washington was a national hero. He was elected President of the United States in 1789, and Martha moved with him to New York City, the nation's first capital. Martha was a warm and popular hostess. She and **Abigail Adams**, the Vice-President's wife, held weekly Friday night receptions open to any "respectable persons." For eight years, Martha helped her husband create a dignified, elegant atmosphere around the presidency. The First Lady and President retired to Mount Vernon after his second term. Martha was in her late 60s, but still hosted an endless stream of family and visitors. When Washington died in 1799, Mrs. Washington spent more and more time in an attic room doing her needlework. She died three years later.

◄ "Steady as a clock, busy as a bee, and cheerful as a cricket" – that's how Martha Washington described herself at home in Mount Vernon, Virginia. She was the first woman to have her picture on paper money (1886) and on a stamp (1902).

Phillis Wheatley

born c. 1753 – died 1784
AFRICAN-AMERICAN POET

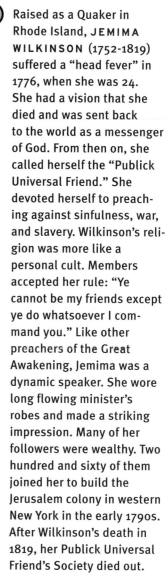

No one knows where or even when the first African-American poet was born. In 1761, Boston merchant John Wheatley bought a young African girl he called Phillis Wheatley from a slave ship. He guessed she was around seven or eight years old, because her baby teeth were falling out. He did not recognize the language she spoke.

Phillis learned to speak and read English within 16 months of her arrival. She was educated along with the Wheatley children and could read the Bible and literary classics by the time she was 12.

Phillis started writing when she was 13. Her love of learning and her strong belief in Christian salvation were important themes in her work. In fact, her first poem to receive public notice was about the death of a Great Awakening preacher. During the 1760s and 1770s Phillis Wheatley's fame as a poet grew. Many people pointed to Phillis as an example of why African-Americans should not be enslaved or considered intellectually inferior.

Phillis was freed by the Wheatleys when she was in her 20s. She suffered from poor health, so they sent her to England in 1773. A religious abolitionist, the Countess of Huntingdon, became the young poet's patron. The countess arranged for Wheatley's book, *Poems on Various Subjects, Religious and Moral* (1773), to be published. *Poems* had an introduction signed by 18 well-known men, including John Hancock. It confirmed that Wheatley was the book's author, in case anyone doubted that a former slave could be a poet.

Phillis Wheatley then returned to Boston. She wrote one more famous work, a poem written to General George Washington. It was published in *Pennsylvania Magazine* in 1776. Shortly after, Wheatley accepted an invitation to visit the general in his Cambridge, Massachusetts, headquarters.

By 1778, Mr. and Mrs. Wheatley had died and Phillis was left without support. Wheatley married a freed slave named John Peters. The couple's children died in infancy. Peters was jailed for debts and Phillis had to work hard in a boardinghouse. She died when she was about 30 years old.

Raised as a Quaker in Rhode Island, JEMIMA WILKINSON (1752-1819) suffered a "head fever" in 1776, when she was 24. She had a vision that she died and was sent back to the world as a messenger of God. From then on, she called herself the "Publick Universal Friend." She devoted herself to preaching against sinfulness, war, and slavery. Wilkinson's religion was more like a personal cult. Members accepted her rule: "Ye cannot be my friends except ye do whatsoever I command you." Like other preachers of the Great Awakening, Jemima was a dynamic speaker. She wore long flowing minister's robes and made a striking impression. Many of her followers were wealthy. Two hundred and sixty of them joined her to build the Jerusalem colony in western New York in the early 1790s. After Wilkinson's death in 1819, her Publick Universal Friend's Society died out.

Growth and Conflict

established, and by the 1880s, both men and women were enrolled in half the nation's colleges. The spread of public schools, especially on the frontier and in the South after the Civil War, increased the demand for teachers. By the 1880s, more than 65 percent of public school teachers were women. Just as some people feared, many educated women wanted more opportunities.

Women filled the pews of churches across the country. Only a few groups, such as the Quakers, allowed women to speak from the pulpit. Yet religious beliefs led many women into reform work. Quakers and some others were opposed to slavery. Middle-class women formed societies to help the poor, to oppose slavery, and to ban the use of alcohol. African-American and working-class women also formed societies for self-improvement and mutual support. Out of these movements came many of the strongest fighters for women's right to vote.

T he United States in the 19th century was more prosperous and complex than in colonial times. Thousands of immigrant women flocked to the cities and factories of the Northeast. The South remained agricultural. Women, especially enslaved women, were needed to work its farms and plantations. Other women were among the pioneers who pushed the nation's boundaries past the Mississippi River. Native American women were often forced from their lands onto reservations.

A Woman's Place is in the Home

Preachers, politicians, journalists, and many women themselves had a picture of the ideal woman. She was a cheerful wife, devoted mother, and self-sacrificing, morally-superior being. She would also buy the many new mass-produced consumer goods. Middle-class and wealthy white women were expected to focus on the "private" life of home and family. Men would take care of the "public" life of business and politics. This division of power and responsibility would last for decades.

Beyond Hearth and Home

Some women gained more independence through education and religion. Women's colleges were

Abolition

When men organized to oppose slavery in the early 1830s, women were not included. White and free African-American women formed their own groups. They wrote, lectured, held prayer vigils, gathered thousands of signatures on petitions, and raised thousands of dollars holding anti-slavery fairs. They were sometimes attacked by pro-slavery mobs or denounced as "unnatural women" by ministers, politicians, and even other abolitionists.

▲ Many African Americans became sharecroppers where they had once worked as slaves. They paid to rent land – leaving little for food, clothing, and shelter.

Women's Rights

At abolition lectures women and their supporters also spoke out for women's rights. In 1848, in Seneca Falls, New York, a group of women's rights activists held the first of many conventions devoted to women's issues. However, in 1861, the battle cries of the Civil War muffled the debate over the "woman question."

Like the Revolution, the Civil War thrust women into new roles, making some more aware of their skills and strengths. North and South, women ran businesses and farms when men left to fight. White and freed African-American women volunteered as military nurses, spies, even soldiers. Others worked in new factory jobs or in government offices for the first time. Still others worked as sales clerks.

The war's end in 1865 left many women feeling shortchanged. African-American women were freed from slavery, but not from poverty. Southern white women had to rebuild their lives with few resources and fewer men; one out of four Confederate soldiers had died. In the North, women who expected to receive the vote for their efforts to end slavery and win the war were soon disappointed.

Whose Suffrage?

Was it more important to get the vote for newly-freed African-American men, or to insist that all women get the vote now, too? This issue would divide the suffrage movement for 20 years.

By 1869, there were two large women's suffrage groups. The conservative American Woman's Suffrage Association (AWSA) backed the Fifteenth Amendment, which gave African-American men the right to vote when it was ratified in 1870. Then AWSA worked to get women's suffrage bills passed in individual states. The more liberal National Woman Suffrage Association (NWSA) opposed the Fifteenth Amendment because it didn't include women. NWSA lobbied for a women's suffrage amendment to the U.S. Constitution. In 1890, the two groups merged

◀ In the 1820s, Lowell, Massachusetts, was considered a model factory town. Single women mill-workers lived in strictly supervised boarding houses. They attended self-improvement lectures, discussed literature, learned languages and music, and published their own magazines – and they worked 12 to 13 hours a day, six days a week for roughly $2!

into the National American Woman Suffrage Association (NAWSA).

Working Women

The Industrial Revolution greatly changed women's lives. They were the first to fill the factory jobs that opened up in the industrial Northeast. No matter what jobs women held, they were paid sometimes only half what their male co-workers made. And improvements in machine technology usually meant people had to work more – and faster – for less money. When working conditions got worse and worse, women were among the first labor organizers and strikers.

Other workers never organized. After the war, most African-American women worked in Southern cities as servants, but some also held the worst and lowest-paying jobs in the tobacco factories. In cities across the country, immigrant women with families did sewing and other piece work at home.

The Industrial Revolution redefined women's work in ways that still have an impact. Beginning then, only labor that involved wages was considered "work." This meant that factory employees or servants were working women, but farm wives and homemakers were not – no matter how heavy their workload. "Working women" represented only 10 percent of all women in the 1840s and only 20 percent by the turn of the century.

America's largest female figure, "Liberty Enlightening the World," stands 152-feet-high, weighs 225 tons, and was dedicated on October 28, 1886.

„ " „ " „ " „ " „ " „ " „

Give me your tired,
* your poor,*
Your huddled masses,
* yearning to breathe free,*
The wretched refuse of
* your teeming shore.*
Send these, the homeless,
* tempest-tost, to me:*
I lift my lamp beside
* the golden door.*

Emma Lazarus was a Sephardic Jewish writer living in New York City. Her poem, "The New Colossus" (1883), was pretty much ignored in her own lifetime. Sixteen years after her death, the poem was inscribed on the Statue of Liberty and the last five lines became famous worldwide.

Louisa May Alcott

born 1832 – died 1888
WRITER

In the rural town of Concord, Massachusetts, 11-year-old Louisa May Alcott wrote wild stories of adventure and exotic places in her "imagination book." But as an adult, her fame would come from writing novels about what she knew best: life at home.

Louisa's father, Bronson Alcott, was a forward-thinking educator and philosopher, but his projects often left the family without much money. As a teenager, Louisa worked as a seamstress and a servant. She thought her writing could help pay the bills, so she moved to Boston in the 1850s. There she made a living teaching school and writing thrillers, sensational stories, romances, and poems. Women's writing was not taken seriously at the time, so Louisa used pen names like A.M. Barnard to help sell her work.

During the Civil War, Alcott went to Washington, D.C., in 1862 to nurse wounded soldiers. A keen observer, she turned her experiences into what became her first successful book, *Hospital Sketches* (1863). After the war, a publisher talked her into writing a novel for young women. She used her own family life for inspiration. *Little Women* (1868–1869) sold over 38,000 copies in its first year. Alcott received $12,000, more money than any American writer at the time. Over the next 10 years, Alcott wrote seven more books based on the characters in *Little Women*.

Susan B. Anthony

born 1820 – died 1906
ABOLITIONIST, SUFFRAGIST

"Failure is impossible," said 86-year-old Susan Brownell Anthony at the last women's suffrage convention she ever attended. She was right. Fourteen years after her death, the Nineteenth Amendment to the United States Constitution was passed in 1920, giving women the right to vote. It is sometimes called the Susan B. Anthony Amendment.

Born in Adams, Massachusetts, Susan was raised as a Quaker and educated at private boarding schools. Susan's father encouraged her to get involved in reform movements to end, or abolish, slavery and to prohibit the sale or use of alcohol.

In 1846 Anthony became headmistress of the Female Department at Canajoharie Academy, near Rochester, New York. She was paid only a quarter of the salary of her male co-workers. Women were not even allowed to speak at teachers' union meetings. The same thing happened at temperance

conventions: Women drove the movement to ban liquor, but men were its public speakers. Anthony was not yet active in the women's rights movement. But she was angry that as a woman she could not speak publicly. Encounters with two other women brought her into the cause that became her famous life's work. In 1850, she heard abolitionist-suffragist **Lucy Stone** speak and was inspired by her message. In 1851, **Amelia Bloomer** introduced Susan to **Elizabeth Cady Stanton**. They formed a personal and political friendship that lasted more than 50 years.

Susan formed the Woman's New York State Temperance Society with Elizabeth as its president. Both women were hardworking abolitionists, though as Susan wrote in 1860, "Many abolitionists have yet to learn the ABCs of woman's rights." Anthony was convinced that women's role in all reform movements was limited because they couldn't vote and had "no purses of their own." Women's rights became her main agenda. She began her long campaign petitioning state and federal legislatures on behalf of women's suffrage and legal status. By 1860, her efforts began to pay off when New York State passed a law improving the property rights of married women. They could now keep what they earned and sue in court.

After the Civil War, Anthony and Stanton had great hopes that both African Americans and women would get the vote. They were quickly disappointed. The Fifteenth Amendment proposed suffrage for African-American men, but not for any women. Some women's suffragists supported the amendment because they believed the rights of the newly freed slaves had to come first. Anthony opposed passage unless it included women. She, along with Stanton, **Lucretia Mott**, and others, formed the National Woman Suffrage Association in 1869 to work for a federal law giving women the vote. Anthony traveled across the country, urging passage of the woman suffrage amendment introduced to Congress in 1868. In 1872, possibly inspired by **Victoria Woodhull**'s

◄ Susan B. Anthony (right) and Elizabeth Cady Stanton. Anthony was an incredible researcher and organizer. As a single woman, she was free to travel widely. Stanton, the mother of seven children, was more house bound, but spent hours writing powerful speeches and pamphlets. In 1868 the two suffragists started publishing *The Revolution*, a weekly women's newspaper.

Suffrage: comes from the Latin word, *suffragium*, meaning vote or ballot. English women who campaigned for the vote were the first to be called suffragettes around 1906. They were not being flattered. Adding the suffix "ette" to a word usually suggests something small, light, or not as good as the real thing. The name stuck, although the more serious *suffragist* was often used in the United States.

speech to Congress, Anthony tried to vote in the presidential elections. She claimed the right to vote because she was a U.S. citizen. Anthony was arrested, jailed, and fined $100, but she refused to pay.

Anthony wanted to make sure that the struggle for women's rights was recorded. She, Stanton, and Matilda Gage began writing the *History of Woman Suffrage* in the 1870s. Four volumes of the 5,000-page work were published in Anthony's lifetime. The last two volumes were published in 1922, 16 years after her death. In 1979, the government issued the Susan B. Anthony silver dollar. It was the first U.S. coin to feature a woman.

• • • • • • • • • • • • • • • • • • • •

 SARAH BAGLEY (?–1847), a worker in the textile mills of Lowell, Massachusetts, started out writing articles like "The Pleasures of Factory Life" for the *Lowell Offering*. Within a few years, she was calling for reform and blasting the mill owners as "driveling cotton lords" in her articles for the pro-labor paper *Voice of Industry*. In the 1840s, new, faster machinery was introduced in the mills. Textile workers had to produce more and their wages were cut. To fight back, Bagley organized the Lowell Female Labor Reform Association in 1844. She recruited 500 members in six months, gathered 2,000 signatures, and testified before the Massachusetts legislature. Bagley and other women described their awful working conditions. They demanded their workday be reduced from 13 hours to 10. The legislature refused to act. Bagley eventually left the mills because of poor health. In 1846 she took a job in the Lowell telegraph office and became the country's first female telegraph operator.

Clara Barton

born 1821 – died 1912
RED CROSS FOUNDER

There were no bandages, no blankets, no food. Clara Barton was shocked by the lack of supplies at the first Battle of Bull Run during the Civil War. She advertised in newspapers for medical supplies. When she got them, Nurse Barton headed to the battlefield on a mule team. Her supplies saved the lives of many soldiers.

Born in Oxford, Massachusetts, Barton was always a hard worker. In 1852, she founded one of the first public schools in New Jersey. When a man was hired as her superior, Barton left the school and got a job in the United States Patent Office in Washington, D.C. She was the first woman hired for a government job, and she was in Washington when war broke out.

In Washington, Barton helped Union soldiers returning from the battlefield. That's when she first realized that medical supplies were needed. An incredible organizer, Barton recruited women to prepare supplies for the front lines. She bypassed government and military authorities and traveled to battlefields such as Antietam, Maryland, and Fredericksburg, Virginia. Clara worked in some of the Civil War's worst battles. She cooked for, gave medical aid to, and comforted the thousands of wounded soldiers she called "my boys." After the war, she helped veterans' families, writing over 60,000 letters to help find missing fathers, sons, and brothers.

In 1868, Barton traveled to Switzerland for a rest. There, she heard about the

▶ "If heaven ever sent out a holy angel, she must be one," said a battlefield doctor about Clara Barton, the Angel of the Battlefield.

International Committee of the Red Cross, an agency that brought medical aid to all sides during wartime. Barton returned home and spent five years drumming up government and public support for a similar group in the United States. The American National Red Cross, which helps people during wars, epidemics, and natural disasters, was formed in 1881. Barton served as its president until she retired in 1904. She published her autobiography, *The Story of My Childhood,* three years later.

☑ Dr. Elizabeth Blackwell

born 1821 – died 1910

DOCTOR, SUFFRAGIST

When Elizabeth Blackwell received her M.D., or doctor of medicine degree in 1849, 20,000 people were there to watch her become the first woman awarded a medical degree in the United States. She did not always get that kind of attention. Blackwell applied to 29 medical schools before Geneva College in New York accepted her. Even there, she was not taken seriously. The college's faculty left the decision about admitting a woman up to the all-male student body. They accepted Blackwell as a joke!

Despite poor treatment from fellow students, Blackwell was an excellent student. But after she received her medical degree, no American hospital would hire her. Dr. Blackwell, who was born in England, returned and worked in a British hospital. She also studied midwifery in France, where she caught an illness from a baby and lost the sight of one eye. This ruined her hopes of becoming a surgeon.

In 1851, Dr. Blackwell returned to New York and tried to set up a private practice. No one would rent office space to a female doctor, so she bought a house and set up her own hospital, the New York Infirmary for Women and Children in 1857.

During the Civil War, Blackwell and **Dorothea Dix** trained women for the Union army medical corps and founded the U.S. Sanitary Commission in 1861. When the war was over, Blackwell established the Women's Medical College of the New York Infirmary in 1868. She returned to England the following year and became a professor at the London School of Medicine for Women.

In the 1840s, **GERTRUDES BARCELÓ** (1800–1852) lived in Santa Fe, New Mexico, where she ran an elegant casino-saloon. The city's top businessmen and politicians – Hispanic, American, and European – flocked to her adobe *sala* to drink and gamble under crystal chandeliers. No matter what people thought about a woman being in the saloon business, La Tules, as she was called, was an excellent businessperson. She gave to the church and to the poor, and once lent the U.S. government $10,000.

Amelia Jenks Bloomer

born 1818 – died 1894

SUFFRAGIST, PUBLISHER

Amelia Jenks Bloomer did not invent "bloomers," the daring women's fashion that bears her name. But she wore them. And she defended the rights of **Elizabeth Cady Stanton** and any other woman to abandon uncomfortable dresses and petticoats for the full-cut pantaloons, or Turkish trousers, worn under a short skirt. Bloomer wrote articles about this outfit in her publication, *The Lily*. *The Lily* was the first newspaper published, edited, and even typeset by women. It featured articles about women's rights and alcohol temperance. It also printed articles about dress reform and women's health, and included patterns for making women's pantaloons. Other newspapers followed up on Amelia's *Lily* articles, and a national craze for "bloomers" started.

People who opposed giving women the vote mocked the outfit. Some religious leaders branded the outfit "devilish."

Bloomer, Stanton, **Susan B. Anthony**, and **Lucy Stone** wore the outfits publicly.

However, people refused to take women wearing pants seriously. Bloomer and others realized their clothing interfered with their reform work, so they abandoned bloomers. Amelia did not abandon her activist work, however. She became president of the Iowa Woman Suffrage Society in 1871.

In the 1860s, the American woman might be wearing almost 15 pounds of clothing. First, there were layers of underwear and petticoats. Then a ribbed whalebone corset was often tied so tightly around a woman's middle that she had trouble breathing. Many fashionable women wore hoop skirts that were almost five feet wide at the bottom. Dress reformers such as journalists **Amelia Bloomer** and **Jane Croly** criticized these styles.

 When Isabelle Boyd was jailed by the Union Army, she hung a picture of Confederate President Jefferson Davis in her cell.

⬟ Belle Boyd ISABELLE BOYD

born 1844 – died 1900

CONFEDERATE SPY

Belle Boyd was 17 years old when the Union army occupied her hometown of Martinsburg, Virginia, in 1861. That year one of the Union soldiers broke into her home. Belle shot and killed him.

Boyd was intensely loyal to the South, but the beautiful, intelligent teenager flirted with the Union soldiers. She passed along military secrets she got from them to the Confederate army. By 1862, Boyd was delivering messages for General Stonewall Jackson. She traveled on horseback, often at night, sometimes riding as far as 15 miles through enemy lines.

On May 23, 1862, Belle Boyd made her most daring run ever. Confederate troops were heading north to drive the Union soldiers out of Front Royal, Virginia, where Boyd was then living with an aunt. Belle discovered that the Union troops planned to destroy nearby bridges to prevent the Confederate Army from advancing. She dashed across the gap between the two armies, in full range of Union riflemen – her fancy white apron made her an easy target. Boyd delivered her warning and became a hero of the Confederacy.

Later that same year, the United States Secretary of War ordered Belle's arrest, and she was jailed in the Old Capitol Prison in Washington, D.C. In March 1864, Boyd sailed for England with messages for Confederate agents there. Her ship ran into a Union naval blockade. Boyd was banished to Canada, under the condition that if she was caught again, she would be executed. Five months later, Belle married the Union naval officer who had captured her ship.

1800s – 1880s

CATHARINE BEECHER (1800–1878) believed in equal education but not equal rights for women. The hardworking writer, educator, and reformer put domestic life at the center of women's world. To be the best wives and mothers, she thought women needed both education and exercise. Catharine and her sister **Harriet Beecher Stowe** wrote *The American Woman's Home* (1869), which gave women useful information about health, hygiene, and child care. Beecher also believed women should take over the teaching profession because they were morally better than men. She founded the American Woman's Educational Association in 1852 to recruit female teachers for Western frontier schools. Later, she also encouraged mill workers to leave their unhealthy jobs to become teachers. By 1870, women held more than 50 percent of the 200,000 teaching jobs.

ELLEN CRAFT (1826–1897), the daughter of a slave and a Georgia plantation owner, was so light-skinned she could pass for white – and did! In 1848, she and her husband William, also a slave, rode a train north from Georgia to freedom. Ellen posed as a sickly white slave owner; William pretended to be her slave. Ellen covered most of her face with a bandage as if she had a toothache. She didn't know how to write, so she wore her arm in a sling to avoid having to sign anything. She also pretended to be slightly deaf. The daring and dangerous plan worked. The Crafts made it to Philadelphia. They later moved to Boston and then England. They became important members of the international abolition movement. After slavery was abolished, the Crafts and their five children returned to Georgia, where they bought a plantation and opened a school to teach trades to freed slaves.

Mary Cassatt

born 1844 – died 1926

PAINTER

Before the 19th century, portraits were usually posed, formal pictures of wealthy people. Mary Cassatt, one of the great Impressionist artists, painted people differently. Her portraits were informal, lively, and emotional. She used her own family members as models. Cassatt's most famous work explored the deep, loving relationship between mother and child.

As a young girl, Mary traveled with her family to Europe, where she was inspired by the art she saw. Determined to become an artist, she moved to Paris in 1866, after studying at the Pennsylvania Academy of the Fine Arts. Cassatt's paintings attracted the attention of Edgar Degas, a well-known French painter. In 1877, he invited her to exhibit her work with a new group of painters called the Impressionists. The Impressionists caused a sensation with their new style of painting. They experimented with light, color, paint, and brush strokes to create impressions, not just realistic pictures, of their subjects. Cassatt was the first and only American artist to hang work in the French Impressionist Exhibitions. She started showing her work in the United States in 1876. Cassatt introduced American art audiences to Impressionism and encouraged American collectors to buy Impressionist paintings. Her art work now hangs in museums such as the National Gallery of Art in Washington, D.C., and the Museum of Fine Arts in Boston.

Fanny Jackson Coppin

born 1837 – died 1913

EDUCATOR

Fanny Marion Jackson was born a slave in Washington, D.C., but was bought out of slavery for $125. Her aunt worked for two years to save enough to buy Fanny's freedom. Fanny herself spent her life helping other African Americans become educated and independent.

When she was 14, Fanny worked as a servant for author George Henry Calvery in Newport, Rhode Island. She was given one hour every other afternoon to pursue her own studies. Fanny took private music lessons and attended a public school for African

Americans so that she could become a teacher to her people. Fanny believed education was a powerful tool that could help end discrimination against African Americans.

In 1860, Jackson entered Oberlin College in Ohio, where she became the college's first African-American student-teacher and one of the first African-American women to receive a college degree. Jackson took a job as a school principal and also taught Greek, Latin, and mathematics at the Institute for Colored Youth in Philadelphia. She stayed at the Institute for 37 years and started programs to train teachers. She also raised thousands of dollars to fund the first program to teach industrial skills to African Americans so they could get higher-paying jobs in different trades. In 1881, Fanny married the Reverend Levi Coppin. They later moved to Cape Town, South Africa, where her husband was a bishop and she worked as a missionary.

++++++++++++++++++

 Almost 4,000,000 slaves were freed after the Civil War. Eighty percent of them were illiterate because of Southern laws against teaching African Americans how to read and write. Many women, such as **Susie King Taylor** and Charlotte Forten Grimké, volunteered to teach former slaves. Grimké, a free and wealthy African American, left the North to teach on the South Carolina Sea Islands, held by the Union Army. By 1869, there were almost 4,500 white and African-American women teaching former slaves. Their lives were often threatened by local people who opposed their work.

Prudence Crandall

born 1803 – died 1890

EDUCATOR, ABOLITIONIST

"My whole life has been one of opposition. I could never find anyone near me to agree with me," Prudence Crandall once said. Certainly the townspeople of Canterbury, Connecticut, did not agree with Crandall's plan to open a school for "Young Ladies and Little Misses of Color." The townspeople hired Crandall in 1831 to run the Canterbury Female Boarding School. When Prudence enrolled Sarah Harris, an African American, parents removed their girls from the school. Crandall closed the whole school rather than expel Sarah. In 1833, she opened a school for African-American girls. Her 20 students came from the Canterbury area as well as Boston and New York.

The just man shall be in eternal remembrance

Went to Prison for Teaching Colored Children.

As a Quaker, Crandall had always been opposed to slavery, but she had not been an active abolitionist. Now, she sought help and advice from abolitionist leaders, who sent contributions to support the school. Townspeople broke school windows and filled the school well with manure. Local storekeepers wouldn't sell her any supplies, and local doctors wouldn't treat her students. Even the local Congregational church refused to admit the African-American students for services.

In 1833, the Connecticut legislature passed a state "black law," making it illegal to teach African Americans from out-of-state. Town officials used the law to shut down Crandall's school. Crandall was arrested and jailed three times before an appeals court overruled the state law.

Since Crandall could not be stopped by law, some people took the law into their own hands. In September 1834, an angry mob overran the boarding school, setting fires, breaking windows and doors, and trashing the classrooms. Crandall and her frightened students hid on the top floor. After the attack, Prudence Crandall closed her school because she did not want her students to be the targets of further violence. She settled in Illinois and continued her work as an abolitionist and educator. In 1886, 52 years after the attack, Connecticut gave Crandall a small pension for the damages done to her school.

+ + + + + + + + + + + + + + + +

New inventions such as the typewriter (1868) and the telephone (1876) opened up new jobs for women. Most businesses, however, refused to hire African American and immigrant women. The first women's secretarial school opened in New York in 1879. By 1880, almost 40% of all office typists and stenographers were women. The Ladies Christian Association, established in New York (1858), and the Young Women's Christian Association (YWCA) in Boston, Massachusetts (1867), offered courses in work skills and boarding houses for young working women.

Jane Croly

born 1829 – died 1901

JOURNALIST

Jane Croly was the first woman columnist whose work was syndicated, or printed in many newspapers. She was also the chief staff writer for a major women's magazine and a drama and literary critic. Still, she was not admitted to the 1868 New York Press Club's reception for the famous English writer Charles Dickens. It was for men only. Croly reacted by founding Sorosis (from the Latin word for "sister"), the first women's club in the United States. By 1869, more than 80 members – authors, poets, teachers, artists, doctors, and a historian – had joined the club to "represent as far as possible the active interests of women."

Croly herself had many active interests. She started writing her column, "Parlor and Side-walk Gossip," in 1855, under the pen name of Jennie June. She managed the women's department of the New York *World* from 1862 to 1872, and was chief staff writer for over 27 years for *Demorest's Monthly*

36

Magazine. Jane Croly was devoted to ideas that improved women's lives. She wrote about the dangers of hoop skirts, the rewards of learning "housewifely arts," and the value of getting a good education. She believed the right to work was even more important than the right to vote. Croly thought employment would bring women equality. In 1889, Jane Croly founded the Women's Press Club of New York and the General Federation of Women's Clubs.

Emily Dickinson

born 1830 – died 1886

POET

"The Soul selects her own Society – /Then – shuts the Door –" Emily Dickinson wrote in one of her 1,775 untitled poems. These lines tell a lot about Emily's own life as a writer and recluse in her Amherst, Massachusetts, home. One of America's finest poets, she spent most of her adult life alone, gardening or writing. When visitors came, Emily often stayed upstairs and spoke to them through the barely open door of her room.

Emily Dickinson came from an upper class, New England family. Her grandfather founded Amherst College. Her father was a lawyer and Congressman. Emily and her sister, Lavinia, lived under his shadow. He did not let the girls buy books or choose their own friends. He sent Emily to **Mary Lyon**'s Mount Holyoke Female Seminary, one of the few times she ever left home.

Dickinson wrote poetry all her life, but was most productive starting in the 1860s. She often wore a white dress and composed poem after poem on little scraps of paper. She wrote about nature, love, longing, and death. Her passionate work explored these great mysteries of life. Many of her poems are short

▶ This daguerreotype of Emily Dickinson is from the Amherst College Library.

In 1871, **ABIGAIL DUNIWAY** (1834–1915) started *The New Northwest*, a weekly newspaper about pioneer women's rights. Duniway had traveled 2,400 miles by wagon train from Illinois to Oregon. There she raised six children, taught school, and ran a store to support the family. She thought of herself as "a general pioneer drudge, with never a penny of my own." She met other women in similar or worse situations. Abigail realized women needed more control over their lives. She traveled throughout the Pacific Northwest, talking about voting rights for women. Duniway organized amendments and petitions and helped pass suffrage bills in Idaho and Washington. She took **Susan B. Anthony** on a 1,000-mile Northwest speaking tour and was elected vice-president of the National Woman Suffrage Association 1884. In 1912, Oregon finally gave women the right to vote. Duniway, 78 years old and in a wheelchair, signed the suffrage amendment with the governor and became Oregon's first registered woman voter.

and some have unusual metaphors and punctuation. Many have their own, almost modern rhythm, unlike the steady meter of poetry popular at the time.

In 1862, Emily Dickinson sent some of her poems to Thomas Wentworth Higginson, the editor of *The Atlantic Monthly*. He discouraged her from publishing her work because it was "too delicate." Though the two became close friends, writing to each other for the next 20 years, Dickinson took Higginson's advice. She did not publish her work. Instead, she sewed her poems into little booklets and hid them in trunks and closets. When Lavinia Dickinson found the poems after Emily's death, she published them in 1890.

 Nineteenth-century women led the way in organizing social reform and charitable groups. One of today's leading institutions, the United Way, was started by Frances Wisebart Jacobs. In the 1870s, Jacobs was President of the Hebrew Benevolent Ladies in Denver, Colorado. There she later founded a hospital and the city's first public kindergarten. Then in 1887, Jacobs created the Charity Organization Society, a group of different charities that worked together to raise and distribute funds. It became the model for the United Way.

🌀 Dorothea Dix

born 1802 – died 1887

HEALTH CARE REFORMER

Mentally ill women were jailed with male criminals. Naked prisoners stood roped and chained in their cells. Dorothea Dix was horrified by what she saw when she arrived to teach Sunday school at a Massachusetts jail in 1841. She started investigating conditions at other state prisons and insane asylums. Eighteen months later she presented her "memorial," or report, to the Massachusetts legislature. After much debate, they voted funds to help the mentally ill. Dix began taking on other states. By 1847, she had traveled more than 30,000 miles investigating and lobbying on behalf of neglected prisoners.

Dix had a direct role in founding 32 new mental hospitals throughout the country. Partly because of her efforts, the number of mental hospitals rose from 13 in 1843 to 123 in 1880. In 1845, Dorothea Dix co-wrote *Remarks on Prisons and Prison Discipline in the United States*. Many institutions eventually adopted some of the reforms she suggested.

In the late 1840s, Dix lobbied Congress to put 12 million acres of public land into a trust fund and then use the money to support programs for the insane. When her efforts failed, Dix left the country. She traveled to Scotland, France, Turkey, and Russia, helping to reform prisons and hospitals there.

Dix had returned home by the time the Civil War began in 1861. Secretary of War Edwin Stanton named her Chief of Nurses for the Union Army. She then formed the Army Nursing Corps and, along with **Dr. Elizabeth Blackwell** in New York, trained volunteer nurses such as **Louisa May Alcott**. Working with Dix was not always easy. She fought with medical administrators and the U.S. Sanitary Commission about nursing duties. And she had strict ideas about who would make a good nurse. She wanted only women who shared her religious beliefs and were plain, over 30 years old, and didn't wear hoop skirts or fancy jewelry.

After the war, Dix continued her hospital and reform work. Her life's work helped lay the groundwork for modern and humane treatment of people in mental hospitals and jails.

∞ Mary Baker Eddy

| born 1821 – died 1910 |

CHRISTIAN SCIENCE FOUNDER

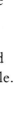

In 1866, Mary Baker Eddy thought she was dying of serious injuries from a fall. She turned to the Bible for comfort and guidance. After reading from the New Testament, Mary believed she understood the method by which Jesus healed people. She also believed her mission was to share this knowledge. In 1879, she established the Mother Church, the First Church of Christ, Scientist, in Boston, Massachusetts.

Widowed by her first husband, and deserted by her second, Mary Baker Eddy moved around New England, living as a guest in people's homes. She started working on *Science and Health*, a book about her Christian Science philosophy of "the superiority of the spiritual over physical power." In *Science and Health*, Eddy explained her belief that good health depends

In the 1800s, many people considered women morally superior to men. Even so, women struggled to gain power in religious organizations. The first female minister of a national church, Antoinette Brown Blackwell, was not ordained until 1853. Three years earlier she had finished theology courses at Oberlin College in Ohio, but was not awarded a divinity degree because she was a woman. Twenty-eight years later, the college finally gave Dr. Blackwell the degree she had earned in 1850.

upon spiritual understanding, rather than just upon standard medical practices. The 456-page book was published in 1875. Over the years, Mary Baker Eddy continually revised her book to make her beliefs clearer. The book went through more than 418 different editions in her lifetime. She personally taught hundreds of students, many of whom were sent out as teachers themselves. But some church members questioned Eddy's methods and authority. The press was sometimes full of bad publicity about church doctrine and attacks on Mrs. Eddy herself. Still, she centralized her leadership in the Mother Church in Boston. In 1908, she established the *Christian Science Monitor*, a newspaper that reflected the church's views and reported objectively on world news events. Mary Baker Eddy died two years later, probably of pneumonia. She left almost $2.5 million to the Christian Science church. There are now about 3,000 Christian Science branches in 57 countries. *Science and Health* has sold over 8,000,000 copies worldwide.

✪ Sarah Edmonds

born 1841 – died 1898

CIVIL WAR SOLDIER

Sarah Edmonds ran away from home when she was a teenager. She disguised herself as a man and became a traveling Bible salesman. When the Civil War broke out, the Union army really needed soldiers. No physical exams were required. Sarah enlisted as Frank Thompson and by June 1861, she was on her way to the front line in Virginia. She served two years, working in a hospital and as a brigade mail carrier. She fought in the battles of Blackburn's Ford and Bull Run, Virginia. Sarah even volunteered for spy duty behind Confederate lines, "disguised" as a woman. In April 1863, Frank deserted, probably to avoid medical attention.

Sarah Edmonds wrote a book about her adventures. But she fictionalized her life story, claiming she was a female nurse, not a male soldier. *Nurse and Spy in the Union Army* was published in 1865 by the same company Frank Thompson had once sold Bibles for. It sold 175,000 copies.

In 1882, Sarah Edmonds applied for veteran's benefits to help support her family. Based on testimonies from her soldier friends, she was awarded a pension of $12 a month.

+ + + + + + + + + + + + + + + + +

 During the Civil War, women set up more than 20,000 relief organizations. Roughly 400 women enlisted as male soldiers in the Union and Confederate armies.

Margaret Fuller

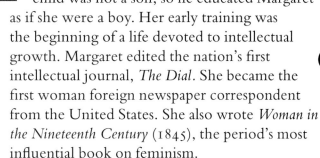

born 1810 – died 1850

AUTHOR, JOURNALIST

Margaret Fuller had an unusual childhood. Her father was disappointed that his firstborn child was not a son, so he educated Margaret as if she were a boy. Her early training was the beginning of a life devoted to intellectual growth. Margaret edited the nation's first intellectual journal, *The Dial*. She became the first woman foreign newspaper correspondent from the United States. She also wrote *Woman in the Nineteenth Century* (1845), the period's most influential book on feminism.

In the late 1820s, Fuller became part of the Massachusetts intellectual circle that included Ralph Waldo Emerson, Henry David Thoreau, and the Alcotts. She began her famous Conversations in Boston in 1839. For five years, Fuller led these lively lecture-discussions, originally for women only. She talked about the major art, education, health, and women's issues with Boston's most notable women.

Fuller was also an enthusiastic supporter of Transcendentalism, a movement that stressed the importance of developing the mind, freeing the spirit, and working toward a perfect society. In 1840, Fuller, Emerson, and a few other Transcendentalists founded *The Dial*. Fuller wrote articles for the journal and then edited it from 1840 to 1842. She moved to New York in 1844 and became the literary critic for the *New York Tribune*. Her newspaper articles created the standards for American arts criticism. She also wrote about politics and economics. In 1846, Fuller traveled to Europe as the *Tribune's* foreign correspondent, where she met the poets Robert and Elizabeth Browning and William Wordsworth, the musician Frederic Chopin, and the Marchesse d'Ossoli, an Italian revolutionary whom Margaret later married.

While the couple were involved in Italy's unsettled politics, Fuller started writing a book about Italian history. She hoped it would be her finest achievement, but she never finished it. In 1850, Margaret, her husband, and their baby fled the trouble in Italy and sailed for the United States. They all died when their boat sank in a storm, just a few hundred feet off the shore of Fire Island, New York.

▲ Margaret Fuller could read Latin when she was seven years old and had learned Greek, French, and Italian by the time she was 14.

1800s – 1880s

Eighteen-year-old JESSIE BENTON FRÉMONT (1824–1902) helped write an adventurous, dramatic report about the Northwest that fired the imaginations of American pioneers. At the time the report was published (1843), Jessie herself had never been farther west than St. Louis, Missouri. Her husband, John Charles Frémont, an army officer, led expeditions into the Far West in the 1840s. The Frémonts worked together: John had the maps and details and Jessie had the literary talent. In 1849, Jessie and her daughter traveled to California, where John had bought land. She wrote about the difficult journey in *A Year of American Travel* (1878). She helped turn their frontier land into a thriving property. Then she helped her husband in his unsuccessful run for president in 1856. By 1873, the Frémonts were bankrupt. Jessie supported the family with her popular articles about Western life. Her work was published in *Atlantic Monthly* and *Harper's*.

⚖ Angelina & Sarah Grimké

born 1805 – died 1879	born 1792 – died 1873

ABOLITIONISTS

The Grimké sisters were born into one of South Carolina's most aristocratic slave-holding families, but they were horrified by the cruelty of slavery. Sarah even broke the law at age 12 by teaching a slave child how to read and write. Both sisters moved North and became two of the greatest abolition speakers.

William Lloyd Garrison printed a letter from Angelina Grimké in his abolitionist newspaper, *The Liberator*. Readers were amazed at the powerful anti-slavery words of a slave owner's daughter. In 1836, the American Anti-Slavery Society invited the sisters to New York to speak.

For the next two years, Sarah and Angelina toured New England and the East delivering their abolitionist message. Their meetings grew from small, women-only "parlor talks" in private homes to large public meetings with both men and women. The Grimkés were among the first women to make speeches on public platforms. Many men booed and whistled during their speeches. Women like **Catharine Beecher** criticized them for stepping out of "women's place." An 1837 Pastoral Letter from the Congregationalist churches called them "unnatural women" who would end up in "shame and ruin." These attitudes convinced the sisters that women's rights were as important as abolition. Angelina wrote that they worked toward "…the breaking of *every* yoke…an emancipation far more glorious than any the world has ever seen."

In 1838, Angelina Grimké became the first woman to speak before a law-making body in the United States when she brought an anti-slavery petition signed by 20,000 women to the Massachusetts State Legislature. That same year, Sarah published *Letters on the Equality of the Sexes*, defending all women's rights to speak out on moral issues.

" " " " " " " " " " " "

💬 *Mine eyes have seen the glory of the coming of the Lord*
He is trampling out the vintage
Where the grapes of wrath are stored.
He hath loosed the fateful lightning
Of His terrible, swift sword;
His truth is marching on!

"The Battle Hymn of the Republic" (1862)

The Atlantic Monthly paid poet-abolitionist-suffragist Julia Ward Howe four dollars for this poem. It became one of the most famous songs of the Civil War.

▲ "I believe it is woman's right to have a voice in all the laws and regulations by which she is to be governed."
– Angelina Grimké (above)

▶ "…whatever is right for a man to do, is right for woman."
– Sarah Grimké, *Letters on the Equality of the Sexes* (1838)

Sarah Josepha Hale

| born 1788 – died 1879 |
| **EDITOR, WRITER** |

"A true woman," Sarah Josepha Hale wrote, was "delicate and timid," and "possessed a sweet dependency." Hale may have been a true woman, but she was also the hard-working first woman editor of a major U.S. magazine. Sarah Josepha Hale was hired as editor of *Ladies Magazine* in Boston in 1828. She wrote most of the articles in the magazine's early days. Her topics included family life, the household duties of women, charity work, and Hale's favorite cause: education for women so they could be better wives and mothers. Sarah had been home-educated, but she supported **Emma Willard**'s and **Mary Lyon**'s schools.

In 1837, Louis Godey bought *Ladies Magazine*, changing its name to *Godey's Lady's Book*. Hale was editor of *Godey's* for almost 40 years. *Godey's* became the largest magazine of its time, with more than 150,000 readers. It ran beautiful color prints of the latest clothes, columns on married women's rights and women in medicine, and advice for women on health and exercise. Hale did not promote equal rights or women's suffrage. Her publishing work supported women's traditional role in the home, but she believed in the "secret, silent influence of women," which made them strong moral forces in the family. Nonetheless, she celebrated women's achievements inside and outside the home in *Woman's Record: or sketches of all distinguished Women, from the Creation to A.D. 1654* (1853). Her book contained 2,500 biographies.

 ++++++++++++++++++

"Mary had a little lamb" became the first words ever recorded when in 1877 Thomas Edison used them with his new invention, the phonograph. The line is from the famous children's poem, originally called *Mary's Lamb* (1830) by its author, Sarah Josepha Hale. Hale also led the movement to make Thanksgiving a national holiday (1863).

1800s – 1880s

Frances Ellen Watkins Harper

born 1825 – died 1911
ABOLITIONIST POET

"I could not rest if I heard the tread/Of a coffle gang to the shambles led/And the mother's shriek of wild despair/Rise like a curse on the trembling air." Frances Harper never rested in her fight for equal rights for African Americans. Throughout the 1850s, she wrote poems and articles and lectured against slavery.

Born in Baltimore, Maryland, Frances Watkins was the daughter of free African-American parents. She worked as a maid and a seamstress, but still found time to write poems. In 1845, her first book of poems, *Forest Leaves*, was published. Her second book, *Poems on Miscellaneous Subjects* (1854), sold 12,000 copies.

In 1854, Frances gave a speech called "Education and the Elevation of the Colored Race" in New Bedford, Massachusetts. For six more years she lectured around the eastern United States, promoting slavery's abolition and women's rights. In 1860, she married Fenton Harper and farmed with him in Ohio until his death in 1864. Frances then returned to lecturing, adding equal education for African Americans and women to her list of causes. She also wrote several books, including *Iola Leroy* (1892), the first novel published by an African-American woman. Watkins was active in many reform organizations, including the National Association of Colored Women, formed in 1896.

+ + + + + + + + + + + + + + + + +

The textile industry which sprang up in the United States in the 1820s depended upon slave and female labor. Enslaved men and women planted and chopped cotton from sunrise to sunset. They had to pick more than 150 pounds a day. In the Northern mills, almost 70 percent of the 58,000 textile workers in the 1830s were women. They worked 12 to 14 hours a day, six days a week, for two dollars and a room. Women workers were among the first to stage "turn-outs" or strikes to protest poor working conditions.

Harriet Hosmer

born 1830 – died c. 1900–1910
SCULPTOR

"Her want of modesty is enough to disgust a dog," an art critic once wrote about the sculptor Harriet Hosmer. The critic was outraged because Hosmer had "casts for the entire *female model* made and exhibited...." She

dared to sculpt the full human body, just as male artists had done for centuries.

Hosmer started her artistic career as a young girl in Watertown, Massachusetts. She scooped up clay from a nearby river-bank and made models. By the time she was a teenager, she had her own sculpture studio at home. Forbidden to study anatomy of the human body in the East because she was a woman, Hosmer moved to St. Louis, where a friend helped her get into classes at Missouri Medical College. In 1852, Harriet moved to Rome, Italy, to study sculpture. Four years later, she became a big success, with her sculpture of Puck, the playful character from English folklore. Hosmer sold *Puck* replicas for $1,000 apiece. In 1856, she sculpted a life-size figure of a robed woman, called Beatrice Cenci, in honor of her Missouri friend. Though she spent most of her working life in Europe in the artistic community that also included **Edmonia Lewis**, Harriet Hosmer is known as one of America's first female sculptors.

◄ Some of Harriet Hosmer's works, such as her bronze statue of Missouri's Senator Thomas Hart Benton (1860) were monumental.

 # Lucy Larcom

born 1824 – died 1893
POET

Lucy Larcom went to work in the Lowell, Massachusetts, textile mills when she was 11 years old. "It was like a young man's pleasure in entering upon business for himself," she later wrote, adding how glad she was to be among "active, interesting girls, whose lives…had principle and purpose distinctly their own." Lucy changed bobbins, the spools that held thread for the spinning frames, from five in the morning until seven at night, six days a week. Unlike most "factory girls" of the 1830s and 1840s who worked for short periods before marrying, Lucy spent several years in the mills. She frequently wrote poems for the *Lowell Offering,* and much of her later work was influenced by her experiences in the mills. In 1846, Larcom left Lowell to teach school in Illinois and attend college herself. She returned to Massachusetts eight years later to teach at Wheaton College. Lucy continued to write poems, which were sentimental and popular. In 1875, *An Idyl of Work,* Larcom's book of blank verse about mill life, was published. Her most famous book was the autobiographical *A New England Girlhood.*

MARGARET KNIGHT (1838–1914) invented a machine in 1868 that made one of the most useful objects in any store or household: the square-bottomed brown paper bag. She patented it in 1870. It was just one of her 27 known patents for things like window sashes, shoe-cutting machines, and auto-motive parts. Margaret got her start when she saw a worker in a New Hampshire textile mill injured by a moving part from his loom. Twelve-year-old Margaret invented a safety device for the loom.

✏ Edmonia Lewis

born 1830 – died c. 1908

SCULPTOR

Edmonia Lewis was one of the first American artists of color to gain widespread recognition for her work. Born near Albany, New York, Lewis had an African-American father and a Chippewa mother. As a young girl, Edmonia lived among the Chippewa, who called her Wildfire. Her brother encouraged her to attend Oberlin College in Ohio. After graduating in 1862, Lewis moved to Boston, where she was praised – and paid – for her sculptures of Civil War figures like John Brown. Lewis used the money to move to Rome, Italy. There she continued to sculpt busts of important figures such as the poet Henry Wadsworth Longfellow and Abraham Lincoln. She also met other sculptors such as **Harriet Hosmer**.

Many of the sculptures Lewis produced in the 1860s and 1870s were inspired by her antislavery beliefs. One of her most famous sculptures, *Forever Free*, shows two freed slaves wearing broken chains to symbolize their emancipation. Another sculpture, *Hagar in the Wilderness*, was inspired by a biblical story about an enslaved woman and by Lewis's sympathy "for all women who have struggled and suffered." In 1876, six of Edmonia Lewis's sculptures were displayed at the Philadelphia Centennial Exposition for the 100th anniversary of the Declaration of Independence. It is thought she remained in Rome for the rest of her life, although there is no exact record of her death.

++++++++++++++++++

Female lawyers were rare in the United States in the 19th century – and the legal profession tried hard to keep it that way. When Myra Bradwell attempted to become a lawyer in Illinois in 1869, she was refused. Her case went all the way to the Supreme Court, which, in 1873, said women were not covered by the Fourteenth Amendment that gave citizens equal protection of the law. The Court left it up to the states to decide which citizens had what rights. Bradwell eventually convinced the Illinois legislature to allow women to become lawyers. Still, when Belva Lockwood won her legal battle to appear before the U.S. Supreme Court, there were only 60 female lawyers practicing in the whole country.

⚖ Belva Lockwood

born 1830 – died 1917

LAWYER

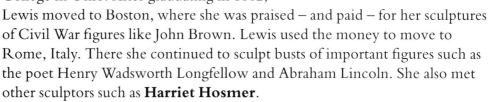

Columbia College Law School refused to admit 39-year old Belva Lockwood because her presence would "distract the attention of the young men." Lockwood got a law degree anyway from Washington, D.C.'s National University Law School in 1873. After graduating, she went on to attract national attention.

In 1876, the U.S. Supreme Court refused to let Lockwood argue a case before it because she was a woman. For three years, Lockwood campaigned for her right to work as a lawyer in the country's highest courts. She drafted a bill and lobbied Congress until it passed legislation in 1879. It said that any female lawyer with a good reputation and three years' practice in state supreme courts could now address the federal Supreme Court. Lockwood became the first woman to do so. Two of the highlights of her legal career were winning $5 million for the Eastern Cherokee in their case against the government and successfully arguing for the right of an African-American lawyer to practice before the Supreme Court.

Throughout her career, Lockwood was also a devoted suffragist. She supported **Victoria Woodhull**'s unsuccessful bid for the presidency in 1872, and ran for president herself in 1884, representing the National Equal Rights Party.

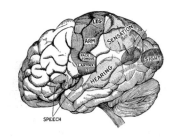

++++++++++++++++++

By 1880, half of the colleges in the United States admitted women and men. Almost one-third of all college graduates were women. Still, some scientists and male reformers complained that too much intellectual work would harm women's reproductive organs. Others thought women's brains were too small for academic study.

🎓 Mary Lyon

born 1797 – died 1849

EDUCATOR

When Mary Lyon wanted to attend Sanderson Academy in Ashfield, Massachusetts, she did not let the fact that she had no money stop her. Instead, she wove two blankets and offered them as payment. The school accepted and Mary enrolled in 1817. Twenty years later, Lyon founded her own school, Mount Holyoke Female Seminary. It was one of the first all-female colleges in the United States.

Lyon became a full-time teacher at the Ipswich Female Seminary in 1828. There, she realized that female education too often depended upon whether men would pay for women's schools.

Lyon began fundraising for her own school in 1834. Her aim was to provide "a solid, extensive, and well-balanced English education [to] prepare ladies to be *educators* of children and youth." She planned to charge low tuition and have students be responsible for cooking and cleaning. This would cut school costs and teach the students to take care of themselves.

Mary raised over $27,000. On November 8, 1837, the Mount Holyoke Female Seminary in South Hadley, Massachusetts, opened its doors to 80 young women. Lyon served as principal for 12 years. Courses at Mount Holyoke included French, music, grammar, algebra, ancient and modern history, philosophy, and sciences. There was even a small laboratory. At the time such a curriculum for women was revolutionary. Today Mount Holyoke College is one of the nation's top women's colleges.

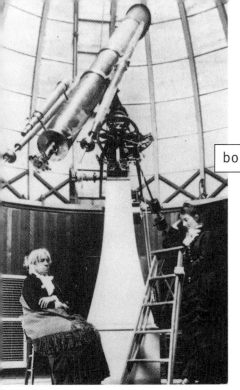

"The eye that directs a needle in the delicate meshes of embroidery, will equally bisect a star with the spider web of the micrometer,"
– Maria Mitchell (above, left), diary entry, 1878.

· · · · · · · · · · · · · · · · · ·

 DOLLEY MADISON (1768–1849) became First Lady in 1809. She had already helped Thomas Jefferson, a widower, entertain during his presidency. Dolley was smart, well-informed, and well-liked. She was also a quick thinker. When 3,000 British troops marched into Washington and set the city on fire in 1814, Dolley saved many valuable items from the White House. Madison rescued the famous Gilbert Stuart painting of George Washington as well as important state documents. She disguised herself as a farm woman and escaped before the British torched the White House.

Maria Mitchell

| born 1818 – died 1889 |
| **ASTRONOMER** |

Maria Mitchell, who lived on tiny Nantucket Island, Massachusetts, loved "sky sweeping," as she called looking at the sky through a telescope. She worked by day as a librarian in the Nantucket Athenaeum, where she could also get books to study mathematics and navigation. But her true work and joy began at night, studying the stars with her father, who had taught her about astronomy. On October 1, 1847, using a two-inch telescope, Mitchell discovered a new comet. People called it "Miss Mitchell's Comet." The King of Denmark gave her a gold medal. And in 1848, Mitchell became the first woman elected to the American Academy of Arts and Sciences.

Travels to Europe followed, where Mitchell met other astronomers and scientists. Her work captured the attention of women leaders. In 1858, a group of them gave her a new, very precise telescope on behalf of "the women of America."

Matthew Vassar offered Mitchell an important post in 1865 as director of the observatory and professor of astronomy at his new school, Vassar Female College in Poughkeepsie, New York. Even better, he gave her a 12-inch telescope, then the third largest telescope in the United States. Mitchell took the job and began a teaching career that lasted more than 20 years. With the help of her Vassar students, she focused most of her studies on the sun, Saturn, and Jupiter. In 1873, Mitchell founded the Association for the Advancement of Women (AAW) to promote women's achievements and help solve some of the challenges they faced.

Lucretia Mott

| born 1793 – died 1880 |
| **ABOLITIONIST, SUFFRAGIST** |

Lucretia Mott, a Quaker minister, practiced what she preached. She was opposed to slavery. She never bought cotton cloth, cane sugar, or any other product of slave labor, and her home was a stop on the Underground Railroad. She was not allowed to attend the first American Anti-Slavery Society convention in 1833 because she was a woman, so she founded and became president of the Philadelphia Female Anti-Slavery Society. Then, when Mott and the other American women representatives were denied seats at the 1840 World Anti-Slavery Convention in London, she joined her new friend **Elizabeth Cady Stanton** in the fight for women's equality. Mott and Stanton were two of the organizers of the first Women's Rights Convention in 1848 at Seneca Falls, New York.

Accompanied by her husband, James Mott, a fellow Quaker, Lucretia crossed the country lecturing on abolition of slavery, equal rights, temperance, and world peace. Some people called Lucretia's public speeches "psalms of life," but others jeered and even physically threatened her. An anti-abolitionist mob once raided a meeting of her Philadelphia anti-slavery society and set the building on fire.

Lucretia Mott was named president of the American Equal Rights Association in 1866, a group devoted to African-American and women's suffrage. She continued to be publicly and privately active until her death at the age of 87.

◉ Annie Oakley PHOEBE ANN MOZEE

born 1860 – died 1926

SHARPSHOOTER

▲ "Annie Oakley" is slang for a ticket punched full of holes. The real Annie was famous for throwing a playing card in the air and riddling it with bullet holes.

Phoebe Ann Mozee was a dead shot even as a child. She helped support her family by shooting game and even earned enough to pay off the mortgage on the family farm outside Cincinnati, Ohio. In 1876, as a teenager, she entered a shooting match with a champion marksman, Frank Butler. She won the match – and a husband. Phoebe changed her name to Annie Oakley and appeared in vaudeville shows with Frank.

Oakley became world-famous when she and Frank joined Buffalo Bill's Wild West Show in 1885. She toured with Buffalo Bill throughout the United States and Europe for more than 15 years. Her skill with a gun was legendary. She could hit a target shooting backward over her shoulder, shoot a dime from between her husband's thumb and fingers, and shoot the flames off revolving candles while standing on a galloping horse. At the request of the Crown Prince of Germany, Oakley once shot the ashes off his cigarette. She continued performing even after being injured in a railroad accident in 1901. Annie Oakley's sharpshooting was captured on film by Thomas Edison in 1894. Irving Berlin later wrote a famous musical, *Annie Get Your Gun,* about the woman many called "Lady Sure Shot."

◉ **ESTHER MORRIS** (1814–1902) invited the political candidates in Wyoming's 1869 election to tea. She got each man to promise that if he won, he would introduce a woman's suffrage bill to the state legislature. Esther claimed women's votes would support law, order, and morality in what was then a rough frontier territory. The Wyoming amendment was passed in 1869, and Morris was appointed America's first woman justice of the peace the following year. She tried 70 cases. None of her decisions was ever overturned by a higher court.

LYDIA E. PINKHAM'S VEGETABLE COMPOUND

Physicians Use it and Prescribe it.

The Weary Woman's Sure Friend.

▲ The Women's Christian Temperance Union backed the use of Lydia E. Pinkham's vegetable compound. They must not have known about one of its ingredients – early batches were 18 percent alcohol!

• • • • • • • • • • • • • • • • •

 VINNIE REAM (1847–1914) was 18 years old when she became the first woman awarded a Congressional sculpture commission. In 1866, she received $10,000 to do a life-size sculpture of recently assassinated President Abraham Lincoln for the rotunda of the Capitol Building in Washington, D.C. Ream went to Italy to choose the marble herself. Though her sculptures were well-received, Ream gave up art in 1878 when she married, in response to her husband's wishes.

$ Lydia E. Pinkham

born 1819 – died 1883

ENTREPRENEUR

"The Greatest Medical Discovery Since the Dawn of History" claimed the label on Lydia E. Pinkham's Vegetable Compound. Pinkham turned a home herbal remedy "for various ills" into a business that would make $300,000 a year.

Pinkham started bottling and selling her compound in 1875, to support her family in Lynn, Massachusetts. She added alcohol to preserve her compound of unicorn root, life root, and other herbs. Pinkham's Vegetable Compound was promoted as a cure for "female complaints" such as menopause and menstrual problems, cramps, headaches, and fatigue. She patented her medicine in 1876 and put her picture on the label. Her three sons acted as her salesmen and found many eager buyers. Lydia Pinkham's became one of the best-known faces of the 19th century.

According to some authorities, Pinkham's Vegetable Compound was only effective because of its alcohol content. But Pinkham's common-sense approach to women's health helped many women, who at the time knew little about the basic facts of health and hygiene. She encouraged her customers to write to her "Department of Advice." She personally answered hundreds of letters, urging good diet, exercise, cleanliness, and, of course, three spoonfuls of the Vegetable Compound a day. She also wrote a booklet on sex and reproduction. Pinkham's product, now called an "herbal compound," is still sold.

⚖ Charlotte E. Ray

born 1850 – died 1911

LAWYER

Charlotte Ray applied to Howard University law school in Washington, D.C., as C.E. Ray to hide the fact that she was a woman and make sure her application got serious consideration. She was accepted. In 1872, Ray graduated and became the first African-American woman lawyer in the United States.

Charlotte's father, Charles Bennett Ray, an abolitionist, Underground Railroad contact, and editor of the *Colored American*, encouraged his daughter to get an education. Charlotte left the family home in New York City and attended the Institution for the Education of Colored Youth in Washington until 1869. Then she worked as a teacher at Howard in the daytime and attended the university's law school at night. An outstanding student, Ray was invited to join the honor society Phi Beta Kappa.

After graduation, Ray became the first woman allowed to practice law in the District of Columbia. Many states refused to let women work as lawyers. In Washington, it was legal, but it wasn't easy being a female lawyer, especially for an African American. Charlotte opened her own law office, but many people were still too prejudiced to bring her their legal business. Without enough clients, Ray was forced to close. She moved back to New York City, taught in the Brooklyn public schools, and worked actively in the National Association of Colored Women and the National Woman Suffrage Association.

⬟ Sacajawea

| born c. 1787 – died c. 1812 |
| **EXPLORER** |

On April 7, 1805, Sacajawea tied her baby to her back and headed out on one of the most important journeys in United States history. She traveled with Meriwether Lewis and William Clark on the United States government's first exploration of the Pacific Northwest.

Sacajawea was a member of the Lemhi band of the Shoshoni tribe who lived in what is now central Idaho. When she was about 13 years old, she was captured in tribal fighting and then either sold or gambled away to Toussaint Charbonneau, a fur trapper. They lived near the Missouri River in what is now North Dakota. Charbonneau was hired as an interpreter for the Lewis and Clark expedition. He brought Sacajawea so she could speak with and

smooth the way with any Shoshoni. For the next year, Sacajawea, Charbonneau, Lewis, and Clark traveled across the Rocky Mountains through the Pacific Northwest and back. It was an 8,000-mile trip. Sacajawea helped negotiate peaceful passage through tribal lands. She showed the explorers which wild foods were edible when supplies ran low. She gathered firewood, cooked, and washed the laundry. She made moccasins and once saved valuable mapping instruments and records when one of the expedition's boats overturned in a storm. Along the way, Sacajawea was reunited with her

◀ This sculpture of Sacajawea by Alice Cooper was the first statue to honor a woman for her daring work. It was dedicated in 1905 by **Susan B. Anthony** and **Dr. Anna Howard Shaw**.

++++++++++++++++++

Explorers, homesteaders, and the discovery of gold in 1848 at Sutter's Mill, California, brought change and suffering to the lives of Native Americans throughout the West. Many were forced to move to reservations in the mid-1800s. Native American women were traditionally in charge of farming tribal lands, which they usually did cooperatively. But the land on reservations was often barren. Missionaries and government agents discouraged communal work and they tried to "re-educate" tribal people with European religious, cultural, and family values. For many Native American women, this meant a loss of power. In the late 1860s, U.S. government treaties with Native American tribes were destroyed or ignored.

brother, who had become chief of the Lemhi. She convinced him to provide horses and guide the explorers down the Clearwater and Columbia Rivers. When the party neared the Pacific in 1806, Sacajawea made her only personal request of the trip. She wanted to see the "great waters" with "the monstrous fish," or whale. Lewis and Clark took Sacajawea and Charbonneau in the canoes headed downriver to the ocean. There they saw the remains of a beached whale.

After the expedition, Sacajawea and her husband returned to North Dakota in 1806. Her death was reported around 1812.

⚖ Elizabeth Cady Stanton

born 1818 – died 1893

ABOLITIONIST, SUFFRAGIST

When she was a child, Elizabeth overheard a widow crying in her father's law office because the law said she had no property rights. Elizabeth got a pair of scissors to cut this unfair law from her father's legal books. Her fight for women's rights had begun.

Elizabeth graduated from **Emma Willard**'s Troy Female Seminary in 1832 and married abolitionist Henry Stanton in 1840. She insisted the word "obey" be taken out of the wedding vows. On their honeymoon, Elizabeth and Henry Stanton attended the World's Anti-Slavery Convention in London, England. Elizabeth was outraged that women delegates, such as **Lucretia Mott**, were not allowed to speak. The women were forced to sit behind a screen in the gallery upstairs.

When Mott and Stanton met again near Seneca Falls, New York, where Stanton lived, they and three other women planned the First Women's Rights Convention to discuss "the social, civil, and religious rights of women." The historic meeting, organized in barely a week, took place in Seneca Falls in July 1848. To the organizers' surprise, 300 people, including 40 men, showed up. Stanton made her first speech: "We hold these truths to be self-evident, that all men *and women* are created equal...." Her Declaration of Sentiments was based on the Declaration of Independence. It listed 18 legal areas where women wanted reform. Stanton also included her boldest demand: the right to vote. Lucretia Mott worried that this was too radical. Henry Stanton thought so too. He left town for the

◄ "The true woman is as yet a dream of the future."
– Elizabeth Cady Stanton said at the International Council of Women, 1888.

weekend when he heard what his wife was proposing, but Stanton stood firm. The suffrage resolution passed by a slim majority.

Stanton wrote articles for the *New York Tribune* and **Amelia Bloomer**'s *The Lily*. When she met **Susan B. Anthony** in 1851, they began an intense working relationship to address women's rights and suffrage, temperance, and the abolition of slavery. In 1863, during the Civil War, the two formed the Women's Loyal National League. The League collected more than 300,000 signatures supporting the Thirteenth Amendment to end slavery.

After the Civil War, the suffrage movement split over whether to link female suffrage with African-American male suffrage. In 1869, Stanton and Anthony formed the National Woman Suffrage Association. The NWSA opposed passage of the Fifteenth Amendment, which gave the vote to African-American men but ignored all women. The amendment passed anyway. The NWSA then lobbied for a constitutional amendment giving women the vote. Stanton and Anthony wrote, lectured, lobbied, and traveled across the country to promote women's suffrage.

Elizabeth Cady Stanton spent the rest of her life fighting for women's rights. She became president of the National American Woman Suffrage Association (NAWSA) in 1890, the group that united the NWSA with **Lucy Stone's** American Woman Suffrage Association. Stanton worked with Anthony on the first volumes of the *History of Woman Suffrage* (1881–1922). She also published *The Woman's Bible* in 1895, criticizing the poor portrayal of women in the Bible.

> " " " " " " " " " "
>
> *Lucy Stoner:* a woman who kept her own last name when she married. It comes from the example set by **Lucy Stone**, who called herself Mrs. Stone after she married Elizabeth Blackwell's brother Henry in 1855. At their wedding, the bride and groom read a protest against current marriage laws that "refuse to recognize the wife as an independent, rational being."

1800S – 1880S

⚖ Lucy Stone

born 1815 – died 1902

ABOLITIONIST, SUFFRAGIST

Even as a child, Lucy Stone doubted the popular idea that men were better than women. She planned to learn Hebrew and Greek so she could read original texts of the Bible and see for herself if passages used to support male authority were properly translated.

Born on the family farm in West Brookfield, Massachusetts, Lucy paid for her own schooling because her father did not believe in educating women. Lucy worked for nine years as a teacher to save the $70 she needed to attend Oberlin College in Ohio. Stone supported herself through college by doing housework and teaching.

In 1847, Stone graduated from Oberlin with honors and became a lecturer for the American Anti-Slavery Society. She was an impressive speaker who drew large audiences to her abolitionist and women's rights lectures. She attracted fellow abolitionist **Susan B. Anthony** to the women's suffrage cause when she spoke at an 1850 Massachusetts convention. Anthony, **Elizabeth Cady Stanton**, and Stone worked for passage of the Thirteenth Amendment outlawing slavery. But the question of the Fifteenth Amendment split them apart and divided the women's rights movement.

All three leaders wanted the Fifteenth Amendment, which gave African-American men the vote, to include all women as well. Stone supported the amendment unconditionally. Anthony and Stanton opposed it if the amendment was not rewritten to include women. Stone and supporters such as **Julia Ward Howe** founded the American Woman Suffrage Association in 1869 to follow their own political agenda. Stone also founded, funded, and edited its weekly newspaper, the *Woman's Journal*. The *Journal* was published for 47 years and was considered "the voice of the woman's movement."

> "*Grief and constant anxiety kill nearly as many women as men die on the battlefield,*" Mary Boykin Chestnut, the wife of a Confederate politician, wrote in her 400,000-word *Diary From Dixie*. Her diary is an important, detailed record of life in the South during and after the Civil War. "*Nothing is left now, but the bare land and debts,*" she concluded.

Harriet Beecher Stowe

born 1811 – died 1896

NOVELIST

"Is this the little woman who made this great war?" President Abraham Lincoln supposedly asked when he met Harriet Beecher Stowe at the White House in 1862. Ten years earlier, Stowe had written the best-seller *Uncle Tom's Cabin*, a story about the injustices of slavery. Her memorable characters, such as the kind, religious slave Uncle Tom and the cruel overseer Simon Legree, became important symbols of the slave system. The book sold over 3,000,000 copies by the outbreak of the Civil War.

Harriet came from a family that gave a lot of thought to moral issues. Her father and seven brothers were respected ministers, while her sister **Catharine Beecher** promoted women's health and domestic education. Harriet taught in her sister's school before marrying a college professor. She bore seven children and wrote short pieces to earn money for her family.

Stowe had read a great deal about slavery. In 1851, she wrote the last chapter of *Uncle Tom's Cabin* first, and worked backward. She said she "worked in a trance," believing she was "the instrument of

God." *Uncle Tom's Cabin* was first published in 40 installments in an anti-slavery newspaper. In 1852, it sold 3,000 copies the first day it appeared in book form. Stowe went on to write more novels, as well as essays, children's books, and biographies.

⊛ Susie King Taylor

born 1848 – died 1912

CIVIL WAR NURSE

Before the Civil War, it was illegal for slaves in the South to learn to read and write. Susie Baker, born a slave in Georgia, had a wise grandmother who made sure she got an education anyway. Susie used her early training to help teach other African Americans, and she later helped soldiers learn to read and write, too.

Susie lived with her grandmother, Dolly Reed, in Savannah, Georgia. She secretly went to a freed woman's house for schooling, her books hidden in a paper wrapping. In 1862, Susie fled to Sea Island, which was controlled by the Union. There she started a school, teaching children during the day and adults at night. That same year she met and married Edward King, a soldier with the U.S. Colored Troops.

Susie King traveled with her husband, working first as a troop laundress and cook. War casualties mounted, and Susie saw how much the troops needed medical care. She quickly started caring for injured soldiers, becoming the first African-American nurse in the Union army. King was a gifted nurse and soon spent most of her time caring for the wounded. She used whatever moments were left to teach the African-American soldiers how to read and write.

After the war, King returned to Savannah and opened a school for the newly freed African Americans. When her husband died, King moved to Boston, Massachusetts, and remarried. She wrote her autobiography, *My Life in Camp with the 33rd United States Colored Troops* (1902). Susie King Taylor, unlike **Sarah Edmonds** and **Harriet Tubman**, received no pension for her important war efforts.

+ + + + + + + + + + + + + + + +

By law, no one in the United States could import slaves after 1808. This had a serious impact on enslaved African-American women. Plantation owners bribed or threatened female slaves into having as many children as possible. Their children born into slavery could be sold off at the owner's whim. Many African-American women and girls were sexually abused by their owners. Some white plantation women also treated these slaves harshly.

1800s – 1880s

⊛ Sojourner Truth ISABELLA BAUMFREE/VAN WAGENER

born c. 1797 – died 1883

ABOLITIONIST, SUFFRAGIST

Sojourner Truth always said her name was a divine inspiration: "The Lord gave me Sojourner because I was to travel up and down the land showin' the people their sins and bein' a sign unto them…and the Lord gave me Truth, because I was to declare truth unto people." Her "declarations" made her one of the great figures of the abolition and women's rights movements.

Isabella Baumfree (Truth's slave name) escaped from slavery in upstate New York. She and two of her children eventually moved to New York City, where she worked as a servant and joined an evangelical religious group. Isabella had always been a mystic and believed she had divine experiences. In 1843, her "voices" told her to take to the road using her new name, Sojourner Truth. She left home with a quarter and a new dress. The 46-year-old woman walked alone through Long Island, New York, and Connecticut, stopping at churches, camp meetings, and street corners to preach God's message. People should love one another, Sojourner Truth told her listeners. She was tall and gaunt and, as some observers remarked, had "the air of a queen." She electrified audiences with her deep, powerful voice and won many people to the anti-slavery movement.

Sojourner Truth visited Northampton, Massachusetts, where she learned about the abolition movement and became one of its strongest advocates. She headed West in 1850, speaking out against slavery, often with Frederick Douglass, another great African-American abolitionist and former slave. Sojourner was often heckled and sometimes even beaten while touring Kansas, Missouri, and Indiana. That same year she had her life story, *Narrative of Sojourner Truth,* written for her. Like most slaves, she had never been taught to read or write. In 1850, she also took up the women's rights cause. Truth was a frequent – and controversial – speaker at women's conventions. Many people, including some women, did not think an African-American woman should speak in public.

In the 1850s, Sojourner Truth and her family settled in Battle Creek, Michigan. During the Civil War, she urged African Americans to fight for the Union and she collected food and clothing for free black soldiers. In 1864, the famous orator was received by President Abraham Lincoln in the White House.

" " " " " " " " " " " "

Q *"That man over there says that women need to be helped into carriages, and lifted over ditches, and have the best place everywhere. Nobody ever helps me into carriages, or over mud puddles or gives me any best place. And a'n't I a woman? Look at me! Look at my arm! I have ploughed, and planted, and gathered into barns, and no man can head me. And a'n't I a woman? I could work as much and eat as much as a man – when I could get it – and bear the lash as well. And a'n't I a woman? I have borne thirteen children and seen 'em most all sold off to slavery, and when I cried out with my mother's grief, none but Jesus heard me. And a'n't I a woman?"*

– Sojourner Truth's speech at the Ohio Women's Rights Convention, 1851

Harriet Tubman

| born 1820 – died 1913 |
| **ABOLITIONIST** |

The words on her gravestone read "Servant of God, Well Done." In her lifetime, Harriet was called General Tubman and Moses because of her daring rescues of more than 300 enslaved African Americans.

Harriet Tubman was born a slave on a plantation in Maryland. Like many slaves, she was overworked, whipped, and abused. When she was only 13 years old, a white overseer hit her in the head with a two-pound weight. Harriet's skull was fractured and she suffered from blackouts for the rest of her life. But she didn't let this stop her from getting what she wanted – freedom, for herself and for others.

In 1849, Tubman escaped to Philadelphia and got a job in a hotel. Within a year, she took on a second, more important job: "conductor" on the Underground Railroad. The Underground Railroad was a secret route of hiding places, or "stations," for slaves escaping to the North and Canada. The system started in 1838 and was run by white and African-American abolitionists. Over the next ten years, Harriet made 19 trips back to Maryland as a conductor. She brought her brothers, sisters, and, in 1857, her aged parents to freedom.

Despite the $40,000 reward slave owners offered for her capture, Harriet kept traveling the Underground Railroad and said she "never lost a passenger." Tubman and her party traveled only at night, especially the longer winter nights, to avoid being seen. They spent days hiding in swamps, forests, barns, and abolitionists' "safe" houses. Harriet and the runaway slaves faced torture or death if they were caught. She once pulled her pistol on a slave who wanted to turn back, thereby endangering the whole group. "You go on or

 DR. MARY EDWARDS WALKER (1832–1919) wanted desperately to work as a surgeon during the Civil War. The Union army was not interested in female doctors, especially ones who smoked and, like **Amelia Bloomer**, wore pants. Dr. Walker worked unofficially in battlefield tent hospitals in Virginia until she finally won an appointment as an army surgeon in 1863. She took risks, often crossing into Confederate territory to care for civilians, and was captured and imprisoned in 1864 in Richmond, Virginia. In 1865, she was awarded the Medal of Honor for her war efforts. She became eccentric in her later years.

1800S – 1880S

◄ Harriet Tubman (far left) with some of the people she helped escape slavery.

die," General Tubman ordered the man. He went on.

Tubman believed God had commanded her to help free the slaves. Her extraordinary faith helped her make quick decisions and face all kinds of dangers. On one trip down South, she saw her former master approaching on a town street. Tubman let loose the chickens she had just bought. As they ran around cackling and flapping, she chased after them, her head bent down. Her master passed right by without seeing her.

During the Civil War, Tubman served as a nurse, a cook, and a spy, crossing Confederate army lines to get information from slaves in South Carolina. At the war's end, she went back to Auburn, New York, where she had bought a small farm from an abolitionist in 1858. Eventually her home became the "Harriet Tubman Home for Indigent Aged Negroes." Tubman petitioned Congress for a pension for her war services. In 1898, she was finally given a $20-a-month pension.

+ + + + + + + + + + + + + + + +

Oberlin College in Ohio opened in 1833. It was founded by abolitionists and was the first college in the United States to admit qualified students of either gender and of any race.

Emma Willard

born 1787 – died 1870

EDUCATOR

When Emma Willard was 13, she taught herself geometry. At the age of 34, she opened the Troy Female Seminary so that other young women could learn mathematics – plus science, history, geography, and all the other courses usually taught only at men's schools.

Emma Hart grew up on a farm in Connecticut. She was encouraged intellectually by her father, with whom she discussed philosophy in between all the farm chores. Emma became a teacher in Middlebury, Vermont, where she met and married Dr. John Willard. To help support the family, Emma founded the Middlebury Female Seminary in 1814, teaching students in her home. Her school was a success. In 1819, she wanted to expand, and she petitioned the legislature in the nearby state of New York for money. Willard's *Plan for Improving Female Education* was an outstanding document that argued for a woman's right to an education, which "should seek to bring its subjects to the perfection of their moral, intellectual, and physical nature." Her *Plan* was respected by people such as John Adams and Thomas Jefferson but was still rejected by the New

◄ Emma Willard was a resourceful teacher. When she ran a school in her home, she cut up potatoes and turnips to show geometric principles.

York State Legislature. In 1821, when the town of Troy, New York, offered to raise $4,000 for her, Emma Willard started her women's school there. Ninety students enrolled. By 1831, the Seminary had over 300 students.

The Troy Female Seminary was unique for its time. Emma Willard developed the courses, the teaching methods, and even wrote many of the textbooks. Many of her students became teachers, spreading the Willard education style throughout the country. Some students, such as **Elizabeth Cady Stanton**, later became leaders in the women's movement, although Emma herself did not embrace the fight for women's political rights. She remained focused on education, traveling throughout the country speaking on behalf of state-supported education for girls.

+ + + + + + + + + + + + + + + + +

Temperance, a movement to ban alcohol sales and saloons, started in the 1820s and 1830s. It grew into one of the nation's largest women's reform movements. Women were drawn to the movement because most of them had no legal protection from the abuse or poverty caused by drunken husbands. Many women and some men felt that liquor was a threat to the family and the cause of many social problems. Most temperance supporters gathered petitions or held meetings. But Carrie Nation brought the movement a lot of publicity. The six-foot-tall woman entered saloons in Kansas and did what she called a "hatchetation." She smashed liquor bottles and barrooms with her ax. Nation was not typical of most temperance workers. She was also thought to have suffered from mental illness.

Frances Willard

born 1839 – died 1898

TEMPERANCE LEADER, SUFFRAGIST

Frances Willard grew up on a farm on the Wisconsin frontier. She had only four years of formal education, but went on to become the country's first female college president and the leader of one of the most powerful reform groups of its time, the Women's Christian Temperance Union (WCTU).

As a young woman, Willard taught in a number of Methodist schools, traveled widely through Europe with a wealthy friend, studied European arts and languages, and read feminist writings by people such as **Margaret Fuller**. In 1870, she was appointed president of a new college, the Evanston College for Ladies, in Illinois. Three years later the college became part of Northwestern University. Frances eventually left the university to work for the temperance movement.

Willard became the star speaker, organizer, and eventually president of the Women's Christian Temperance Union, formed in 1874. The organization soon had over 200,000 members. Frances saw the WCTU as a perfect platform from which to launch crusades for a variety of health, education, and social reforms, as well as for women's right to vote. (She was a member of **Lucy Stone**'s American Woman Suffrage Association.)

▲ "Do Everything!" was Frances Willard's personal motto. "For God and Home and Native Land," was the one she coined for the Women's Christian Temperance Union.

+ + + + + + + + + + + + + + + +

Western settlement provided opportunities for some women. The U.S. government's Homestead Acts of 1860 and 1890 gave men and women each 320 acres of land to build on. Women could hold the land titles in their own names. But this was all at the expense of Native American people. Helen Hunt Jackson's book *A Century of Dishonor* (1881) reported on unjust government tribal policies. Jackson created more of a public stir about the "Indian question" when she published her book *Ramona* in 1884. Her novel about a young Native American girl's hard life in California was a huge success.

Frances Willard served as WCTU president for almost 20 years, from 1879 to 1898. She was a genius at organizing and helped turn the WCTU into a powerful national institution that developed social programs and pressured politicians for reform. Willard created 39 departments, each with a specific focus such as suffrage (headed by **Dr. Anna Howard Shaw**), prison reform, health and hygiene, and labor law reform. Each department had a leader at the national WCTU level. The national union also supervised 57 state unions, who in turn supervised 10,000 local unions. Willard herself often traveled as many as 20,000 miles a year, crisscrossing the country, attending WCTU conventions and giving stirring speeches, encouraging women to join all the WCTU efforts. Willard called her program Home Protection. She claimed prohibition, the vote, and all the other WCTU reform agendas were necessary to protect women's traditional roles as homemaker, wife, and mother.

Linking temperance with suffrage did cause some problems. When Willard invited **Susan B. Anthony** to speak at the 1881 WCTU convention, some conservative members walked out because they did not share Anthony's suffragist views. When Willard tried to create a new political party by merging Home Protection and The National Prohibition Party, members of each group balked. Some WCTU women wanted to avoid politics, while many prohibitionists weren't interested in women's suffrage. Throughout it all, the powerful liquor industry fought against giving women the vote. They were afraid that female temperance voters would pass prohibition laws.

Sarah Winnemucca THOC·ME·TONY

born c. 1844 – died 1891

NATIVE AMERICAN ACTIVIST

She negotiated, lectured, wrote a book, and met with President Rutherford B. Hayes on behalf of her people, the Paiute of Nevada. Fluent in three tribal languages, as well as Spanish and English, Sarah Winnemucca had worked as an interpreter and peacekeeper among the Paiute, the United States army, and Bureau of Indian Affairs (BIA) agents in the 1860s and 1870s. In 1878, she also served as a spy for the army, traveling over 100 miles alone to rescue her father, held captive by the Bannock tribe. She relayed important information to the army, then at war with the Bannock.

Though Winnemucca had helped the U.S. government, she could not stop it from taking the Paiute's tribal land. In the dead of winter, the Paiute were forced to move onto a Washington reservation. Winnemucca protested to President Rutherford B. Hayes and Secretary of the Interior Carl Schurz in 1880. Schurz promised the Paiute would be given their own land. Corrupt BIA agents refused to honor that promise. Sarah Winnemucca went on a lecture tour to publicize the sufferings of her people and fight for policy reform. She wrote an enormously successful book, *Life Among the Piutes* (1883), and gathered hundreds of signatures on a petition to the government to give her tribe their own land. Congress passed a bill ordering it done, but no one executed the order.

Ⓢ Victoria Woodhull

| born 1838 – died 1927 |

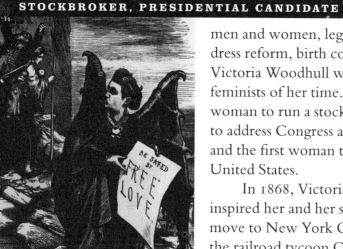

STOCKBROKER, PRESIDENTIAL CANDIDATE

Her enemies called her Mrs. Satan, because of her views on free love, equal moral standards for men and women, legalized prostitution, dress reform, birth control, and socialism. Victoria Woodhull was one of the most radical feminists of her time. She was also the first woman to run a stock brokerage firm, the first to address Congress about female suffrage, and the first woman to run for president of the United States.

In 1868, Victoria had a vision, which inspired her and her sister Tennessee Claflin to move to New York City. There they met the railroad tycoon Cornelius Vanderbilt, who shared their interest in spiritualism. In 1870, he financially backed the sisters when they opened Woodhull, Claflin & Company, a Wall Street stock brokerage. Their company reportedly made nearly half a million dollars in its first year. Woodhull used some of the money to publish *Woodhull & Claflin's Weekly* to promote her radical views.

Woodhull used her personal charm to convince a Congressman to let her address the House Judiciary Committee in 1871. She argued that women's suffrage was already protected by the Constitution because the existing amendments about voting and citizenship did not specify gender. Therefore, women, as citizens, should be allowed to vote. **Susan B. Anthony** invited Victoria Woodhull to join the National Woman Suffrage Association. She was a fiery speaker for the NWSA, and even challenged Anthony for leadership of the group.

Lucy Stone and the more conservative American Woman Suffrage Association were put off by Woodhull's radical feminism. Woodhull formed a new "people's party" for the 1872 election and ran for president. **Belva Lockwood** was among her supporters, but Woodhull had lost the support of the women's suffrage movement. She also lost the election.

+ + + + + + + + + + + + + + + + +

Thousands of young Chinese women came to the United States from the 1840s through 1880s and were forced to work as prostitutes in West Coast towns. Chinese women came to be stereotyped as sex objects.

In the 1800s, almost 90 percent of the Chinese people in the United States were men. They had come to work in the West building the railroads or the mines. Employers discouraged them from bringing their families or from marrying and settling in the United States. Prostitution businesses opened to provide Chinese women for these Chinese workers. Some of the women had been kidnapped in China, some had been tricked into thinking a husband awaited them. Some had been sold by their families.

The Rights of Women

Labor Leaders and Social Housekeepers

Many women revolted against these awful conditions. With little support from the male-dominated labor unions, they called strikes, marched on picket lines, and fought for their rights. Women labor leaders found new, if sometimes uneasy, partners in the middle and upper-class women who saw themselves as the nation's "social housekeepers." They believed women were responsible for making sure the nation, in its race to become modern, industrialized, and rich, did not sacrifice the health and morals of its citizens. Through women's clubs and associations and settlement houses, they sponsored programs for "working girls" and provided charity for the poor. Many social reformers turned to politics to fight for minimum wages, shorter work weeks, child labor laws, and industry safety standards. There was often class prejudice between white working women and women from other classes, but there was also often support. Women of color, however, were forced to form their own organizations. And many reform and labor women realized they needed something more to achieve their goals. They needed the vote.

A s one century ended and another began, the United States experienced all kinds of growth – and growing pains. This had a big impact on women.

By 1900, only one-third of the nation still worked on farms. Forty percent of Americans lived in cities, with thousands of new immigrants arriving daily. The railroad, oil, and steel companies thrived. The textile and garment industries grew more powerful. As businesses got bigger and richer, workers were squeezed tighter and tighter by pay cuts and the high cost of food and housing. This was especially true for women, because they were already paid less than men.

Many of the millions of working women were recent immigrants from Eastern Europe who had settled throughout the Northeast and Midwest. They worked long hours in unsafe or unhealthy factories, meat-packing plants, and steam laundries. They sewed everything from hats to shoes in cramped, airless sweatshops. And when they finished their 12-to-14 hour days, most of them went home to overcrowded tenements, where a whole family might be crammed into a tiny 300-square-foot apartment with no running water. For women of color, jobs and housing options were usually even worse.

▲ The March 3, 1913 suffrage demonstration in Washington, D.C. Marchers were heckled and harrassed by people in the crowd, mostly men. The police did nothing. Soldiers had to restore order.

The Winning Plan

By the time suffragist leader **Susan B. Anthony** died in 1906, the drive to get women the vote had become

very complicated. The National American Woman Suffrage Association (NAWSA) was still divided over whether to win the vote state-by-state or launch a national campaign. Some white suffragists did not want to join efforts with African-American women, because they feared offending the Southern politicians whose support they needed. Other suffragists remained racist, claiming that if women could vote, that would help support white supremacy over African-American and immigrant voters.

Despite all these issues, the women's suffrage movement became more powerful than ever in the early 1900s. It attracted a broad group of middle-class women, young college graduates, and reformers. It gained national attention as suffragists became bolder, louder, and more visibile. They gave speeches on street corners and at state fairs, they marched in suffrage parades, and they pressured politicians. Public support grew. NAWSA president **Carrie Chapman Catt** put her "winning plan" into action. NAWSA members worked at all local, state, and federal levels, building on the voting power women had already won in several states. By 1917, **Alice Paul's** radical National Woman's Party (NWP), was picketing the White House. The suffrage movement seemed unstoppable, but, once again, war crowded women off the front page.

World War I and Victory for Women

The United States entered World War I in 1917, bringing new opportunities for women. Thousands of nurses and ambulance drivers volunteered for the Red Cross overseas. At home, women worked in steel mills and on streetcars. They manufactured everything from airplanes to explosives. Many women became government clerical workers. Women learned new skills and received better wages than ever before, although most of these opportunities were not open to African-American women.

◄ The Women's Trade Union League brought together women in labor unions and in the women's rights movement. The WTUL demonstrated, printed fliers, supported strikers, and put some of its socially prominent members on the picket lines.

HELLO! THIS IS LIBERTY SPEAKING— BILLIONS OF DOLLARS ARE NEEDED AND NEEDED **NOW**

▲ During World War I (1914–1918), women filled jobs left by men gone off to fight. After the war, women were expected to return home or to unskilled, lower-paying jobs.

World War I also helped the final push to get women the vote. Leaders of the NAWSA realized that if women were active, public supporters of the war effort, President Woodrow Wilson might help the suffrage movement. They were right. President Wilson eventually urged Congress to pass the Susan B. Anthony (or Nineteenth) Amendent. In January 1918, it passed the House of Representatives with the exact number of votes needed. In June 1919 the Senate finally approved the amendment. In less than a year, it was ratified in 35 of the 36 states needed to make it law. The battlelines were then drawn in Tennessee, the remaining state most likely to approve of the amendment. Suffragists and anti-suffragists flooded into Nashville to lobby for their cause. The outcome hinged on whether a young state representative, Harry Burn, cast a "yea" or a "nay." His mother sent him a reminder to "...be a good boy and help Mrs. Catt put 'Rat' in ratification." Burn voted for the amendment, and on August 26, 1920, nearly 26 million American women finally got the right to vote.

New Women in A New Age

Once women could vote, their influence as a group began to change. Some of the old suffrage networks drifted apart. Many people now worried that labor leaders, pacifists, and feminists were a radical threat to the "American way of life." Women who had been hailed for their reform work or labor leadership were at best ignored. More often they were denounced and sometimes jailed or deported. The Roaring Twenties with its flappers, jazz clubs, consumer culture, and arts movements such as the Harlem Renaissance, also ushered in much public discussion about the "new woman." For many women, this meant being independent, educated, employed, but not necessarily feminist.

Jane Addams

born 1860 – died 1935

SETTLEMENT HOUSE FOUNDER

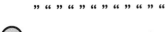

Settlement houses: city community centers, often set up by women college graduates, to help people in need. Many of these people were new immigrants. The settlement movement was a response to growing industrialism which brought workers to the cities. It helped create the whole field of social work. From 1890 to 1910, more than 400 settlement houses opened. Places like **Jane Addams**'s Hull House in Chicago or Lillian Wald's Henry Street Settlement in New York City offered education, health, and cultural programs. Wald opened the country's first city playground (shown below). Many settlement workers were important activists in the political fight for improved working conditions, especially for women and children.

In the late 1880s, Chicago was a bustling city, full of industry and opportunity – but not for the poor or the immigrants who made up 75 percent of the city's population. Jane Addams founded Hull House in 1889 to help provide care, education, and opportunity for this unserved group of Americans.

After receiving her degree from Illinois's Rockford Female Seminary in 1882, Addams toured European cities, where she was moved by the poverty she saw. But she was inspired by her visit to a settlement house in London. Once back in Chicago, she used her own money to open a settlement in Hull House, an old mansion right in the middle of a crowded immigrant neighborhood. Addams and her supporters moved into the mansion. Within a few years, Hull House offered education programs, work training, child care, and arts programs to thousands of people. Addams encouraged hard-working, reform-minded women like **Julia Lathrop** and **Florence Kelley** to work for Hull House. Addams herself was not above delivering a baby or even getting a job as a garbage inspector to improve services in the neighborhood. Hull House grew until it included 13 buildings and a summer camp near Lake Geneva, Wisconsin. As the settlement house expanded, so did Addams's work in social reform. She campaigned for workers' rights and for the rights of children. Addams helped establish the country's first juvenile court in 1899. She also was a popular lecturer and wrote many articles and books, including her popular autobiography, *Twenty Years at Hull House* (1910).

▲ In addition to her work at Hull House, Jane Addams served as vice-president of the National American Woman's Suffrage Association (1911–1914). Addams, along with **Elizabeth Gurley Flynn** and others, also founded the American Civil Liberties Union in 1920.

Nellie Bly ELIZABETH COCHRANE SEAMAN

born c. 1865–67 – died 1922

JOURNALIST

Investigative journalism was a man's business – until Nellie Bly came along. Born Elizabeth Cochrane Seaman, Bly got her pen name from a popular song. Her writing career took off in 1885 when she wrote an angry response to the *Pittsburgh Dispatch*'s article "What Girls Are Good For." The newspaper then hired the young writer. Nellie wrote about slum life and conditions for "working girls" in Pittsburgh, Pennsylvania. But it was Bly's investigative pieces that got people calling her "the best reporter in America."

In 1887, Nellie took a job with the *New York World* newspaper. She wrote her stories from firsthand experience. One of her first articles exposed conditions in a New York mental institution. Bly faked insanity and got herself committed to the asylum on Blackwell's Island. Her story prompted a grand jury investigation of the institution, which resulted in better patient care. Bly also pretended to shoplift, so she would be arrested and could accurately write about life in jail.

Always looking for a challenge, Nellie Bly decided to beat the record of Phileas Fogg, the fictitious hero of Jules Verne's *Around the World in 80 Days*. She sailed from Hoboken, New Jersey, on November 14, 1889, and traveled around the world by boat, train, even rickshaw. Seventy-two days, six hours, and 11 minutes later, on January 25, 1890, Bly arrived in New York City, where she was greeted by fireworks and a parade.

◀ Nellie Bly recorded her experience in *Nellie Bly's Book: Around the World in Seventy-two Days* (1890).

1890s – 1920s

HARRIET STANTON BLATCH (1856–1940) walked in the footsteps of her mother, **Elizabeth Cady Stanton**, in the march toward suffrage. Blatch formed the Equality League of Self-Supporting Women in 1907. She believed working women should demand their political rights because they contributed to the country's economy. In one year, 19,000 women – from factory workers to professional women to fashionable society ladies – became League members. Blatch organized the first women's suffrage parade in the United States, despite the objections of the conservative National American Woman Suffrage Association. They thought a parade would be "undignified" and "would set women suffrage back fifty years." Blatch proved them wrong. The march, staged in New York City on May 21, 1910, attracted a lot of attention and favorable press coverage. Outdoor demonstrations became an important tactic in women's struggle for the vote.

▲ Annie Jump Cannon was famous for her studies of stellar spectra, or the characteristics of stars.

+ + + + + + + + + + + + + + + + +

The pioneer settling of the West and the Midwest changed the lives of Native Americans forever. By the 1890s, almost all tribal members were forced to live on reservations. Survival was difficult. Some Native American women began to sell goods like rugs and baskets that they had traditionally made for their own use. Mountain Wolf Woman, a Winnebago born in Wisconsin in 1884, became a basket weaver to help support her family. In 1957, she dictated her autobiography, in Winnebago and in English, to an anthropologist. *Mountain Wolf Woman, Sister of Crashing Thunder* was published in 1958 and is an important record of Native American life and the impact of white culture.

Annie Jump Cannon

born 1863 – died 1941
ASTRONOMER

Annie Jump Cannon had her head in the stars. That's why she discovered over 300 rare stars and classified nearly 400,000 stars in her lifetime.

After graduating from Wellesley College in Massachusetts, Cannon got a job as assistant astronomer at the Harvard College Observatory in 1896. There she met Williamina Fleming, a former maid who learned astronomy when her employer, a Harvard professor, asked her to work for him in the Observatory because his male assistants did such a poor job. Fleming and Cannon set out to tackle the huge project of recording, classifying, and cataloging stars. Annie Jump Cannon developed a way to classify stars by their temperature. Her pioneering system was adopted by astronomers everywhere. Cannon published her findings, a classification of around 225,000 stars, in the nine-volume *Henry Draper Catalogue* published between 1918 and 1924. No other astronomer before or since has ever produced such a large body of work. Cannon, a member of the National Woman's Party, became the first woman to receive an honorary degree from England's Oxford University (1925). She won a medal from the National Academy of Sciences in 1931 and the **Ellen Richards** prize from the Society to Aid Scientific Research by Women in 1932.

Willa Cather

born 1873 – died 1947
NOVELIST

"Most of the basic material a writer works with is acquired before the age of fifteen," Willa Cather once said. So it's not surprising that her most popular novels were set in Nebraska's Great Plains, where the writer grew up.

When Willa was nine, her father moved the family from their comfortable Virginia farm to the frontier town of Red Cloud, Nebraska. Willa felt painfully uprooted, but also inspired by the prairie's wide-open spaces and the struggles of the Swedish, Russian, and German immigrants to make new lives in a new environment. This had a strong influence on her writing.

Cather attended the University of Nebraska in Lincoln, where she cut her hair short and preferred to be called "William." After graduating in 1895, she worked as a journalist in Lincoln and then in Pittsburgh, Pennsylvania, before turning to teaching. Cather published a few collections of poetry and short stories, then moved to New York in 1906 to become editor of *McClure's*

Magazine. There, she made a name for herself and for *McClure*'s. Her first novel, *Alexander's Bridge*, was published in 1912. Cather then quit editing and became a full-time writer – and a successful one. In *O Pioneers!* (1913), she wrote, "There are only two or three human stories, and they go on repeating themselves as fiercely as if they had never happened before." This was true for the author's work. Many of her novels, such as *My Antonía* (1918) and *One of Ours* (1922), which won the Pulitzer Prize, deal with similar themes: the spirit and values of the pioneer tradition, the relationship between achievement and satisfaction, and the tension between the immigrants' old world customs and their new frontier experiences. Later, Cather became fascinated with the Southwest and wrote bestsellers such as *Death Comes for the Archbishop*, published in 1927. Cather is considered a master writer of the American frontier and is known for her portrayal of strong women.

 In 1915, women could vote in only 13 states. Most of these states were in the West and Midwest. None of them was in the eastern part of the United States, where the original fight for liberty, the Revolutionary War, had started. The anti-suffrage movement included men, women, and the powerful liquor industry, which thought women would vote to ban alcohol.

⚖ Carrie Chapman Catt

born 1859 – died 1947

SUFFRAGIST

When Carrie Chapman married her second husband, George Catt, in 1890, their marriage contract guaranteed that Carrie would be free at least four months a year to do her women's suffrage work. And work she did. Catt's Winning Plan helped secure passage of the Nineteenth Amendment giving women the vote.

Catt was an experienced suffrage campaigner by the time she was elected president of the National American Woman Suffrage Association (NAWSA) in 1900. Five years earlier, under NAWSA President **Susan B. Anthony**, Catt had created and headed an Organization Committee to direct NAWSA's campaigns around the country. As NAWSA president, Catt was a careful planner and an imaginative leader. She raised funds, opened new NAWSA branches, and was a powerful speaker. But she resigned from the office in 1904 when George Catt became ill. She was succeeded by **Dr. Anna Howard Shaw**.

Over the next few years, Catt continued her suffrage work internationally and in New York state. In 1915, the NAWSA re-elected her president. The group had weakened

◄ Carrie Chapman Catt (right) and Dr. Anna Howard Shaw.

Some women took to the air, some to the water. From 1921 to 1925, **GERTRUDE EDERLE** (b. 1906) set national and international swimming records and won Olympic swimming medals. In 1926, the 19 year old from Queens, New York, became the first woman to swim across the English Channel. Her time – 14 hours and 31 minutes – was almost two hours faster than any man's record.

under Dr. Shaw's leadership and a radical suffrage group led by **Alice Paul** had split away. Catt brought new energy and new professionalism to the group. She hired a board of directors, reorganized national headquarters, set up a group to lobby Congress, and came up with her Winning Plan. The plan focused NAWSA efforts on two fronts: getting state legislatures to give women the right to vote, and using the voting power in these states to pressure Congress to pass a federal amendment. NAWSA membership ballooned from 100,000 to over 2,000,000 by 1917.

Even during World War I, Catt kept up the suffrage momentum. She had founded the Woman's Peace Party with **Jane Addams** in 1915. But when the United States entered the war in 1917, Catt encouraged women to be part of the war effort at home. She thought this would make women look patriotic and help the suffrage movement. Catt herself served on the Woman's Committee of the Council of National Defense. Still, she didn't stop what she called her "red-hot never-ceasing campaign" to get women the vote. Catt's Winning Plan succeeded: on August 26, 1920, the amendment passed, giving women the right to vote. Next she helped NAWSA become the League of Women Voters, so that women would be active, informed voters. As Carrie Chapman Catt wrote, the "vote has been costly. Prize it."

Bessie Coleman

born 1893 – died 1926

PILOT

When Bessie Coleman was barred from aviation schools because she was an African American, she didn't let that ground her dreams of learning to fly. Instead, Bessie learned French and headed to Europe, where she became the world's first licensed African-American woman pilot.

Bessie Coleman was the 12th of 13 children in a sharecropper family in Atlanta, Texas. She picked cotton and did laundry to help the family and tried to save enough money for college. Eventually Bessie moved to Chicago and worked as a manicurist. She was inspired by stories she heard about Eugene Jacques Bullard, an African American who had flown with the French Army during World War I. Coleman's own flying adventures began in France, too. Toward the end of the war, she traveled there with a unit of the Red Cross. In 1921, ten months after her first lesson, Bessie Coleman became a licensed pilot.

Coleman returned home in 1922 and worked in air shows across the United States. She performed daredevil flying stunts like loops, twirls, and figure eights. She also lectured on flying. But her real aviation goal was to create a flight school for African Americans. Before she could make this happen, Coleman died in an airplane crash in a Florida exhibition in 1926.

Isadora Duncan

born 1878 – died 1927

MODERN DANCER

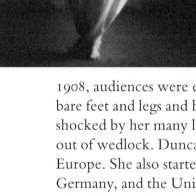

"Toe walking deforms the feet, and corsets deform the body," said the dancer Isadora Duncan, explaining why she rejected classical ballet and developed her own style of dancing. Duncan also found ballet's precise movements did not allow her as much expression as she wanted. She created her own free style, based on natural and spontaneous movement. Duncan was one of the first to develop what is now called modern dance.

Isadora was born into a poor Irish-American family in San Francisco, California. She started teaching other children dance when she was six years old, and by 1896 had joined the Augustin Daly Theater Company in New York. But Duncan felt frustrated as an artist and began giving dance performances in private homes. At the turn of the century, Isadora went to Europe, where her innovative style was a sensation in England, France, Hungary, and Germany. However, when she toured the United States in 1908, audiences were either uninterested in her free style or appalled by her bare feet and legs and her flowing, revealing costumes. They were also shocked by her many love affairs and by the fact that Isadora had two children out of wedlock. Duncan returned to her more appreciative audiences in Europe. She also started dancing schools for children in Russia, France, Germany, and the United States. In 1927, Isadora Duncan was killed instantly when her scarf caught in the wheels of a sports car in which she was riding.

1890s – 1920s

" " " " " " " " " " " "

Feminism: In the 1890s, people started referring to the movement for women's equal rights as feminism. An English journal, the *Athenaeum,* is credited as being the first to print the words *feminism* and *feminist,* in 1895. Many feminists believed in personal freedom and equal rights as citizens and workers for all people. Not all suffragists were feminists, but some women who belonged to **Alice Paul**'s National Woman's Party called themselves feminists. So did women such as **Crystal Eastman**, **Elizabeth Gurley Flynn**, and **Charlotte Perkins Gilman** who belonged to a weekly New York study group called Heterodoxy, started in 1912. Heterodoxy members included artists, intellectuals, and labor organizers. To join, a woman should "not be orthodox [traditional] in her opinions."

Crystal Eastman

born 1881 – died 1928

LABOR LAWYER

Crystal Eastman was exposed to reform ideas at an early age. Her mother, Annis Eastman, was a preacher and strong advocate of women's rights in upstate New York, where the Eastmans lived. Crystal decided the best way to bring about reform was to change laws, so she became a lawyer.

Eastman was an authority on labor law and fought to improve work conditions. She was the only female member of the New York State Employers' Liability Commission, which looked at workers' compensation. Her book *Work Accidents & the Law* (1910) contributed to the passage of U.S. worker-safety laws. Eastman was a radical suffragist. She believed women should have all the legal and social rights and employment opportunities men had. And she picketed, demonstrated, and confronted politicians to get these things. She helped **Alice Paul** launch the Congressional Union for Woman Suffrage in 1913. In 1919, she read the opening statements at the first Feminist Congress in New York.

Eastman was also a hard-working pacifist. She helped found the Woman's Peace Party in 1914, and when the United States entered World War I in 1917, Crystal Eastman organized the Civil Liberties Bureau to help conscientious objectors, people who refused to serve in the armed forces because of their religious or moral beliefs.

++++++++++++++++++

At the turn of the century, many rural women hauled water from a pump for cooking and cleaning. Outhouses were common. Many city families lived in tenement apartments without kitchens or bathrooms. Women cooked on sooty coal stoves in the living room and drew cold water from sinks outside in the hallway. The toilet was often in the basement. Almost everybody who washed clothes did it by hand in a washtub with a hand-cranked clothes wringer. But by the end of the 1920s, the majority of American homes had indoor plumbing and electricity. This, along with packaged food and ready-to-wear clothes, changed the lives of everyone, especially women.

Fannie Farmer

born 1857 – died 1915

NUTRITIONIST

Fannie Farmer was born into a poor family in Boston, Massachusetts. When she was 16, she suffered a stroke that paralyzed her left leg. Fannie dropped out of school, did household work, and discovered she had a special knack for cooking.

Farmer enrolled in a two-year course at the Boston Cooking School in 1887. By 1894, Farmer was named head of the school. At the same time, she wrote the *Boston Cooking School Cook Book* and found a publisher who would print it if Farmer paid for the first edition. The book was published in 1896,

◀ This picture of a woman in a Chicago tenement is by a famous American photographer, Lewis Hine. It is from the George Eastman House Collection.

and was an instant hit. No one had ever clearly written out the ingredients, directions, and precise measurements for such great recipes. Fannie Farmer's recipes were popular not just because they were flavorful but because they were healthy, too. Farmer understood that with a proper diet people "will be able to do better mental and physical work, and disease will be less frequent." A hundred years later, Fannie Farmer's book, updated as *The Fannie Farmer Cookbook*, is still in print and has sold more than 4,000,000 copies.

$ Elizabeth Gurley Flynn

born 1890 – died 1964

LABOR LEADER

In 1906, 16-year-old Elizabeth Gurley Flynn delivered a speech to a large crowd at the Harlem Socialist Club in New York. Flynn spoke about "the right of every woman to be a wife, a mother, a worker, a citizen." She exercised each of those rights in her lifetime.

Elizabeth was the daughter of a socialist father and a feminist mother. In 1900, her Irish working-class family moved from Concord, New Hampshire, to the Bronx, New York. There Elizabeth met anarchist **Emma Goldman**. She dropped out of high school and became a fiery speaker, often on street corners, for the Industrial Workers of the World. The IWW was a radical labor reform group that tried to unite workers of all industries and nationalities to fight for better wages and working conditions. Flynn's work took her across the country, to wherever there was a workers' strike. Between 1906 and 1926, she helped organize 20 strikes. Flynn was arrested 15 times for her labor activity.

In 1920, Flynn, along with **Jane Addams** and others, founded the American Civil Liberties Union (ACLU). The ACLU expelled Flynn in 1937 when she joined the Communist Party. She said the party offered "the full opportunity for women to become free and equal citizens." Flynn got caught in the 1950s wave of anti-Communism. When she was 65, she was sent to jail for three years for advocating the overthrow of the government. In 1961, Flynn became the first woman to chair the American Communist Party.

More than 10,000 mill workers in Lawrence, Massachusetts, walked out in 1912. At the town railroad station, state troopers clubbed women strikers who were trying to send their hungry children to another city. **Elizabeth Gurley Flynn** was arrested in the 1913 silk workers' strike in Paterson, New Jersey. Women strikers withstood abuse and poverty but helped win many labor reforms.

1890s – 1920s

Charlotte Perkins Gilman

born 1860 – died 1935

WRITER

"Is our present way of organizing home life, based on the economic dependence of women on men, the best way to maintain the individual in health and happiness?" Charlotte Perkins Gilman asked in her famous book, *Women and Economics*. Based on her personal and professional life, Gilman's answer was clearly, "No."

Charlotte grew up in Hartford, Connecticut, and in 1884, married a painter, Charles W. Stetson. They had a daughter. After several years, Charlotte found her role as a housewife so depressing she had a nervous breakdown. A doctor recommended that Charlotte never write or paint, two things she loved to do, and instead devote herself to her family. This cure didn't work. Charlotte moved West on her own. When she arrived in California, Gilman began writing poems and short stories. Her story, "The Yellow Wall-Paper" (1892) showed the collapse of a young woman's mental and physical health because of her home life. It remains one of Gilman's most well-known and widely read works.

Charlotte also started lecturing on women's issues, economics, suffrage, and social reform. She traveled cross-country, visiting other reform leaders such as **Jane Addams** at Hull House. When *Women and Economics* was published in 1898, it confirmed Gilman's reputation as one of the great social thinkers of the time. In her book, Charlotte called for radical changes in women's roles. She suggested new, public forms of child care, communal kitchens, and communal laundries, so that women would be freer to work outside the home.

ISABELLA STEWART GARDNER (c. 1840–1924) was wild. She once walked a lion down a main street in Boston. She was shocking. Her gowns were low-cut, and her wit was biting. She was social. She knew everyone from the boxer John L. Sullivan to the famous portrait painter John Sargent. And she was rich. Isabella married a wealthy man and inherited $2.75 million from her father. In 1891, Gardner found her life's work. She started buying art. As one of the first great American collectors, Gardner bought works by European masters such as Rembrandt and Vermeer. Then she went to Italy, bought floors, balconies, walls, and statues from old buildings, shipped them to Boston, and had them re-assembled to create an Italian palace she called Fenway Court. Gardner lived in Fenway Court and opened it as a museum in 1903.

Emma Goldman

born 1869 – died 1940

ANARCHIST

"Demand work. If they do not give you work, demand bread. If they deny you both, take the bread. It is your sacred right!" Emma Goldman told hundreds of unhappy, jobless workers in New York City in 1893. The crowd went wild. Red Emma was arrested.

Goldman was one of the most famous radical speakers of her time. She supported the anarchist movement, which promoted cooperative equality without government. Goldman spoke out against capitalism, war, and discrimination. Her enemies called her Red Emma, associating her with foreign socialism and Russian communism.

Goldman had emigrated to the United States from Russia in 1885 and went to work in a factory in Rochester, New York, then moved to New York City. There she met a fellow radical, Alexander Berkman, and joined the anarchist effort. In 1889, Berkman was jailed for trying to kill a rich steel mill owner during a Pittsburgh strike. After that, Goldman was often followed by the police. She was jailed several times for her fiery speeches.

Emma Goldman traveled around the country lecturing on birth control, women's rights, and labor issues. From 1906 to 1917, she published *Mother Earth*, a magazine that promoted ideas on women's political and sexual

freedom. Goldman gathered many followers and many enemies. The government tried to link her to the killing of President William McKinley in 1901, because the assassin said he was a follower of Goldman's. In 1917, Goldman was sentenced to two years in jail for speaking out against drafting soldiers for World War I. In 1919, she and 248 other people considered "subversive" were deported to the Soviet Union. J. Edgar Hoover, who handled her deportation for the U.S. Justice Department, called Emma Goldman "the most dangerous woman in America."

+ + + + + + + + + + + + + + + + + +

Factory and mill work by the beginning of the 20th century was not only low-paying, it was dangerous. The chemicals used in making matches rotted workers' jawbones. Cotton mill workers developed tuberculosis from all the lint in the air. Many factory workers were exposed to paint fumes and toxic dust. Around 1908, Dr. Alice Hamilton, a bacteriologist (and sister of **Edith Hamilton**), started researching these problems. She introduced the field of industrial medicine in the United States. Her books, surveys, and reports on poisons in industry helped bring about new safety laws in the workplace. In 1919, Alice Hamilton became Harvard University's first woman professor.

1890s – 1920s

Mother Jones's motto was "Pray for the dead and fight like hell for the living." This is also the slogan of the modern liberal magazine *Mother Jones*. Jones is shown here with President Calvin Coolidge.

$ Mother Jones MARY HARRIS JONES

born 1830 – died 1930

LABOR LEADER

Mary Harris Jones did not become a labor activist until she was almost 50. By 1867, she had already lost her husband and four children to yellow fever. Then her dressmaking business had burned down in the great Chicago fire of 1871. When Mary walked through her ruined neighborhood, she stopped at a Knights of Labor meeting hall and found her life's work: labor agitation.

For more than 50 years, Mother Jones goaded workers to strike for better working conditions and a living wage. Railroad workers, coal and copper miners, textile and streetcar workers called this tough Irish-American woman "Mother." She joined them in the dangerous, violent labor battles that were fought across the United States. Jones helped convince workers in West Virginia and Pennsylvania to join the United Mine Workers. She organized miners' wives into "mop-and-broom brigades" to prevent strikebreakers from entering the mines. Jones got a job in a cotton mill to investigate working conditions for children. She saw young children who had lost fingers or hands in dangerous machinery or become deformed because of their jobs. In 1903, Mother Jones organized the Crusade of the Mill Children and marched with them from Pennsylvania to President Theodore Roosevelt's summer home on Long Island. He refused to see Mother Jones, but the publicity brought national attention to the children's status. Union officials did not always approve, but Mother Jones's sensational acts helped keep labor struggles in the headlines and in the public eye.

Jovita Idar de Juarez

born 1885 – died 1946
JOURNALIST

In the early 20th century, Mexicans and Mexican Americans living in Texas and other places were often poorly treated. Whether looking for an education, a job, or simple legal justice, they faced discrimination. Jovita Idar de Juarez, a Mexican American from South Texas, went to work on the problem.

Jovita had taught school before turning to journalism to publicize the poverty and prejudice that affected many Mexicans and Mexican Americans. She wrote articles on education and on preserving Mexican heritage for Spanish-language publications, including newspapers owned by her father. In 1911, Juarez helped organize the First Mexican Congress in Laredo, Texas. Mexican-American leaders attended and addressed the important issues of their community. The Mexican Feminist League grew out of this Congress and Juarez was elected its first president. The league focused much of its efforts on educating children of the poor and working towards equal rights for women. Jovita Idar de Juarez also organized a medical relief group, the White Cross, to help people injured in the Mexican Revolution (1911).

Helen Keller

born 1880 – died 1968
EDUCATOR

W-a-t-e-r. Anne Sullivan held Helen Keller's hand under a water pump and tapped the five letters from the manual alphabet into the little girl's hand. The word opened up a new world for Helen Keller.

A childhood disease had left Helen deaf, blind, mute, and unable to communicate with anyone. Anne Sullivan changed all that. She had trained at the Perkins Institution for the Blind in Boston. In 1887, Anne, just 20 herself, went to the Kellers' Alabama home to work with seven-year-old Helen. Anne and Helen lived together for 50 years, until Sullivan's death. Anne taught Helen to read Braille, to use the manual alphabet, and to feel sign language.

▼ Helen Keller (left) with Annie Sullivan.

1890s – 1920s

Keller grew to be a determined young woman. She learned to speak by feeling and imitating mouth movements. She enrolled in Radcliffe College in Massachusetts, graduating in 1904. Her language skills were remarkable: she learned French, German, Greek, and Latin. Keller became one of the first people to write articles about blindness for major magazines. Traveling with Sullivan as her translator, Keller helped organize 30 state commissions for the blind and lectured in support of the American Foundation for the Blind. She also donated $2 million to the foundation. In 1962, the story of Anne Sullivan and Helen Keller's relationship was made into an Oscar-winning film, *The Miracle Worker.* The next year, Helen Keller was awarded the Presidential Medal of Freedom.

+ + + + + + + + + + + + + + + + +

On March 25, 1911, a fire broke out on the eighth floor of the Triangle Shirtwaist Company's New York building. It quickly spread because the floors were soaked in sewing machine oil and the air was filled with cotton dust. The workers, mostly Jewish and Italian women, were trapped because the company had locked all the stairway doors from the outside. The only terrible choice was burn to death or jump to death. One hundred and fifty women, girls, and men died in the disaster. Eight thousand people attended their funerals. Company owners were found not guilty of any crimes and collected $65,000 in property insurance.

$ Florence Kelley

born 1859 – died 1932

LABOR ACTIVIST

Florence Kelley was an activist who fought to protect women and children who worked long hours for little pay. A member of **Jane Addams**'s group, Kelley brought together Hull House and the Illinois Women's Alliance so they could lobby for laws for shorter hours and higher pay. Kelley also became the first state factory inspector in Illinois.

Florence Kelley was born in Philadelphia, Pennsylvania. She attended Cornell University in Ithaca, New York, and then graduate school in Zurich, Switzerland, because women in the United States were usually barred from postgraduate study. While she was in Europe, she was exposed to socialist ideas, which deeply influenced her. She also translated into English an important

THE NEW YORK HERALD.

NEW YORK, SUNDAY, MARCH 26, 1911.—112 PAGES.—BY THE NEW YORK HERALD COMPANY.   PRICE FIVE CENTS.

NE HUNDRED AND FIFTY PERISH IN FACTORY FIRE;
WOMEN AND GIRLS, TRAPPED IN TEN STORY BUILDING,
LOST IN FLAMES OR HURL THEMSELVES TO DEATH

IDENTIFYING BODIES OF THOSE WHO JUMPED TO THE SIDEWALK.

omed Victims Dashed

BUILDING AT NORTHWEST CORNER OF EAST WASHINGTON PLACE AND GREENE STREET, THE THREE TOP FLOORS IN WHICH LOSS OF LIFE OCCURRED, WERE COMPLETELY DESTROYED.

Only One Fire Escape to Lofts Occupied by

book, *The Condition of the Working Class in England* by German socialist Friedrich Engels.

Kelley returned to the United States in 1886. She joined Lillian Wald's Henry Street Settlement in New York and became head of the National Consumers League (NCL) in 1899. The league used two of the most powerful weapons available to women: publicity and the boycott. Under Kelley's direction, the NCL asked people not to shop at department stores where young women worked under terrible conditions. Forced to stand up to 12 hours a day, these saleswomen worked six days a week, only to take home $6. The NCL also discouraged people from buying goods made by child labor or in sweatshops. Florence Kelley led the league's battle for minimum wage and shorter working hour laws. She also helped set up the United States Children's Bureau, which **Julia Lathrop** headed.

💲 Rose Knox

born 1857 – died 1950

INDUSTRIALIST

When Rose Markward Knox's husband died in 1908, her friends told her to sell the gelatine company the Knoxes had built together. But Rose ignored them. She kept the company and turned it into a million-dollar business by 1935.

Born in Mansfield, Ohio, Rose Markward and her family moved to Gloversville, New York, when she was in her 20s. There she worked in a glove factory and married Charles Knox in 1883. Seven years later the couple combined their savings and invested it in a gelatine business. Gelatine was a by-product of the Gloversville factories that prepared animal skins. Rose studied the different ways gelatine could be used. She wrote a booklet called *Dainty Desserts* in 1896, and soon the orange Knox box was a popular item in thousands of homes. After her husband's death in 1908, Rose took control of the Knox's company. She promoted gelatine with recipes in her 1917 booklet *Food Economy* and in a newspaper column, "Mrs. Knox Says." Rose Knox ran her company in what she called "a woman's way." She changed the work week from five and a half days to five days a week. Then she created two-week vacations and sick leave for her workers. Knox became the first woman member of the American Grocery Manufacturers' Association and, in 1929, its first woman director. She retired as president of the Knox company in 1947, at the age of 90.

+ + + + + + + + + + + + + + + + + +

At first, the American Federation of Labor ignored women workers as "unskilled labor." But women workers, especially immigrant women, were skilled labor organizers. They called many of the nation's "turn-outs," or strikes, against low wages, long hours, salary cuts, unsafe factories, and sex discrimination. In November 1909, the International Ladies Garment Workers Union led a strike of almost 30,000 New York workers for 13 long weeks. Women picketers of this Great Uprising were beaten and jailed.

1890s – 1920s

🌀 Julia Lathrop

born 1858 – died 1932

CHILD WELFARE ACTIVIST

Julia Lathrop received a special request from President William Howard Taft in 1912. He asked her to be the director of the United States Children's Bureau. This federal agency was designed by **Florence Kelley** and Lillian Wald to protect the welfare of children and enforce child labor laws. Lathrop gladly took the job.

Lathrop had already spent years working for social causes. In 1890, she lived at **Jane Addams**'s Hull House and did pioneering investigative work on state institutions for the poor or sick. Three years later, she became the first woman appointed to the Illinois Board of Charities. She made a name for herself by inspecting poorhouses and mental institutions – and writing a grim report about the horrible conditions she saw. Concerned about children's treatment within the legal system, Lathrop also helped establish the nation's first juvenile court (1899). She was a founder of the Chicago School of Civics and Philanthropy, which became the University of Chicago's School of Social Service Administration. There she trained the next generation of reformers.

An active director of the Children's Bureau, Lathrop ordered studies of the death rate of babies and proposed education programs for mothers. She campaigned for passage of the Sheppard-Towner Act (1921), which became the first federal health and welfare program. The Act funded medical care for poor women and their children. Though the Children's Bureau had few resources when it was created, Lathrop turned it into an effective government agency.

” “ ” “ ” “ ” “ ” “ ” “

🔍 *Sweatshops* were workrooms often set up on a floor of a city tenement building. Some sweatshops spilled out onto roofs, halls, or fire escapes. A contractor called a middleman would get a job order from a store or business and then hire men and women to produce the order in these sweatshops. This was particularly true in the garment or clothing industry. Sweatshop seamstresses, many of them immigrants, worked 14 to 16 hours a day, sometimes for as little as $3 a week. Sweatshops are still operated today. Many of them make their profits by paying workers, often women, very little money and offering no benefits.

◄ Child laborers in a factory

Mary Elizabeth Lease

born 1850 – died 1933

POPULIST PARTY LEADER

"Raise less corn and more hell!" Mary Lease shouted to the thousands of Kansas farmers in the crowd. The farmers were suffering because crop prices were low and the shipping costs of bringing their crops to market were high. They were ready to listen to Lease's message about corrupt government and greedy railroad tycoons.

Mary Lease was a lively and popular public speaker. She got her start in 1885 by rallying support in the United States for the Irish National League's independence movement. This led to her interest in workers' rights. Mary joined the Union Labor Party in Wichita, Kansas, where she lived. She worked for the Kansas Farmers' Alliance, a cooperative formed to improve the economic status of farmers.

By the turn of the century, many people in the United States were unhappy with the wide financial gap between big business owners and the working class. Many farm and factory workers joined the Populist Party (also known as the People's Party) to run their own candidates for political office. Mary Lease was a big hit at Populist rallies all over the West and South. In 1890, she made 161 speeches in Kansas alone, speaking against both Democrats and Republicans. She attacked what she saw as "a government of Wall Street, by Wall Street, and for Wall Street." As a result, Kansas elected independent candidates for Congress. Lease was appointed president of the Kansas State Board of Charities in 1893. After leaving that position in 1894, she moved to New York and continued her activist work there.

▲ Mary Elizabeth Lease's enemies called her the "Kansas Python."

+ + + + + + + + + + + + + + + +

At the turn of the century, over 50 percent of working Americans labored on farms or in the agricultural industry. In the West, many women of color worked in the fish, fruit, and vegetable canneries or picked crops in the field. These low-paying jobs were often the only ones open to them because of discrimination or language barriers.

1890S – 1920S

▸ Queen Liliuokalani actively worked for islanders' rights after the Hawaiian monarchy was destroyed. She also wrote about her life and Hawaiian history, and composed over 200 songs, including the popular "Aloha Oe."

⚖ Queen Liliuokalani

born 1838 – died 1917

QUEEN OF HAWAII

"Hear me for my downtrodden people! Their form of government is as dear to them as yours is precious to you," Queen Liliuokalani of Hawaii wrote in 1898. But the monarchy, dear to most Hawaiians, had been overthrown five years earlier when the pineapple and sugar industries and the United States Marines forced Liliuokalani to give up her throne.

Born Liliu Kamakaeha, the future queen grew up in Honolulu and attended missionary boarding school. She married an American sea captain in 1862. As part of the royal family, she traveled all over the world, meeting people such as the Queen of England and U.S. President Grover Cleveland. In 1877, Liliu was named the next heir to the throne and after that was called by her royal name, Liliuokalani. In 1891, when her brother, the king, died, she became the first ruling queen of Hawaii.

Queen Liliuokalani inherited economic problems and a constitution forced on the island by the United States in 1887. Two years after she became queen, white business leaders such as Sanford B. Dole overthrew Liliuokalani's government so they could control the Hawaiian sugar industry. Then they asked the United States for protection. U.S. troops were sent to Hawaii and Liliuokalani was dethroned. Her people revolted, so she was put under house arrest in the Royal Palace. In 1895, Queen Liliuokalani officially gave up her title, but still believed in "Hawaii for Hawaiians." She led the Oni pa'a (Stand Firm) movement against the occupation of Hawaii. Despite the islanders' protests, the U.S. government claimed Hawaii as part of its territory in 1898. It became a state in 1959.

Juliette Gordon Low

born 1860 – died 1927

GIRL SCOUTS FOUNDER

In 1912, several young girls, all dressed alike in bloomers and stockings and white blouses, were eager to pass the "tenderfoot" test. If they could tie knots, knew their governor and mayor, and knew the history of the American flag and how to fly it, they could join either the Pink Carnation or the White Rose patrols. They could become the first Girl Scouts of the United States of America.

Founded by Juliette Low of Savannah, Georgia, the Girl Scouts were originally called the Girl Guides, just like the groups Juliette had already formed in England and Scotland. Juliette Gordon Low was married to an American who lived in England. She spent time in both the United States and Great Britain, where she met Sir Robert Baden-Powell. Baden-Powell was the founder of the English Boy Scouts. His sister, Agnes, had started a similiar group called the Girl Guides. The Baden-Powells encouraged Low to start Girl Guide troops, too. In 1912, several years after her husband's death, she returned to Savannah, bringing the Girl Guide movement with her. Low's group quickly became a popular national organization and by 1915, the group had changed its name to the Girl Scouts. The scouts eventually changed their bloomers, too, and started wearing the familiar green uniforms that have been updated several times. Low served as first president of the Girl Scouts. She traveled across the country promoting this active new option for girls and raising funds for the organization until her retirement in 1919.

▼ Juliette Gordon Low (standing, center) and Girl Scouts in the mid-1920s. There are now more than 3.5 million Girl Scouts in the United States. They sold over 165,000,000 boxes of Girl Scout cookies in 1994.

1890s – 1920s

✏️ Edna St. Vincent Millay

born 1892 – died 1950

POET

"My candle burns at both ends;/ It will not last the night;/But, ah, my foes, and, oh, my friends –/It gives a lovely light." When a young, Maine-born poet wrote these lines, many people living in the Roaring Twenties understood what she meant. The author, Edna St. Vincent Millay, was the first woman to receive the Pulitzer Prize in Poetry (1923). She was a popular artist and symbol of her time.

When Edna was 19, she published a poem called "Renascence" in a collection. The poem won the attention of poetry critics and Edna got a scholarship to Vassar College in Poughkeepsie, New York. She graduated in 1917 and moved to New York City's Greenwich Village. The Village was the center of the artistic community. Millay, who was spirited, independent, and sometimes called "the spokes*man* [italics added] for the new woman," fit right in. Her apartment was often crammed with other writers, actors, artists, and political revolutionaries. Millay published her first book, *Renascence and Other Poems*, and wrote plays for the famous and innovative Provincetown Players. But like many other artists, she did not make much money. To support herself, Millay wrote popular fiction and poetry under the name Nancy Boyd.

Millay won the Pulitzer Prize for her poetry collection, *Ballad of the Harpweaver*. It included some of her finest sonnets, a type of 14-line rhythmic poem. That same year, she married Jan Boissevain, a Dutch businessman, and in 1925, they moved to a farmhouse in Austerlitz, New York, where Edna continued to write poetry and even opera. Millay's *The King's Henchman*, staged by New York's Metropolitan Opera Company, was the most successful American opera of its time. Her upstate farm is now the famous Millay Artist Colony, a retreat for writers and painters.

" " " " " " " " " " " " "

🔍 *Flappers:* Young women who had short, bobbed haircuts, wore short dresses and make-up, danced in nightclubs, and sometimes even smoked cigarettes or drank alcohol. Some people considered them sexy. Some thought they were shocking. Flappers became the symbol of the "Roaring Twenties." They were the signs of a new American emphasis on youth and on a public role for the "new woman" who could now vote and often had her own paycheck.

⚖️ Alice Paul

born 1885 – died 1977

SUFFRAGIST, LAWYER

On March 3, 1913, the day before President Woodrow Wilson's inauguration, 5,000 women marched down Pennsylvania Avenue in Washington, D.C. They carried flags and banners or rode on floats, all decorated with the same message: Give women the vote. At the head of the parade was 28-year-old New Jersey Quaker and activist Alice Paul.

Paul and other young activists such as **Crystal Eastman** had organized the march. It was the largest of its kind at the time and a part of their work for the Congressional Committee of the National American Woman Suffrage Association (NAWSA). NAWSA's Congressional Committee was supposed to

organize the drive for a federal suffrage amendment. Paul felt NAWSA and its president, **Dr. Anna Howard Shaw**, were not aggressive enough. She favored a more radical type of protest, like the ones she had seen while attending graduate school in England. There she was jailed several times for organizing working women into trade unions and demonstrating with militant women suffragists. In England, Paul waged hunger strikes and was once painfully force-fed by tubes through her nose for almost a month.

Paul split from NAWSA in 1913 and formed what eventually became the National Woman's Party (NWP) in 1917. She held the Democrats in Congress responsible for not acting on a suffrage amendment. NWP lobbied against electing Democratic candidates everywhere. Using protest marches and other forms of direct action, members of the group, including Paul, were repeatedly jailed for their militancy. That did not stop them. "Once you put your hand to the plough you don't remove it until you get to the end of the row," Paul declared.

In January 1917, the NWP stepped up its campaign to urge presidential support for the **Susan B. Anthony** constitutional amendment to give women the right to vote. Members picketed the White House daily and more than 265 of them were arrested. To discredit her, Alice Paul was jailed in solitary confinement in the psychiatric ward of a prison. But when the press published reports of the horrible conditions in the prison, national sympathy and support forced President Wilson to pardon all the suffragists. Two months later, he came out in favor of the suffrage amendment. Paul and her radical efforts and other suffragists' lobbying and organizing were both key to passage (1919) and ratification (1920) of the Nineteenth Amendment, which gave women the right to vote. Paul continued her feminist work throughout her life. She wrote the first Equal Rights Amendment, called it the **Lucretia Mott** amendment, and got it introduced in Congress in 1923.

+ + + + + + + + + + + + + + + + +

 Carrie Chapman Catt and the leaders of the National American Woman Suffrage Association did not approve of the radical methods of the National Woman's Party. NWP members still picketed the White House for several months during World War I.

☒ Annie Smith Peck

born 1850 – died 1935

MOUNTAINEER

When she reached the top of Mount Huascarán in the Peruvian Andes on September 2, 1908, Annie Smith Peck became the first mountaineer, male or female, to scale the 21,812-foot peak. She was 57 years old.

Born and raised in Providence, Rhode Island, Peck graduated from the University of Michigan and taught in colleges. Pursuing advanced degrees, she was the first woman admitted to the American School of Classical Studies in Athens, Greece, in 1885.

On a trip to the Swiss Alps in 1885, the sight of the Matterhorn aroused her interest in mountain climbing. After practicing smaller climbs, she tackled her first big mountain, Mount Shasta (14,380 feet) in California, in 1888. When she finally climbed the Matterhorn in 1895, she was only the third woman to make the ascent. Her outfit – knickerbockers, or short trousers, and a tunic – created almost as much news as her achievement.

Peck climbed mountains, including Mount Orizaba in Mexico, for the next 37 years. At 18,314 feet, Orizaba was the highest point in the Western Hemisphere reached by a woman at the time (1897). In 1911, Peck did her part for suffrage by planting a "Votes for Women" flag when she became the first person to reach the summit of Mount Coropuna in Peru. Peck raised money for her equipment and expeditions by lecturing and writing magazine articles and books. She made her last climb, of New Hampshire's Mount Madison, at the age of 82.

☑ Dr. Mary Engle Pennington

born 1872 – died 1952

SCIENTIST

At the turn of the century, getting food from the farm to the market to the dining room table was sometimes risky business. Things such as meat and dairy products spoiled easily. Chemist Mary Engle Pennington helped make sitting down to eat satisfying *and* safe. She helped develop refrigeration.

Pennington earned a doctorate in chemistry from the University of Pennsylvania in 1895 and opened her own laboratory in Philadelphia. She developed guidelines for milk inspection that were adopted by health boards throughout the country. By 1905, Pennington had started researching a new type of food preservation, refrigeration. She applied for a civil service job

"Oh beautiful for spacious skies, for amber waves of grain for purple mountains' majesty..."

Katherine Lee Bates wrote "America the Beautiful" in 1893 after climbing more than 14,000 feet up Pikes Peak in Colorado.

under the name M.E. Pennington for fear the government would not hire a woman scientist, and got a job working in refrigeration research. She had become the first chief of the U.S. Food Research Laboratory by the time Department of Agriculture officials realized they hadn't hired a man. Pennington helped develop refrigeration until it became the standard method of food shipping and storage. Her research helped in building railroad refrigerator cars that were used for decades. After leaving the department in 1919, Dr. Pennington continued her work on food preservation, especially in frozen foods.

 # Mary Pickford GLADYS MARY SMITH

born 1893 – died 1979

ACTOR

Mary Pickford was famous for her sweet face and golden curls. But it was hard work and talent that made her a stage and film star.

As a child, Mary appeared in the stage version of **Harriet Beecher Stowe**'s *Uncle Tom's Cabin*. When she was 16, she started working with D.W. Griffith, the famous Hollywood director. By the time she was 23, Pickford had appeared in dozens of plays and movies and had become the first movie star to form her own film production company. In 1919, Pickford made an excellent business move. She, Griffith, and actors Charlie Chaplin and Douglas Fairbanks, Sr., organized the United Artists Corporation so they could control ownership and distribution of their films. A year later, Fairbanks became Pickford's second husband, and they bought Pickfair, an estate in Beverly Hills, California.

Mary Pickford worked steadily through the 1920s and early 1930s, making nearly 200 silent films and four "talkies." She received an Academy Award in 1929 for *Coquette*, her first talking picture. Pickford retired from acting in 1933, and three years later became vice-president of United Artists. She also produced several films and wrote four books, including her autobiography. After her long career as one of the most famous women in Hollywood, Mary Pickford died a recluse at Pickfair. Her assets were worth $50 million.

◄ Mary Pickford's nickname, America's Sweetheart, came from her stage and screen roles. Mary played two famously sweet female characters, Rebecca of Sunnybrook Farm and Pollyanna.

 The Hollywood film industry started around 1913. By the 1920s, movie stars were important influences on American culture. Screenwriters were often women. Many films featured working women, although these movies were usually about romance and marriage. Movies showed women what they should do and wear to be "glamorous." But the industry's idea of glamour did not apply to women of African, Asian, Native American, or Hispanic descent. They rarely appeared in these films, although African-American women were cast as servants.

1890s – 1920s

✓ Dr. Susan La Flesche Picotte

born 1865 – died 1915

DOCTOR, OMAHA LEADER

Dr. Susan La Flesche Picotte is said to have treated all 1,300 members of her Omaha tribe sometime during her 25 years as a doctor. The first Native American woman to earn a medical degree, Picotte was a tireless advocate for better health care for her people.

Susan came from a remarkable family. Her father, Joseph La Flesche, was chief of the Omaha. Her sister, Susette La Flesche, was a famous writer and lecturer on Native American rights who brought women such as Helen Hunt Jackson into the cause. Susan graduated at the head of her class at Woman's Medical College in Philadelphia before she was even 24. She returned to the Omaha reservation in Nebraska to practice medicine, and a few years later, married Henry Picotte.

Dr. Susan Picotte became an unofficial leader of the Omaha. She opened up a medical practice and treated both Native American and white patients. She chaired the local board of health and fought for sanitation improvements. She also traveled to Washington, D.C., to lobby for a ban on liquor sales on the reservation. Liquor, introduced by white settlers, had caused many social and health problems among the Native American tribes. In 1913, Picotte established a modern hospital in Walthill, a reservation town.

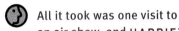

All it took was one visit to an air show, and **HARRIET QUIMBY** (c. 1875–1912) was hooked. She secretly enrolled at the Moisant School of Aviation in Hempstead, New York, and wore a heavy cap and veil for her flying lessons. On August 1, 1911, Harriet passed her flying test and was issued a pilot's license from the Aero Club of America. She became the first woman in the United States, and only the second woman in the world, licensed to fly.

On April 16, 1912, she became the first woman to fly across the English Channel. Through heavy fog, with no visibility, Quimby used only a compass to guide her French Blériot monoplane safely from Dover, England, to Hardelot, France, in 30 minutes. A few months later, she wasn't as lucky. Quimby's plane flipped during an air show over Dorchester Bay in Massachusetts. Harriet and her co-pilot, who were not strapped in, plunged 6,000 feet to their deaths.

⚖ Jeannette Rankin

born 1880 – died 1973

U.S. REPRESENTATIVE

Jeannette Rankin was a politician and a pacifist. She was the first woman elected to Congress and but she did not give up her anti-war stand when she took her seat in the U.S. House of Representatives in 1917.

A Republican, Rankin represented her home state of Montana, one of the few states that allowed women to vote. As a member of Congress, Rankin fought for passage of a federal suffrage amendment and also introduced several bills that supported the rights of women and children. In 1917, she voted against entering World War I, declaring, "I want to stand by my country, but I cannot vote for war." This vote assured her loss in the next election. Rankin spent the next several years as a social worker and lobbyist for peace with **Jane Addams** and **Florence Kelley**.

In 1940, Montana re-elected Rankin to the House of Representatives. She voted her conscience again. In 1941, on the day after the bombing of Pearl Harbor, Rankin was the only Congressional member who voted against a declaration of war. She was not re-elected.

For the rest of her life, Jeannette Rankin lobbied and lectured for women's rights and other social issues. One of her final acts as a peace activist came in 1968, when Rankin was 87 years old. She led 5,000 women in a Jeannette Rankin Brigade in a march on Washington, D.C., to protest U.S. involvement in the Vietnam War.

++++++++++++++++

 Some women were against United States involvement in World War I. Radicals such as **Emma Goldman** opposed a war they did not think would help the working class. The Woman's Peace Party, founded in 1915 by **Jane Addams**, **Carrie Chapman Catt**, **Crystal Eastman**, **Charlotte Perkins Gilman**, **Jeannette Rankin**, and others, continued its pacifist work, although Catt withdrew support during World War I. Many thought people who were anti-war were unpatriotic. Jane Addams's campaign for peace cost her support for Hull House, but won her the 1931 Nobel Peace Prize. Many other women lost their jobs, friends, or reputations for taking a stand against war.

1890s – 1920s

⌖ Ellen Swallow Richards

born 1842 – died 1911
CHEMIST

Nicknamed "Ellencyclopedia," Ellen Swallow Richards lived up to her reputation. Richards studied astronomy with **Maria Mitchell** at Vassar College and was the first woman admitted to the Massachusetts Institute of Technology (MIT). She was also the first woman elected to the American Institute of Mining and Metallurgical Engineers, and the person who established home economics as a serious course of study.

Richards distinguished herself at MIT by analyzing public water systems and by helping establish a Women's Laboratory there in 1876. At the laboratory, Richards taught women chemistry, biology, and mineralogy. She and her students also did research and analysis for private industry. Richards published their findings in works such as *The Chemistry of Cooking and Cleaning* (1882). She joined the faculty of MIT in 1884, and for the next 27 years developed the scope and techniques of sanitary engineering, the study of water, air, and sewerage.

Richards strongly believed that scientific research should have practical applications, and that the home was key to a strong society. These two beliefs merged into a new field called home economics. Richards was a leader in this field, which pioneered the teaching of health, hygiene, and sanitation issues in schools and women's study groups and their application in homes and service institutions across the United States. She was among the founders of what became the American Association of University Women (1882).

+ + + + + + + + + + + + + + + + +

The World's Columbian Exposition of 1893 celebrated Christopher Columbus's trip to America. It also celebrated women's achievements. Many of the 27 million people who attended the Chicago fair visited the Women's Building. The building was designed by Sophia Hayden and featured a huge mural by **Mary Cassatt**. The international exhibit had been assembled by women from 47 countries, although it did not focus much attention on working class and African-American women. There was a library with 4,000 books by women, a women's invention hall, and a food kitchen run by **Ellen Swallow Richards**. There was also a World's Congress of Representative Women, where women crowded in to hear 500 speakers such as **Susan B. Anthony, Lucy Stone, Dr. Anna Howard Shaw, Francis Willard, Jane Addams, Fanny Coppin**, and **Frances Watkins Harper**.

⌬ Margaret Sanger

born 1879 – died 1966
BIRTH CONTROL ACTIVIST, FEMINIST

Margaret Sanger, the founder of what became the Planned Parenthood Federation of America, devoted her life to providing information about birth control. She was the first to use the term.

Born into a family of 11 children and little money, Margaret saw how difficult life was for her hard-working mother, who died at age 49. When she later worked as a nurse in a New York City immigrant neighborhood in the 1910s, she saw many women whose health was endangered by too many pregnancies. She saw many parents who could not afford to feed and care for all their children. Sanger became convinced of the need for family planning.

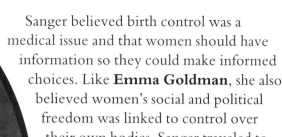

Sanger believed birth control was a medical issue and that women should have information so they could make informed choices. Like **Emma Goldman**, she also believed women's social and political freedom was linked to control over their own bodies. Sanger traveled to Europe in 1913 to gather information about contraceptives from doctors and government clinics. When she returned, she published her findings in a magazine, *The Woman Rebel*, and started the National Birth Control League. Sanger started her crusade at a time when it was illegal to give out any information about contraceptives. She was charged with sending obscene materials through the mail.

In 1916, Sanger opened the country's first birth control clinic in Brooklyn, New York. Hundreds of women lined up to learn about family planning and receive a copy of Sanger's pamphlet "What Every Girl Should Know." The clinic was shut down and Sanger was arrested and jailed for 30 days. She continued to be arrested for such activities throughout the 1930s. But the public became more and more sympathetic to her message. Her efforts later helped change the laws, so that at least doctors could distribute contraceptives. Margaret Sanger's Birth Control League underwent several changes, and in 1942, became the Planned Parenthood Federation of America, still operating today. In 1952, Sanger got Katherine McCormick, a wealthy scientist and feminist, to fund research to develop an oral contraceptive. "The pill," as it was called, was first sold in 1960. It had a major impact on women's lives.

" " " " " " " " " " " "

Mother's Day: Anna Jarvis of Philadelphia started the International Mother's Day Association in 1912 to get Congress to set aside a day to honor mothers. In 1914 President Woodrow Wilson issued a proclamation declaring the second Sunday in May Mother's Day, a national holiday. Below is "Mother and Child" (c. 1899) by **Mary Cassatt**, who often used mothers and their children as the subjects of her paintings.

1890s – 1920s

⚖ Dr. Anna Howard Shaw

born 1847 – died 1919
MINISTER, SUFFRAGIST, DOCTOR

As a lonely young farm girl living in northern Michigan, Anna Howard practiced preaching by giving sermons to the trees in the woods. Years later, Shaw became a minister, a doctor, and one of the most persuasive speakers of the women's suffrage movement. Shaw left the harsh life on the frontier farm and eventually worked her way through college. She earned degrees in theology and medicine from Boston University. In 1880, she became the first woman ordained in the Methodist Protestant Church.

Dr. Shaw began to think that being a pastor or a doctor was not doing enough to change women's lives. She turned to the temperance and suffrage movements, which became her life's work. Her friend **Frances Willard**

appointed Shaw head of the Franchise (suffrage) Department of the Women's Christian Temperance Union in 1888. **Susan B. Anthony** was so impressed when she heard Dr. Shaw give a speech that she convinced Shaw to join her suffrage group. Anthony's group eventually merged with **Lucy Stone**'s suffrage group to form the National American Woman Suffrage Association (NAWSA). Dr. Shaw served as NAWSA vice-president from 1892 to 1904 and then president from 1904 to 1915. Although she was an inspiring speaker, Shaw was a poor manager. In 1915, Dr. Shaw quietly resigned, and **Carrie Chapman Catt** became president of NAWSA. Shaw continued her spirited suffrage lectures. When the United States entered World War I in 1917, she was named head of the Woman's Committee of the U.S. Council of National Defense. She was awarded the Distinguished Service Medal in 1919.

Bessie Smith

born 1894 – died 1937

BLUES SINGER

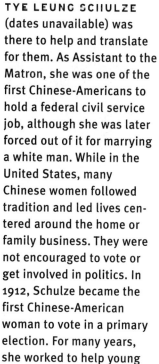

When Bessie Smith sang, "Nobody Knows You When You're Down and Out," she was singing about her own experiences with poverty, oppression, love, and heartbreak.

Bessie was born and raised in Chattanooga, Tennessee. Not much is known of her early life except that she was very poor. Her career may have started as early as 1910, when she toured with the famed blues singer Gertrude (Ma) Rainey. Smith traveled through the South singing in bars, theaters, and tent shows for several years. In 1923, she made her first records, *Down Hearted Blues* and *Gulf Coast Blues*, which were immediate hits. *Down Hearted Blues* sold 2 million copies. Her recordings and live performances were very successful, and Smith became one of the highest-paid woman entertainers. In 1929, she also appeared in *St. Louis Blues*, now a classic film of the era.

During her career, Smith struggled with alcohol and personal problems but never stopped singing. Her powerful voice, perfect rhythmic sense, and ability to improvise made her one of the country's greatest blues singers. She was an important influence on other great singers such as Billie Holiday and Mahalia Jackson and recorded with jazz greats such as Louis Armstrong and Benny Goodman.

▲ Nicknamed the "Empress of the Blues," Bessie Smith made 160 recordings during her 18-year career.

Many Asian immigrants arrived at Angel Island in San Francisco Bay. In 1910, TYE LEUNG SCHULZE (dates unavailable) was there to help and translate for them. As Assistant to the Matron, she was one of the first Chinese-Americans to hold a federal civil service job, although she was later forced out of it for marrying a white man. While in the United States, many Chinese women followed tradition and led lives centered around the home or family business. They were not encouraged to vote or get involved in politics. In 1912, Schulze became the first Chinese-American woman to vote in a primary election. For many years, she worked to help young Chinese women out of forced prostitution. She also fought to have the owners of prostitution houses prosecuted for their crimes and was an important activist in the Chinese-American community.

1890s – 1920s

Nettie Stevens

| born 1861 – died 1912 |
| **BIOLOGIST** |

Biologist Nettie Stevens's greatest achievement came from a discovery she made studying a beetle. Through experiments with the *Tenebrio molitor* beetle, Stevens identified x and y chromosomes. She explained their role in determining the sex of an embryo (an xx combination produces a female, xy a male).

Born in Cavendish, Vermont, Stevens graduated from Stanford University in California in 1899. In 1903, she got her doctoral degree in biology from Bryn Mawr College in Pennsylvania, where she remained as a researcher for the rest of her career. Stevens's research into the way cells replace themselves led her to a study of embryos and chromosomes. In 1905, she published a paper that detailed the findings from her beetle experiments. Another researcher, Edmund B. Wilson, also made a similar discovery at the same time, confirming Stevens's discovery.

Ida Tarbell

| born 1857 – died 1944 |
| **JOURNALIST** |

During her lifetime career as a journalist, Ida Tarbell wrote about women's role both in the French Revolution and in the labor movement in the United States (though she did not support the suffrage movement). She wrote profiles of famous men from Napoleon Bonaparte to Abraham Lincoln to Benito Mussolini. But it was her investigative reporting on John D. Rockefeller and the Standard Oil Company that brought her national fame and a new name: "muckraker."

Tarbell's *The History of the Standard Oil Company* (1904) led the muckraking, or investigative reporting, trend that exposed corruption and secret deals in big business. Ida was the perfect reporter to write about the Standard Oil Company for *McClure's Magazine* in 1900. Already a popular journalist, she had been raised in Pennsylvania near Standard Oil's headquarters.

Tarbell spent two years researching the giant company's business practices, and discovered a shady system of deals, especially with railroad

When it came to the full figure, many people thought Lillian Russell was the ideal. Russell was a popular star of stage shows and musicals in the 1880s and the 1890s. She was five feet six inches tall and weighed around 160 pounds. Russell set a desirable standard of beauty at the time.

◄ A political cartoon showing Ida Tarbell (on horse, center) on a crusade.

companies. Standard Oil made these deals to get rid of any competition and give Rockefeller a monopoly, or 90 percent-control of the U.S. oil-refining industry. Rockefeller made over $40 million a year – and there was no income tax then! Tarbell exposed everything in 19 *McClure's* articles. Readers were outraged. Tarbell's pioneering work led to anti-trust laws to prevent such unfair business practices.

Mary Church Terrell

born 1863 – died 1954

NACW, NAACP FOUNDER

In 1879, Mary Church enrolled at Oberlin College in Ohio to get an education, and to disprove any ideas that African Americans were intellectually inferior.

Mary got a master's degree in mathematics and learned Greek, Latin, French, and German. Back in Memphis, Tennessee, her millionaire father disapproved of women working, but Church got a job anyway. She taught first at Wilberforce University in Ohio and then in Washington, D.C., in 1887. Because married women weren't allowed to teach, Mary was forced to resign when she wed Robert Terrell in 1891. A year later, a friend of Mary's and **Ida B. Wells**'s was lynched in Memphis. Mary Terrell and the famous orator Frederick Douglass went to see President Benjamin Harrison to share their concern about the rise in racial violence. He listened, but said nothing in his public speeches. Terrell organized African-American women's clubs to fight for equality. She also worked for women's suffrage.

In 1896, Mary Church Terrell was elected president of the

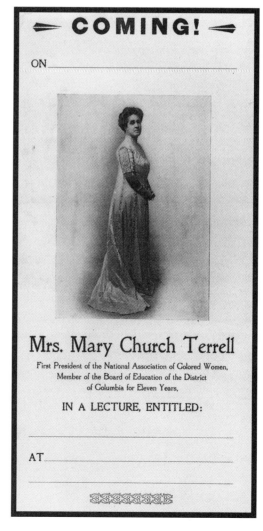

COMING!

ON _____

Mrs. Mary Church Terrell

First President of the National Association of Colored Women,
Member of the Board of Education of the District
of Columbia for Eleven Years,

IN A LECTURE, ENTITLED:

_____

AT _____

 The motto of the General Federation of Women's Clubs was "unity in diversity" – but no African-American members were allowed. African-American women formed their own clubs. In 1896, the National Association of Colored Women (NACW) incorporated more than 36 of these clubs. By 1917, there were more than 50,000 NACW members. **Jovita Idar de Juarez** did similar organizing among Mexican-American women. There was prejudice in the suffrage movement, too. The National American Woman's Suffrage Association (NAWSA) and even the more radical National Women's Party did not want to anger white Southern suffragists by actively working with African-American suffragists. By the turn of the century, African-American women had formed their own suffrage organizations throughout the country, although some leaders still worked with the NAWSA.

1890s – 1920s

National Association of Colored Women (NACW), one of the most powerful African-American women's organizations in the country. As president, Terrell crossed the country, lecturing on African-American history, establishing kindergartens and day care centers, and setting up women's suffrage chapters. In 1909, she, along with **Jane Addams** and Ida B. Wells, became one of the founding members of the National Association for the Advancement of Colored People (NAACP). Terrell fought for her rights as an African American and as a woman throughout her life. She sued the American Association of University Women in 1949 because they tried to deny her admission. Even at 90 years of age, Mary Terrell was picketing Washington, D.C. restaurants that refused to serve African Americans, taking her suit all the way to the U.S. Supreme Court. In 1953, the Court ruled that discrimination based on race in public places in Washington was illegal.

MAGGIE LENA WALKER (1867–1934) started out poor and ended up as the country's first woman bank president. She was born in Richmond, Virginia, in 1867, just after the Civil War. Her mother, a former slave, insisted Maggie go to school. Walker joined the Independent Order of St. Luke Society, which helped with health care and burials for its members, many of whom had been slaves. Walker built up the organization, bought an office building, and opened a bank in 1903. Walker was president of the St. Luke Penny Savings Bank. She became head of the board of directors when it merged with other African-American banks and became the Consolidated Bank and Trust Company. Maggie Walker encouraged African-American women to manage their money and was active in many social service groups.

Madame C.J. Walker SARAH BREEDLOVE

born 1867 – died 1919

ENTREPRENEUR

Sarah Breedlove was an orphan in Louisiana at six, a wife in Mississippi at 14, and a widow and mother in Missouri at 20. By the time she died at 52, she was a millionaire with a cosmetics factory in Indianapolis, a mansion in Harlem, and a villa in upstate New York.

Sarah worked as a laundress in St. Louis for almost 18 years. In 1905, she had a dream. It gave her the idea for a special formula for grooming African-American women's hair. She created what came to be called the Walker System. It included a shampoo, her grooming formula, brushing, and hot iron combs. The result was a smooth, shiny hair-do. Sarah started doing door-to-door sales and the style caught on. In 1906, Breedlove moved to Denver, married newspaperman Charles Walker, and started calling herself Madame C.J. Walker.

Madame Walker hired and trained a staff of agents she called "beauty culturists" to sell her products. In 1910, she opened a manufacturing plant in Indianapolis. With 3,000–5,000 female employees, it was the country's largest African-American-owned business. Walker agents, dressed in long black skirts and white blouses, made beauty house calls all across the United States. Many of the hygiene rules that Madame Walker insisted her employees follow later became part of laws governing the cosmetology industry.

Madame C.J. Walker's Harlem mansion was often filled with leading African-American artists, writers, and intellectuals. She was generous with her money, contributing to the National Association for the Advancement of Colored People (NAACP) and **Mary McLeod Bethune**'s school.

Ida B. Wells

born 1862 – died 1931

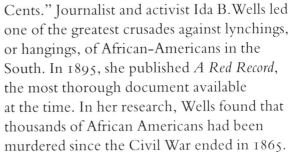

JOURNALIST, CIVIL RIGHTS ACTIVIST

▸ Ida B. Wells was forcibly removed from a train when she refused to sit in the "colored only" section. The 18 year old sued the Chesapeake & Ohio Railroad and was awarded $500, but the Tennessee Supreme Court later overturned the decision.

+ + + + + + + + + + + + + + + +

An estimated 500,000 African Americans moved from the South to northern cities during the Great Migration of 1915 to 1920. Many moved to New York City, increasing the African-American population by over 65 percent and establishing Harlem as one of the cultural centers of the world. African-American women found more job opportunities in the North, especially during World War I. They earned more cooking, working in factories, or working for the railroad companies than they did as servants or cotton pickers in the South. Still, many were paid only half of what northern white women earned. They were also given the lowest level or hardest jobs.

The sign read, "Southern Horrors. Lynch Law in all its Phases. Miss Ida B. Wells. Price, Fifteen Cents." Journalist and activist Ida B. Wells led one of the greatest crusades against lynchings, or hangings, of African-Americans in the South. In 1895, she published *A Red Record*, the most thorough document available at the time. In her research, Wells found that thousands of African Americans had been murdered since the Civil War ended in 1865.

Ida Wells's parents were slaves in Holly Springs, Mississippi. They died when she was 14, and Ida raised her five siblings while she attended Rust University, a school for freed African Americans. Then Ida taught school while she studied at Fisk University in Nashville, Tennessee. In 1891, Wells wrote articles protesting the poor conditions of schools for African-American children. As a result, she was fired from her teaching job by the all-white school board.

She quickly became co-owner of the Memphis *Free Speech* newspaper and wrote about the rising violence against African-American men and women. "Nobody in this section of the country believes the threadbare lie that Negro men rape white women," she proclaimed. That was the excuse Southerners used to lynch African-American men. When three of Wells's friends were lynched outside of Memphis in 1892, the journalist stepped up her campaign. Her exhaustive research showed white men were lynching people either because African-American businesses were cutting into their profits or because they feared African Americans would take their jobs. Ida Wells urged African Americans to leave Memphis and move to the Oklahoma Territory. Thousands did. Memphis became a dangerous place for Ida, even if she was carrying a pistol for protection. An angry mob ransacked her newspaper office and then hoped to lynch her. Wells left for New York City. There she continued her crusade, writing articles for the *New York Age* and speaking all across the country.

Wells married Ferdinand L. Barnett in 1895 and moved to Chicago. She worked with **Jane Addams**, continued her fight for the rights of African Americans, and worked for women's suffrage. She was secretary of the National Afro-American Council from 1898 to 1902, and later formed the Negro Fellowship League. When **Mary Church Terrell** and other leaders formed the National Association for the Advancement of Colored People in 1910, Ida B. Wells did not support their efforts. The NAACP was not radical enough for her.

Edith Wharton

| born 1862 – died 1937 |
| **WRITER** |

"There are two ways of spreading light: to be the candle or the mirror that reflects it," wrote Edith Wharton. Edith was both a candle and a mirror. Her life showed that women could pursue careers outside family and home life. Her writing reflected the social world of her time.

Edith Newbold Jones was born into a wealthy, high-society family in New York City. In 1885, Edith married Edward Wharton, a rich Boston banker. They traveled the social loop of the time: Boston; New York; Newport, Rhode Island, and Europe.

Edith began to write seriously after she was married, perhaps because her marriage was not satisfying. Like many women of her time, she first wrote stories and poems for magazines, especially *Scribners Magazine.* Then, in 1897, Wharton re-decorated her Newport mansion and co-wrote a book on interior decorating. She called it *The Decoration of Houses.* It sold quite well. Wharton began writing even more, although she did not publish her first novel until she was 40. When *The House of Mirth* was published in 1905, critics and readers recognized Edith Wharton's strong talents. She used her own social world as inspiration and wrote about the conflict between what people feel they *should* do and what they really *want* to do.

The Whartons moved to France in 1910, where Edith spent the rest of her life. She continued to produce successful novels like *Ethan Frome* (1911), now considered an American classic. In 1921, Edith Wharton became the first woman to win the Pulitzer Prize for fiction for *The Age of Innocence.*

Wealthy and middle-class families hired domestic help to do the cooking, cleaning, laundry, and child care. Many young, single, immigrant women worked as live-in servants. They worked 10- to 14-hour days and had little free time. African-American women, many of whom were married, worked equally hard, often for less pay. Most refused to live in. They wanted to be with their own families, and living with their employers reminded many of the days of slavery. By 1900, domestic service paid almost the same as factory work, but it was considered more menial.

1890s – 1920s

Hard Times, Tough Choices

reality, many couples needed the woman's salary to get by. Families suffered because of this bias against married women working.

Unemployed single women were often ignored by welfare agencies which mainly helped male heads of households during the Depression. Without jobs or family support, many single women ended up homeless and hungry.

Women of color were the first to be laid off when businesses shut down. To survive, many were forced to do home work, such as sewing, for very little money. And because so many people needed work at any wage, women who did household work in other people's homes found their low wages cut even lower.

The Depression was the final blow for many rural women and their families in the Midwest. Several years of drought had killed their crops, turning farmland into a "dust bowl." Many farmers couldn't pay their mortgages and lost everything they owned. Thousands of men, women, and children headed West looking for jobs on California's fertile farms. What they found was low-paying, grueling migrant work – or nothing at all.

The hardships of the Great Depression and the great demands of World War II pushed women's issues to the background, but women created new roles for themselves throughout the 1930s and 1940s. Female pilots tested the limits of aviation. Female movie stars were larger than life on the silver screen. Female athletes set records on tennis courts, on golf courses, and in Olympic stadiums. And the women's reform machine cranked back up to help deal with the nation's economic and social problems.

Surviving the Great Depression

After the stock market crashed on October 29, 1929, women in the United States had fewer job options but more political opportunities.

During the Great Depression that followed the crash, one out of four workers was unemployed. Many businesses and state governments would not hire married women because they believed men, followed by single women, should get available jobs. The Economy Act of 1932 said if a husband and wife both worked for the federal government and cutbacks were necessary, the wife had to be laid off. In

Getting into Politics

Because of the great poverty and suffering during the Depression, more and more people began to agree with reforms women's groups had championed for decades. When Democrat Franklin Delano Roosevelt (FDR) became president in 1933, the federal government took a more active role in people's lives. FDR called his plan the New Deal. It included health, education, and welfare programs, and laws to protect workers. The New Deal incorporated many of the reforms women's groups had lobbied for. And when First Lady **Eleanor Roosevelt** moved into the White House, she brought her strong network of women reformers, social workers, and activists with her. Women were appointed to key positions in the Democratic Party and in New Deal federal agencies such as the Social Security Board, which oversaw old-age insurance, and the Works Progress Administration (WPA), which created jobs and education programs. Under FDR, the country had its first woman cabinet member, Frances Perkins, the Secretary of Labor.

Though the New Deal brought relief to millions, it did not always do so fairly. Men were still given priority for jobs and government aid. Government relief agencies favored white people. New labor laws usually didn't protect household or agricultural workers, many of whom were African-American and Hispanic-American women. And most job-training programs still taught women "domestic" skills, such as sewing, rather than training them for higher-paying jobs.

Movie Stars and Model Moms

In the 1930s, millions of people paid their 10¢ admission and went to a movie to escape the misery of the Depression. This was the Golden Age of Hollywood. Movies featured popular female stars playing characters who were lovable screwballs, glamorous heroines, or tough, sophisticated career women.

Meanwhile, ads from this period encouraged women to keep their homes and themselves beautiful to preserve family life. Movies and ads showed women who were white, well-groomed,

▶ Actor-dancer Ginger Rogers, star of 1930s movie musicals

Women are doing a big job on the Pennsylvania Railroad

Pennsylvania Railroad
Serving the Nation

▲ During World War II (1941–1945), business and government appealed to women's patriotism to fill the gaps left by servicemen.

and sure of a happy ending. They ignored the fact that most American women struggled with work, raising families, and even basic survival.

Women at War

The United States entered World War II after the Japanese attacked Pearl Harbor on December 7, 1941. Women joined the war effort. They were praised for holding war bond drives to raise money and for volunteering for the armed forces or the Red Cross. When men headed overseas to battlefronts, many women took their jobs in factories and defense plants. The high unemployment of the 1930s gave way to a worker shortage in the 1940s. By 1942, the government's War Manpower Commission actively recruited women, single and married, to fill manufacturing jobs at higher salaries than they had ever earned.

Women, however, still did not have equal standing in the labor unions that were becoming more powerful. They were also more likely to hold industry's unskilled, lower-paying jobs. When the war ended, women were expected to go home and raise families, making way for returning military men. Many women did not want to give up their jobs. Others couldn't really afford not to work. But most industrial jobs were once again considered "men's work." Women again took home the smaller paychecks of clerical or service workers. And many women did settle into the roles of "Mrs." and "mom" as the suburban nuclear family became *the* approved social unit.

99

Berenice Abbott

▲ ABC Auto School, Harlem, New York, a 1938 photo by Berenice Abbott.

PHOTOGRAPHER

"Photography helps people to see," Berenice Abbott once said in an interview. Her startling black-and-white photos showed human beings, architecture, even science, in ways no one had ever seen.

Abbott, a native of Ohio, moved to New York and then Europe to study sculpture in the 1920s. She became part of the lively Paris art scene and worked as an assistant to the famous photographer Man Ray. Then Abbott opened her own portrait studio, where she photographed well-known people like the Irish writer James Joyce and the American poet **Edna St. Vincent Millay**.

Abbott returned to the United States in 1929, just as the Great Depression hit. She was hired by the government's Federal Art Project and turned her keen eye to the New York landscape, shooting everything from bridges to barber shops. Her collection, called *Changing New York*, is an important document of how this city destroyed the old and built the new during the 1930s. Berenice Abbott became well-known because of the series and was hired to teach at the city's New School for Social Research in 1935. In the 1950s, working with the Massachusetts Institute of Technology in Cambridge, Abbott pioneered new techniques and new technology for photographing scientific subjects such as water waves and light beams.

Dr. Hattie Alexander

PEDIATRICIAN, MICROBIOLOGIST

Before 1939, babies who got meningitis, an infection that inflames the membranes around the brain and spinal cord, faced certain death. That year their odds changed when Dr. Hattie Alexander developed an antiserum that worked against the disease. The death rate for children and adults with meningitis dropped sharply.

After Alexander graduated from college in 1923, she worked as a scientist studying bacteria for the federal and Maryland public health services before she was admitted to Johns Hopkins medical school in Baltimore,

Maryland. An outstanding student, Alexander received her medical degree in 1930 and went to work at Babies Hospital at Columbia-Presbyterian medical center in New York City. There she headed the microbiology laboratory. At Babies Hospital, Dr. Alexander saw infants die every day from meningitis. She worked years to find a cure, often with a partner, Dr. Michael Heidelberger. Her discovery of an antibody that could fight meningitis made her famous – and saved thousands of lives starting in the 1940s. Dr. Alexander became the first woman president of the American Pediatric Society in 1964.

Marian Anderson

born 1902 – died 1993

OPERA SINGER

When Marian Anderson sang an opera in Salzburg, Austria, in 1935, the great Italian conductor Arturo Toscanini said, "What I heard today one is privileged to hear only in a hundred years." When she sang in Town Hall in New York the same year, *The New York Times* called it "music making that probed too deep for words." But when Marian Anderson wanted to sing at Constitution Hall in Washington, D.C., in 1939, the Daughters of the American Revolution (DAR), who owned the hall, said no. People were outraged that one of America's greatest opera singers was not allowed to sing because of her color. First Lady **Eleanor Roosevelt** resigned from the DAR and arranged a concert for Anderson at the Lincoln Memorial.

Marian got her early training at a Baptist church in Philadelphia. Her range was so great that she could sing all four of the major voice parts: bass, alto, tenor, and soprano. She won several scholarships, and in 1925, beat 300 other singers to win a chance to sing with the New York Philharmonic Orchestra. Her performance was outstanding and for the next few years Anderson toured Europe, where she was hailed as one of the great voices of the century. Marian Anderson continued to perform and win awards in the United States after the Lincoln Memorial concert. In 1955, she became the first African American to sing with the famous Metropolitan Opera in New York. Her performances and recordings were legendary and earned her the Presidential Medal of Freedom in 1963 and a Lifetime Achievement Grammy award in 1991.

◄ Marian Anderson sang for an audience of 75,000 at her famous 1939 concert in front of the Lincoln Memorial in Washington, D.C.

During the 1930s and 1940s, several talented African-American women singers, many with church choir or gospel backgrounds, stirred music audiences from opera halls to jazz clubs. Like **Ella Fitzgerald**, jazz legend Sarah Vaughan got her start at Harlem's Apollo Theater. Vaughan, called "The Divine One" because of her incredible voice, was an innovative jazz singer. Also in the jazz world were Mary Lou Williams, a pianist and composer who wrote arrangements for Louis Armstrong and Duke Ellington, among others; and the great jazz-blues singer Billie Holiday.

1930s – 1940s

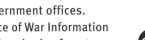 Mary Anderson

born 1872 – died 1964

LABOR LEADER, GOVERNMENT OFFICIAL

"Wage rates should be based on occupation and not on sex" was one of Mary Anderson's mottos. For 24 years, she headed the Women's Bureau of the U.S. Department of Labor, working through two world wars and the Great Depression to make this idea a reality.

Anderson knew a lot about personal full employment. She came to Michigan from Sweden when she was 16 and started washing dishes at a boarding house for $1.50 a week. In 1892, she moved to Chicago to work in a shoe factory. Mary stitched shoes and boots for 18 years. When she wasn't at her machine, she was at the union hall, organizing other workers. Anderson eventually became a national organizer for the Women's Trade Union League. During World War I, she worked for the War Department agency that monitored the working conditions of women who filled job gaps left by men serving in the army. In 1920, President Woodrow Wilson made the agency a permanent bureau of the U.S. Department of Labor. Mary Anderson became the first president of this Women's Bureau. Under her direction, the bureau investigated women's working conditions, lobbied for labor laws, and made sure women were included in the 1938 Fair Labor Standards Act. Anderson's efforts were encouraged by Secretary of Labor **Frances Perkins** and First Lady **Eleanor Roosevelt.**

+ + + + + + + + + + + + + + + +

During World War II, 6,000,000 women joined the war work effort. Some worked outside the home for the first time. Others left lower-paying domestic jobs, such as housekeeping, for higher-paying work in defense factories, shipyards, railroad companies, and government offices. The Office of War Information printed hundreds of posters to encourage women to get jobs, making "Rosie the Riveter" a popular image. However, the government did not fund day-care centers until 1943 and there were never enough. The Women's Bureau found that in 1944, 16 percent of working mothers still had no child care.

 Dorothy Arzner

born 1900 – died 1979

FILM DIRECTOR

Hollywood had its Golden Age in the 1930s. Female stars were everywhere – but there was only one female director, Dorothy Arzner.

Arzner met plenty of movie people when she waited tables in her father's Hollywood cafe, but she decided to go into medicine. After working as a World War I ambulance driver, Arzner returned to California and got a job as a typist in Paramount Studios' script department. Dorothy worked her way up to film editor. Her creative edit of a bullfight scene in *Blood and Sand* (1922), starring movie idol Rudolph Valentino, established Arzner as one of the star editors of silent film. In 1927, Paramount Studios finally let Arzner do what she wanted to do: direct. Her debut movie, *Fashions for Women,* was a big hit and launched Arzner as a Hollywood director. And she was an

innovative one. Arzner was among the first directors to use theme music in films and the first to use overhead microphones. While filming *The Wild Party* (1929), Paramount's first movie with sound, she hung a mike from a fishing pole over the actors' heads. Her techniques became film standards. During her career, Dorothy Arzner worked with stars such as **Katharine Hepburn**, making films with strong, independent female leads. She also shot training films for **Oveta Culp Hobby** and the Women's Army Corps from 1943 to 1945.

🎓 Mary McLeod Bethune

born 1875 – died 1955

EDUCATOR

"The drums of Africa still beat in my heart," Mary McLeod Bethune once said. "They will not let me rest while there is a single Negro boy or girl without a chance to prove his worth." Mary, the daughter of former slaves in South Carolina, didn't rest until she got an education herself and then helped thousands of other African Americans do the same.

Mary attended the first school for African-American children in her town. Then she got scholarships to Scotia Seminary in Concord, North Carolina, and to Moody Bible Institute in Chicago. In 1904, she moved to Daytona Beach, Florida, where many African Americans had moved to work in

+ + + + + + + + + + + + + + + + +

Like many African Americans, Native Americans also organized during the 1940s. Native American women joined The National Congress of American Indians (NCAI), which was founded in 1944 to protect the interests of tribes all across the country. In 1945, NCAI ruled that at least one woman should be elected to the executive council every year.

1930s – 1940s

◀ Mary McLeod Bethune served as vice-president of the National Association for the Advancement of Colored People (NAACP) from 1940 until her death in 1955.

+ + + + + + + + + + + + + + + + +

 Brenda Starr, one of the first comic strips to feature a professional woman, was the first one created by a woman artist. It started running in 1940 and was printed in the Sunday funnies of the *Chicago Tribune-New York News* chain. Fans of the fearless, red-haired, twinkle-eyed reporter made the comic strip so popular it became a daily and still runs today. Early on in her career, *Brenda Starr's* creator had changed her name from Dalia to Dale Messick so she could get ahead in the man's world of newspaper comics.

the big hotels or to build the Florida East Coast Railway. Bethune only had $1.50 to her name, but she had a big dream: to open her own school. She rented an old cottage, used packing crates for chairs and desks, and opened the Daytona Normal and Industrial Institute for Negro Girls. Five students were enrolled. Two years later, there were 250 students, four teachers, and night classes for adults. In 1923, the school merged with the Cookman Institute for Men and became Bethune-Cookman College. Mary McLeod Bethune served as its president for many years. She raised funds for Bethune-Cookman, gaining support from women such as **Eleanor Roosevelt** and **Madame C.J. Walker**. She also was president of the National Association of Colored Women from 1924 to 1928. In 1935, Bethune founded the National Council of Negro Women to fight racism and sexism. The next year, President Franklin D. Roosevelt made her head of the Office of Minority Affairs of the National Youth Administration. Bethune was the first African-American woman to hold a government job at this level. As part of FDR's "Black Cabinet," she was responsible for the education of 600,000 African-American children across the country.

Margaret Bourke-White

born 1906 – died 1971
PHOTOGRAPHER

Margaret Bourke-White took her camera wherever she went: the tops of New York skyscrapers, the bottom of South African mines, across the American South, and into German concentration camps. She was one of the first – and best – photojournalists.

Bourke-White became one of four staff photographers of a new photo

magazine, *Life,* in 1936. She was already known for her striking architectural photos, for the first industrial photographs of the Soviet Union and Germany, and for her heartbreaking photos of poor Southern sharecroppers in the United States. These last photos, a joint project with her second husband, novelist Erskine Caldwell, were collected into a famous book, *You Have Seen Their Faces* (1937).

In 1941, Bourke-White scooped the world with photos from the Soviet Union, which had just been invaded by Germany. Women rarely did war reporting, but Bourke-White insisted on covering World War II for *Life*. Her camera clicked all over Europe and the Soviet Union. She flew on bombing missions and was torpedoed on a boat off North Africa. She became the U.S. Army's first woman war correspondent in 1942 and traveled with General Patton's army. Her chilling photographs of the liberation of Nazi concentration camps shocked the world.

Bourke-White remained with *Life* magazine for 33 years, covering newsworthy events worldwide, and once again served as a war correspondent during the Korean War.

Pearl S. Buck

born 1892 – died 1973

WRITER

Pearl Sydenstricker Buck, the first woman to win the Nobel Prize for literature (1938), was born in West Virginia but lived in eastern China for part of her childhood. She used her writing to encourage greater understanding between the people of her native and adopted cultures.

Pearl, the daughter of American missionaries, lived her first eight years in China and returned to the United States in 1900. After she graduated college, she went back to China to teach English. Many of her stories, such as *The Good Earth*, are set there. That novel tells the story of Wang Lung, a Chinese peasant whose deep love of the land pulls him through years of hardship and struggle. It won the 1932 Pulitzer Prize, sold over 2 million copies, and was made into a play and later an Academy Award-winning film. Buck wrote more than 40 novels and hundreds of short stories and essays and a book on feminism called *Of Men and Women* (1941). In 1941, she founded the East-West Association, which promoted cultural understanding. She also started two organizations to care for unwanted children: Welcome House (1949), an adoption agency for Asian-American children, and the Pearl S. Buck Foundation (1963).

+ + + + + + + + + + + + + + + + + +

Despite **Pearl S. Buck**'s efforts to inform Americans about China, Chinese people were ignored or stereotyped in popular American culture. In fact, the film version of Buck's *The Good Earth,* used non-Asian actors wearing make-up.

Hollywood usually cast Anna May Wong, a famous actor who made more than 80 films in her 37-year career, as a dragon lady or exotic but obedient "china doll."

⊛ Jacqueline Cochran

born c. 1910 – died 1980

AVIATOR

May 1953. The F-86 Sabre soared up to 45,000 feet, then the pilot turned the jet's nose toward the earth and began her dive. Hundreds of people heard the loud *boom* – Jackie Cochran had just become the first woman to break the sound barrier!

Jackie Cochran broke a lot of barriers in her lifetime. She worked her way out of childhood poverty in Florida by becoming a beautician. Jackie thought she could sell more beauty products if she flew instead of driving from city to city. Within three weeks of her first flying lesson, Cochran had a private pilot's license. Two years later, in 1934, she also opened her own successful cosmetics business in California, but flying had become her real love. "When I paid for my first lesson," Cochran recalled, "a beauty operator ceased to exist, and an aviator was born."

World War II broke out in Europe and in 1941, Cochran flew a United States bomber to England. After the U.S. joined the war, President Franklin D. Roosevelt asked Cochran how women pilots could help the war effort. Their talk led to the founding of the Women Airforce Service Pilots (WASP) in 1943, with Cochran as director. One thousand and seventy-eight women joined the group. WASPs were not allowed to fly in combat, but their service was invaluable: they taught student pilots, towed target planes for soldiers training as gunners, and delivered war planes within the United States and Canada. Cochran was awarded the Distinguished Service Medal, won the Harmon trophy for outstanding female pilot 15 times, and broke over 200 aviation records in her career. On May 4, 1964, she became the fastest woman alive when she flew 1,429 mph in a Super Star jet.

💬 *Airline hostesses:* the country's first flight attendants. In 1930, the first hostesses were nurses. They could be no taller than 5′ 4″ and no heavier than 115 pounds. They had to have a "pleasant personality," "unquestionable family background," and be "well-proportioned," according to one airline's rules. And, of course, they were young and single. Airlines wanted their hostesses to seem friendly and reassuring to passengers. Even though airline hostesses, like other women at the time, were considered the "weaker sex," they still did everything from carrying luggage to cleaning the plane cabin to serving lunch. Some even helped push the plane into the hangar!

Bette Davis

born 1908 – died 1989

FILM ACTOR

"Fasten your seat belts – it's going to be a bumpy night," Bette Davis warned in *All About Eve* (1950), an Academy Award-winning film about ruthless actresses. She could have been talking about her own life and career.

Ruth Elizabeth Davis was born in Lowell, the Massachusetts mill town. She moved to New York in 1928 and studied first at the John Murray Anderson Dramatic School and later studied dance under **Martha Graham**. In 1930, Davis made the move to Hollywood – and failed her first screen test with a major studio. She finally signed with Warner Brothers studio and started making movies, often second-rate ones. But in 1935, Davis won an Academy Award for her role in *Dangerous*. Three years later, Warner suspend-

ed the outspoken movie star because she refused to work in a new film whose script she thought was "atrocious." That same year, she won a second Oscar for *Jezebel*. Bette, who was once considered unsexy and droopy-eyed, now was a box-office hit. Women audiences especially liked her because she often played tough, independent characters.

In 1941, Bette Davis became the first woman to head the Academy of Motion Picture Arts and Sciences, the professional organization that awards the Oscars. Davis continued working in film and television, and in 1977, became the first woman to receive the famous American Film Institute Life Achievement Award.

+ + + + + + + + + + + + + + + + +

Actor Hattie McDaniel, who played the role of Mammy in the 1939 film classic *Gone with the Wind,* was the first African American to win an Academy Award. McDaniel acted in more than 20 films and later on in television, becoming a wealthy woman. But like most women of color, she found very few roles open to her. McDaniel usually played a maid or servant, but did so with distinct style and out-spokenness. She once said, "It's better to get $7,000 a week for playing a servant than $7 a week for being one."

1930s – 1940s

Molly Dewson MARY

born 1874 – died 1962

POLITICAL ACTIVIST

When Molly (Mary) Dewson was a senior at Wellesley College in 1897, her class predicted she would someday become President of the United States. Although this prediction never came true, she at least got into President Franklin Roosevelt's inner circle and became head of the Women's Division of the Democratic National Committee in 1933.

After graduating college, Molly worked on the Domestic Reform Committee of the Women's Educational and Industrial Union. Her job was to find ways to make housework a paying job for women. Her report for the National Consumers' League led to the 1912 Massachusetts minimum wage act for women and children, the first of its kind in the country. During the 1920s, Dewson was an important figure in the New York reform and suffrage movements. **Eleanor Roosevelt** asked her to enlist and organize women in the Democratic Party. In 1932, Dewson was named head of the Women's Division of the Democratic National Committee. Five years later, she became vice-president of the entire committee. Dewson fought for women to hold half the seats on the party platform committee. She campaigned for **Frances Perkins**'s successful approval as Secretary of Labor. Dewson took on an even bigger workload when she became the first woman member of the Social Security Board in 1937.

Katherine Dunham

born 1910

ANTHROPOLOGIST, CHOREOGRAPHER

Katherine Dunham loved studying people and customs from different countries. She also loved dancing. As a University of Chicago student, Dunham won a $2,400 travel fellowship and found a way to bring her two loves together. Dunham studied dance and anthropology on Caribbean islands such as Jamaica, Martinique, Trinidad, and especially Haiti. She saw that many of the island dances had African origins. Dunham returned to the United States and created dance pieces, based on what she had seen, to share important black cultural history. Around 1939, she formed her own dance company with all African-American dancers. It toured all over the world. Some of her most famous African-Caribbean pieces for the dance troupe include *Tropics and le Jazz Hot – From Haiti to*

Harlem (1940) and *Caribbean Rhapsody* (1950). In 1938, she became dance director of the Federal Theater Project.

Katherine Dunham's work in plays such as *Cabin in the Sky* (1940), in movies such as *Stormy Weather* (1943), and with symphony orchestras and New York's Metropolitan Opera introduced audiences to a wide range of Caribbean, African, and African-American movements and rhythms. She has received many awards, including the Kennedy Center Honor (1983) and the Capezio Dance Award (1991). When Dunham retired from performing in the 1960s, she founded the Katherine Dunham Center in East St. Louis, Missouri, to teach young African Americans their roots through dance. She also kept a home in Haiti. Her love for that island and its people sparked her 1992 hunger strike against the U.S. government's poor treatment of Haitian refugees. Dunham stopped eating for 47 days, ending her fast only when the exiled Haitian president personally asked her to. Eighty-two-year-old Katherine had shown the world her body still had power to speak for the people – just as it had when she danced.

☺ Amelia Earhart

born 1897 – died c. 1937

AVIATOR

In 1928, Amelia Earhart boarded a three-engine propeller seaplane called the *Friendship* as a standby co-pilot and passenger and became the first woman to fly across the Atlantic Ocean. Unlike the male pilot and mechanic, Earhart was not paid for the trip. But she didn't care because she was where she wanted to be – up in the air.

Earhart achieved many "firsts," including speed and altitude records, during her nine years as a pilot, and was active in opening aviation to women. Born in Kansas, Earhart had been a social worker and

+ + + + + + + + + + + + + + + + +

Amelia Earhart, or AE, as she liked to be called, was the first president of the Ninety-Nines (99s), a female pilots' organization founded in 1929. The group was named for the number of women pilots (out of a total of 126 licensed at the time) who paid $1 each to join. Ruth Nichols, **Jacqueline Cochran**, and Kathryn Cheung, the first Chinese woman in America to get a pilot's license, were among the early members. The Ninety-Nines sponsored races and other activities to show that women were capable and talented fliers. Newspapers called them Flying Flappers and Petticoat Pilots. There are now about 6,400 Ninety-Nines members from all over the world.

1930s – 1940s

nurse before turning her passion for flying into a career. In the early 1920s, she flew in air shows, which were very popular at the time. After the *Friendship* flight, Amelia met and married publisher George Putnam in 1931. Putnam managed Earhart's career, which was really taking off. In 1932, she became the first woman to fly solo across the Atlantic Ocean. Amelia flew alone through dangerous thunderstorms and fog in her Lockheed Vega on the 2,026-mile flight from Newfoundland to Ireland. She still set a transatlantic record, crossing in 14 hours and 56 minutes. Earhart was awarded the U.S. Distinguished Flying Cross. Three years later, in 1935, she became the first person to fly solo from Hawaii to California, a 2,400-mile trip over the Pacific Ocean.

Earhart's last flight was her most ambitious. In 1937, she and her co-pilot, Fred Noonan, took off from Miami, Florida, in a twin-engine Lockheed Electra. They were headed on a 27,000-mile trip around the world at the equator, but on July 2, the plane disappeared over the Pacific Ocean. Earhart and Noonan were never seen again. George Putnam was finally forced to open the letter Amelia had once left him in case she never returned. In it she wrote: "Please know I am quite aware of the hazards. I want to do it because I want to do it. Women must try to do things as men have tried. When they fail, their failure must be but a challenge to others."

+ + + + + + + + + + + + + + + + +

In the 1920s, the United States was racially segregated – legally in some places, unofficially in others. White audiences could drop into a Harlem, New York, nightclub far more easily than well-known African-American entertainers could tour cross-country. Performers like **Ella Fitzgerald** sometimes had to play two shows in towns they visited – one for a white audience and another for a black audience. When African-American artists traveled, they had to look hard for hotels, restaurants, and other facilities that would serve them.

Ella Fitzgerald

Ella Fitzgerald is one of the greatest jazz singers of all time. She was voted best female vocalist in *Down Beat* music magazine every year from 1953 through the mid-1970s. She won 12 Grammy Awards. And in 1992, she was awarded the Presidential Medal of Freedom.

Ella's big break came at the famous Apollo Theater in Harlem, New York, when she was 15. She sang on amateur night and got a wild round of applause. She also got the attention of bandleader Chick Webb, who signed her on as a singer. In 1938, Fitzgerald and Webb had their first big hit together, "A-Tisket A-Tasket," a new and jazzy version of an old nursery rhyme. When Webb died in 1939, Fitzgerald became the band's leader for a while. In 1942, she went solo. Often called the "First Lady of Song," she used her voice like a musical instrument. Fitzgerald could sing everything from blues to ballads to scat, the improvised, nonsense-syllable jazz

born 1918 – died 1996

JAZZ SINGER

she made famous. In 1946, Fitzgerald started singing on Jazz at the Philharmonic tours and traveled all over the world. Fitzgerald worked with great composers like Duke Ellington, Irving Berlin, Cole Porter, and George Gershwin. She has recorded over 2,000 songs on more than 70 albums.

Martha Graham

born 1894 – died 1991

DANCER, CHOREOGRAPHER

"Nothing is more revealing than movement," Martha Graham once stated. Her fascination with the way movement communicates truth beyond words was Graham's main source of inspiration as a dancer, choreographer, and the Mother of Modern Dance.

In 1916, in Los Angeles, California, Graham became a student of Ruth St. Denis, an innovative dancer and the co-founder of the first major dance school in the United States. By 1920, Graham was studying dance in New York City. She joined the *Greenwich Village Follies* in 1923, but left to explore her own dancing style, and founded the Martha Graham School of Contemporary Dance in 1929. Graham's style was new and daring. She rejected the pointed toe of classical ballet for a more modern dance that acknowledged the body, breathing, and gravity. Her arrangement of dance movements was based on the idea of contraction and release of the torso, or trunk of the body. Graham choreographed a lot of tight, contracted motions, followed by letting the body in motion open up. Many contemporary dance pieces just had dancers tell a story, such as *Romeo and Juliet*, with their movements. Graham's dances told what was going on inside her characters, what sparked their inner spirit. She used dance to explore mood, emotion, and expression far beyond what was common in dance at the time.

From 1928 until 1938, Graham choreographed many dance pieces based on political issues. They included *Revolt*, *Immigrant*, *Four Insincerities*, and *Heretic*. Graham also created pieces about great women, such as **Emily Dickinson**, the Bronte sisters, and Joan of Arc. Greek myths were another important source for her work. *Clytemnestra*, created in 1958, was her greatest Greek performance.

Martha Graham retired from performing in 1970, at the age of 76. She continued choreographing, creating more than 150 pieces in her lifetime, and was director of the Martha Graham Dance Company. Graham received many awards, including the 1976 Presidential Medal of Freedom and a National Medal for the Arts in 1985.

▶ Martha Graham had a far-reaching effect on dancers and dance education, as well as on noted dancer-choreographers such as **Agnes de Mille** and **Twyla Tharp.** Her students have included everyone from **Maya Angelou** to **Bette Davis** to **Madonna.**

1930s – 1940s

☯ Edith Hamilton

born 1867 – died 1963
WRITER

"All things are to be examined and called into question," Edith Hamilton wrote in *The Greek Way*, published in 1930 when Edith was 63. Hamilton herself always questioned what she saw. Her curious mind led her to write many eye-opening books about history and literature.

Edith and her sister **Alice Hamilton** grew up in Indiana, and were taught Latin, Greek, French, and German at home. Edith went to Bryn Mawr College in Pennsylvania, where she continued studying Latin and Greek. In 1895, she became the first woman to attend the University of Munich in Germany. She then became headmistress of the Bryn Mawr Girls' School in Baltimore. When she quit in 1922, Edith admitted she had never liked that job. Five years later, her love of classical studies brought her work she did like.

A friend of Hamilton's talked her into writing some articles about ancient Greek drama and culture for *Theatre Arts Monthly* magazine. That was the beginning of Hamilton's new career. Her writing style appealed to scholars and general readers. Her book *The Greek Way* was a huge success. Hamilton made ancient Greek culture seem rich and alive. She did the same thing with *The Roman Way* (1932) and then explored the world of the Bible in *Prophets of Israel* (1936). Hamilton was elected to the American Institute of Arts and Letters in 1955, and was made an honorary citizen of Athens, Greece, in 1957.

+ + + + + + + + + + + + + + + + +

🌐 Mae West made more than $450,000 a year by 1935, for her tough, sexy film and stage roles. She had the second highest income in America at the time. During World War II, the military's inflatable life preserver was called a "Mae West" after the movie star's legendary figure.

☯ Edith Head

born c. 1907 – died 1981
COSTUME DESIGNER

Edith Head got her big chance to be a costume designer through Cecil B. de Mille, a Hollywood director famous for his extravagant films. He asked her to make a costume for an elephant! It was the beginning of Head's long, distinguished career that included 35 nominations and eight Academy Awards for best costume design.

Edith Head had several college degrees and had attended art school in Los Angeles when she heard about a design job at the Paramount movie studios in 1923. She showed some fashion designs and was hired. Head was a sketch artist for years, working her way up in the design department, where she designed Mae West's clothes for *She Done Him Wrong* (1933). In 1938, Head was made Paramount's Chief Designer. She was the first woman to be in charge of a design department at a major film studio. In 1949, Head won her first Academy Award for designing the clothes in *The Heiress*, a Victorian-era drama. The following year she won two Oscars, one for the modern *All About Eve*, starring **Bette Davis**, and another for the biblical love story, *Samson and Delilah*. In 1967, Edith Head moved to Universal Studios as chief designer. She won her last Oscar in 1973 for *The Sting*, a movie about two con men in the 1920s. Her broad range of film work showed Edith Head could design costumes for just about any time, place, or character.

Katharine Hepburn

| born 1909 |
| **ACTOR** |

When Katharine Hepburn moved from acting in New York theaters to acting in Hollywood films in the 1930s, she brought along her own style – and attitude. Quick, witty, and determined to move ahead, Hepburn wanted to be paid well and left alone: no interviews, no autographs. She wanted respect as an actor and complete privacy as an individual. And she worked hard to get it all, declaring, "without discipline, there's no life at all."

Hepburn was born into a wealthy Hartford, Connecticut, family. After attending Bryn Mawr College in Pennsylvania, where her interest in acting grew, she moved to New York City in 1928, hoping for a stage career. Katherine was soon on her way to Hollywood, where her third film, *Morning Glory* (1933), won her an Academy Award. That same year, she created a popular portrayal of Jo March in a film of **Louisa May Alcott**'s *Little Women*. In 1942, Hepburn and Spencer Tracy made their first movie together, *Woman of the Year*. They became one of Hollywood's most famous couples, onscreen and off, making eight more films together. Hepburn's highly stylized acting method together with Tracy's more naturalistic approach had exciting chemistry and box-office appeal.

Katharine Hepburn portrayed strong, spirited women in almost every movie she made. She played a missionary traveling down a dangerous river with a drunk boat captain in the famous *African Queen*. She played a queen at war with her husband in *The Lion in Winter*, which won her another Academy Award in 1968. She also won Academy Awards for playing the role of a mother in *Guess Who's Coming to Dinner?* (1967) and in *On Golden Pond* (1981). Hepburn continues to work in film and television.

" " " " " " " " " " " "

Pinup girl: a photo of a young, beautiful woman that soldiers "pinned-up" wherever they were stationed. The women pictured were in sexy poses and were symbols of the American Way of Life that soldiers were supposed to be defending. Movie star Betty Grable, with her blonde hair, long legs, and wholesome look, was the most popular pinup girl of World War II. Fox movie studios had her legs insured for $1 million. Grable herself made $300,000 a year in the 1940s.

1930s – 1940s

✪ Oveta Culp Hobby

born 1905 – died 1995
WAC DIRECTOR, CABINET MEMBER

During World War II, Congress decided that women were suitable for about 54 different army jobs. When Oveta Culp Hobby became the first director of the Women's Auxiliary Army Corps in 1942, she added 185 more jobs to the list, just about everything short of combat duty.

The Women's Army Corps (WAC), as it was called from 1943 on, was a regular part of the United States Army. Colonel Hobby was appointed by President Franklin D. Roosevelt to recruit women for the war effort. Nearly 100,000 women enlisted who fit WAC requirements: good health, good character, and no children under age 14. They worked in clerical jobs, as nurses, or as supply officers. Seventeen thousand WACs served overseas. Hobby received the U.S. Army Distinguished Service Award for her work. She was the first woman so honored.

After the war, Hobby became co-publisher (with her husband) of the *Houston Post* newspaper, and became active in state and national politics. Hobby was a key campaigner during Dwight D. Eisenhower's 1952 bid for the presidency. In 1953, he named Oveta Culp Hobby head of the U.S. Department of Health, Education, and Welfare (HEW). She was the second American woman, after **Frances Perkins**, named to a cabinet office.

+ + + + + + + + + + + + + + + + +

 The U.S. Office of War information appealed to women's patriotism during World War II. Nearly 350,000 white, African-American, Native American, Chinese-American, and Hispanic-American women answered the call and enrolled in women's branches of the Army, Navy, Coast Guard, and Marines. Most worked as clerks, in supply offices, or as nurses. Under **Jacqueline Cochran**, 1,000 women pilots joined the WASPS.

✏ Malvina Hoffman

born 1885 – died 1966
SCULPTOR

The famous French sculptor Auguste Rodin once told his student Malvina Hoffman to study anatomy. She took his advice and went on to become one of the era's most productive sculptors.

Born and raised in New York, Hoffman first went to Paris in 1910 to study with Rodin. She came to know many of the artists in the cultural scene of the 1920s, from writer and art collector **Gertrude Stein** to ballerina Anna Pavlova. Hoffman sculpted several dance-related pieces, inspired by Pavlova and others, which won awards and

brought Hoffman to the attention of the art world. She sculpted several monuments and also worked in crayon portraits.

In 1930, Chicago's Field Museum of Natural History hired Hoffman to sculpt a series of works to show the different racial types of people. Hoffman traveled around the world for two years meeting people from Africa, Asia, Europe, the Pacific Islands, and North America. She talked to anthropologists and made models. The result of all her research was a collection of 25 full-figure sculptures and 85 busts. Most were cast in bronze, and a few sculpted from marble or stone. It was one of the largest sculpture commissions ever assigned to a woman.

Dr. Karen Horney

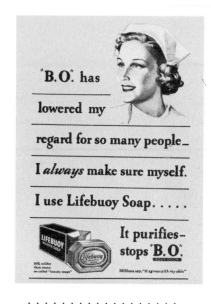

| born 1885– died 1952 |
| PSYCHOANALYST |

Born near Hamburg, Germany, Karen Danielssen Horney had a very strict father who taught her that a woman's role was to serve men. She challenged his ideas by studying and developing a new view of women's psychology.

Karen got her medical degree from the University of Berlin in 1911. She married and had three daughters. Conflicts among her different roles as physician, wife, and mother led to depression and sparked her interest in psychoanalysis. At that time, it was a fairly new field of study pioneered by Dr. Sigmund Freud. Psychoanalysts explore the sources of people's mental problems and behavior. By 1919, Dr. Horney was a teacher at the Berlin Psychoanalytic Institute. She began studying women's problems and how they were treated. Horney attacked Freud's idea that "anatomy was destiny," that a woman's gender dictated how she should best live. Horney pointed out how social and cultural expectations play an important role in women's mental health. She wrote that "women see themselves in the way that their men's wishes demand of them." Horney was criticized for these radical ideas.

Horney moved to Chicago in 1932 and worked at the Institute for Psychoanalysis and then went to New York City to work at the Psychoanalytic Institute. When she published *New Ways in Psychoanalysis* in 1939, again attacking Freud and his ideas about women, the human sex drive, and death, she was expelled from the New York institute. Two years later, she founded the Association for the Advancement of Psychoanalysis. Dr. Horney was one of the first psychoanalysts to recognize the connections between women's mental illness and sexism and changes caused by industrialization.

From the 1920s on, advertisers began to connect women's self-image with what they bought. At the same time, psychology, especially Sigmund Freud's ideas about women, became an important part of American culture.

1930s – 1940s

🖊 Zora Neale Hurston

| born 1903 – died 1960 |
| **WRITER, ANTHROPOLOGIST** |

Zora Neale Hurston was born and raised in Eatonville, Florida, the first incorporated all-black town in the United States. She studied at Howard University, and then moved to New York City in 1925. Three years later she became the first African-American graduate of Barnard College, where she had studied anthropology under the same professor who taught **Margaret Mead**. Hurston then traveled throughout the southern United States, Jamaica, and Haiti, collecting folklore, the legends and beliefs handed down through generations. Her book *Mules and Men* (1935) was a study of folkways, shared ways of thinking and behaving, among African Americans in Florida. A mix of anthropological and travel writing, *Tell My Horse* (1938) captures what Hurston saw in Haiti.

Hurston's most popular book was a novel, *Their Eyes Were Watching God*, published in 1937. Hurston wrote many other books, most of which were set in African-American communities not linked to the white world. The main characters of many of Hurston's books were women trying to create meaningful lives for themselves. She used dialect and folklore in her stories, which some other Harlem Renaissance writers thought was demeaning. Despite her successes, Hurston's work was pretty much forgotten by the time she died in poverty in a welfare home in Fort Pierce, Florida. Today, thanks to the efforts of writers such as **Alice Walker**, Hurston is recognized as one of America's great and influential storytellers.

++++++++++++++++++

 Congress and President Roosevelt created the Works Progress Administration (WPA) in 1935 to help put some of the 9 million unemployed Americans back to work. The WPA was not specifically designed to help women, but some artists such as **Berenice Abbott** and **Augusta Savage** were hired by the WPA's Federal Art Project. **Zora Neale Hurston** did work for the WPA's Federal Writers' Project. **Katherine Dunham** worked for the Federal Theater Project.

📖 Dorothea Lange

| born c. 1895 – died 1965 |
| **PHOTOGRAPHER** |

Dorothea Lange's most famous photographs told the harsh story of the 1930s Great Depression and the drought that turned parts of the Midwest into the Dust Bowl. Her photographs helped spur the federal government into taking action.

Lange was a portrait photographer in San Francisco shooting mostly well-to-do people when the Depression hit. Her business slowed down and her

▶ Dorothea Lange's "Migrant Mother, Nipomo, California" (1936).

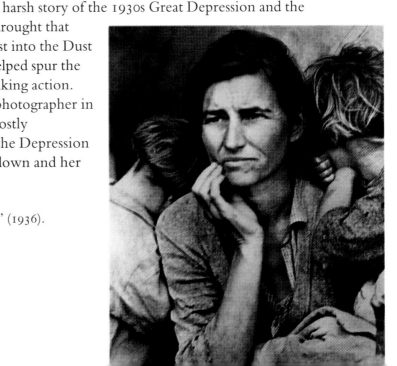

interests shifted to the streets where thousands of unemployed people stood on breadlines. A university social economist was impressed by Lange's photographs of the effects of the Depression on people. Lange and Professor Paul Taylor started documenting the lives of people who had moved to California looking for work. Their report, which included Lange's photographs, helped secure federal money to build the first sanitary facilities for migrants.

In 1935, Lange was hired by the federal agency that would become the Farm Security Administration (FSA). Lange's job was to document the impact of the Depression on rural people and to show what the FSA was doing for them. Her sympathetic but bleak photographs appeared in newspapers, books, and magazines. They had an enormous effect on the public and helped create support for government programs. During the summers of 1936–38, Lange spent time with farm people in Oklahoma and other midwestern and southern Dust Bowl areas. Many were leaving their farms, which had been wiped out by drought or by competition from larger farm corporations with more machinery. Lange recorded their hardships in her book, *An American Exodus: a Record of Human Erosion*, published in 1939. During World War II, Lange worked for the Office of War Information. In the 1950s, she turned toward the everyday, intimate aspects of family life, but continued to take some assignments.

Margaret Mead

born 1901 – died 1978

ANTHROPOLOGIST

How does culture influence people's personalities? Margaret Mead devoted her life to finding an answer to this question.

Margaret studied anthropology at Barnard College in New York. As part of her graduate fieldwork, 23-year-old Mead traveled alone to the Pacific Islands in 1925. She studied 50 young Samoan teenagers, learning their language and living as they did. When she returned to the United States, Mead wrote up her study and added comparisons between teenage island life and the lives of young Americans. Mead's *Coming of Age in Samoa* was published in 1928 and became an immediate bestseller. Mead showed that anthropology could be presented in a way that was interesting to ordinary readers. She also showed that adolescent rebellion and social roles based on sex were not the same everywhere. Although much of her work focused on societies where there was no

+ + + + + + + + + + + + + + + + + +

The United States entered World War II after the Japanese attack on Pearl Harbor in December 1941. The U.S. government decided that Japanese, even Japanese Americans, living in this country were a threat to national security. In 1942, over 110,000 of these men, women, and children were forced to leave everything they owned and move to "relocation camps" in California, Oregon, and Washington. Many of them were second and third generation Japanese Americans. **Dorothea Lange** photographed these camps, which were under guard and surrounded by barbed wire. Many of her photographs were not published because the government thought she was too sympathetic toward the internees. In 1988, Congress approved the Civil Liberties Act which awarded $20,000 to each person who had been forced into a relocation camp, as partial compensation for the injustice.

1930s – 1940s

industry, after World War II, she included American culture in her studies. Mead was particularly interested in how "progress" changed "primitive" societies and how men's and women's roles were defined across cultures.

Margaret Mead was curator of ethnology (the study of human cultures) at New York's American Museum of Natural History from 1926 to 1969. In 1961, she headed President John F. Kennedy's Commission on the Status of Women. Her tombstone spells out her life's mission: "To cherish the life of the world."

+ + + + + + + + + + + + + + + +

By the end of the 19th century, almost 20% of American women remained single. By 1930, there was a new emphasis on women finding fulfillment only through marriage, and only 5% of American women remained single. Most women college graduates hoped to become wives, even if it meant giving up hopes of careers outside the home.

Agnes de Mille

born 1905 – died 1993
CHOREOGRAPHER

Agnes de Mille's family tried to discourage her interest in dance, but Agnes refused to listen. Instead, she secretly practiced ballet steps in her bedroom. After graduating from the University of California in 1927, she headed for the dance studios and stages of New York and then Europe.

De Mille, who was influenced by the work of her close friend **Martha Graham**, combined precise choreography with American country or folk dance in her modern dances. She performed the role of Cowgirl in her first big hit, a ballet she choreographed called *Rodeo* (1942). The next year one of de Mille's greatest accomplishments was staged. She created all the dances for the musical play *Oklahoma!* It was one of the first theater productions to successfully weave singing and dancing through a dramatic plot.

Agnes de Mille became one of America's leading choreographers, creating dances for other Broadway musicals such as *Carousel* (1945), *Brigadoon* (1947), and *Gentlemen Prefer Blondes* (1949). De Mille also created the dances for the film versions of many of these plays.

De Mille received the Kennedy Center Career Achievement Award in 1980 and the National Medal for the Arts in 1986. She also wrote books on dance and several autobiographies, including *Reprieve* (1981), which describes her struggle to regain her abilities after a stroke.

ⓢ Luisa Moreno

born 1907 – died c. 1990

LABOR ORGANIZER

As a labor organizer, Luisa Moreno dedicated her entire life to only one cause: the rights of workers. Although she worked with laborers from many ethnic groups, Moreno focused on helping Mexican Americans.

Born into a wealthy Guatemalan family, Moreno came to the United States in 1928 and studied at the College of the Holy Names in Oakland, California. She later moved to New York, married a Mexican artist, and had a baby. Then she took a job in a New York City sweatshop to help support her family. In the 1930s, she began to organize other Hispanic garment factory workers, urging them to unionize.

Moreno returned to California when World War II started. She got a job putting processed food in cans. She kept organizing, encouraging other Hispanics to join the United Cannery, Agricultural, Packing, and Allied Workers of America (UCAPAWA) union. In 1938, Moreno helped launch the National Council of the Spanish Speaking People, the first Mexican-American civil rights organization for workers. El Congreso, as the group was also called, was active from 1938 to 1941 and had over 70,000 members. Moreno also served as national vice-president for the UCAPAWA from 1937 to 1950. In 1943, Moreno was part of a union team that won a wage increase for women working at the California Sanitary Canning Company. During the "anti-Red" panic of the 1950s, Moreno was accused of being a Communist and deported, or forced to leave the country. She continued organizing workers in Mexico, Cuba, and Guatemala.

+ + + + + + + + + + + + + + + + +

 By the 1940s, nearly 75% of the workers in California's canneries were women, many of them Hispanic.

1930s – 1940s

🎨 Georgia O'Keeffe

born 1887 – died 1986

ARTIST

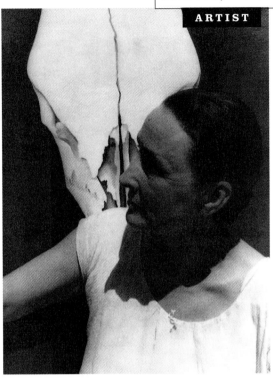

▲ Georgia O'Keeffe was fascinated by the play of light and the forms of flowers, bones, shells, rocks, and landscapes. This fascination inspired many paintings.

Artist Georgia O'Keeffe captured not only a unique quality of light, color, and space in her paintings but also a very deep, personal relationship with nature.

Born in Sun Prairie, Wisconsin, O'Keeffe knew she wanted to be an artist by the time she was 13. In 1904, she attended the Art Institute of Chicago and then the Art Students League in New York City. After art school, she supported herself as an advertising illustrator and art teacher. In 1916, a friend showed O'Keeffe's work to Alfred Stieglitz, a well-known photographer and important figure in the art world. Stieglitz exhibited O'Keeffe's work at his famous 291 Gallery, and introduced her to other people in the New York art scene. They were married in 1924.

O'Keeffe's first paintings were abstracts based on shape and light. Her work slowly evolved into paintings of recognizable objects viewed from unusual angles or distances. She did a famous series of large, sensual flower paintings so that "even busy New Yorkers will take time to see what I see of flowers." During a visit to New Mexico in 1929, O'Keeffe fell in love with the Southwest countryside and returned every summer to paint for the next 17 years. After her husband's death in 1946, she settled in New Mexico. The starkness of the desert landscape held a special attraction for her. Her paintings of skulls and bones, crosses, adobes, and desert scenes are among her most famous works.

Georgia O'Keeffe received a Gold Medal from the National Institute of Arts and Letters in 1970, and was awarded the Medal of Freedom in 1977. Although she lost most of her eyesight later in life, she continued to paint and sculpt until her death.

⚖️ Frances Perkins

born 1880 – died 1965

SECRETARY OF LABOR

In 1911, Frances Perkins saw the young women workers trapped in the Triangle Shirtwaist Factory fire leap to their deaths right in front of her. Perkins, already involved in suffrage and social reform, was outraged. From that point on, she devoted her life to fighting for the health and safety rights of American workers.

 First woman Cabinet member Francis Perkins, with FDR (front, center).

Perkins, with the New York Committee on Safety, pushed for new regulations to prevent another Triangle fire. She lobbied the New York state legislature for a law limiting women's workday to nine hours. In 1919, she became the first woman named to the N.Y. Industrial Commission. When President Franklin D. Roosevelt (FDR) appointed Perkins Secretary of Labor in 1933, she became the first woman to serve as a Cabinet member. Now she could work for labor on a national scale. She kept the job longer than any other labor secretary.

Perkins was part of a women's social reform-political network that was championed by **Eleanor Roosevelt** and included women such as **Mary Anderson** and **Molly Dewson**. Like other women in government, she had to defend her job as well as her goals. Some labor leaders objected to Frances's appointment because she came from "outside" the unions. Some people objected to a woman holding what they thought of as a "man's job."

When Perkins took office, the country was in a depression. Industry had slowed to almost a stop. Fifteen million people were unemployed. During the 12 years (1933–1945) Perkins was secretary of labor, she helped establish major New Deal programs. These included the Federal Emergency Relief Administration (1933), the first program for unemployment relief, and the National Recovery Administration (1933), the agency charged with establishing fair business practices and seeing that workers were able to bargain collectively, as a group or union, for their rights. Perkins reorganized the Department of Labor to make it more effective and efficient. But she didn't spend all her time in the office. Secretary Perkins visited steel plants and dockyards. She met with everybody from factory workers to FDR.

Frances Perkins believed working people had the right to a fair wage, decent hours, and benefits if they lost their jobs and when they retired. Her work toward these goals had a powerful impact on the federal government's role in the economy, which is still part of today's policy. Secretary Perkins lobbied for the the Social Security Act of 1935 and the Fair Labor Standards

+ + + + + + + + + + + + + + + + +

During the Great Depression, many businesses and state governments would not hire married women. They believed men and then single women should get available jobs. The federal government even passed the Economy Act of 1932, which said if a husband and wife both worked for the federal government and cutbacks were necessary, the wife had to be laid off. In reality, many couples needed the woman's salary to get by, and families suffered because of this bias against married women.

Act (1938). The latter abolished child labor and created labor laws and standards, including a minimum wage and a maximum 40-hour work week. The Women's and Children's Bureaus and Bureau of Labor Statistics thrived within Perkins's Department of Labor.

After Roosevelt's death in 1945, Perkins resigned from the Cabinet, saying "I am grateful to God for having lived in these times." But she did not retire. She worked for President Harry Truman, wrote a book about the Roosevelt years, and lectured and gave seminars until her death at 85.

Eleanor Roosevelt ANNA ELEANOR

born 1884 – died 1962

FIRST LADY, SOCIAL REFORMER

"It is not fair to ask of others what you are not willing to do yourself," First Lady Eleanor Roosevelt wrote in her newspaper column, "My Day." By that standard, Eleanor was one of the fairest women of her time.

Born into a wealthy upper-class family in New York City, Eleanor was orphaned when she was ten years old. She was raised by her aunts and grandmother and sent off to boarding school in England when she was 15. A shy, serious young woman who was considered homely, Eleanor later returned to New York. There she worked at settlement houses and investigated sweatshops for the National Consumers' League before she married her cousin, Franklin Delano Roosevelt (FDR), in 1905. Eleanor and FDR had six children together, one of whom died as a baby. They nearly divorced in 1918, when Eleanor discovered her husband's affair with a staff member. The Roosevelts stayed together and Eleanor convinced FDR to remain in politics after he was paralyzed by polio in 1921.

When FDR was first elected president in 1933 during the height of the Great Depression, Eleanor Roosevelt was there, ready to bring women into the political circle and change the role of First Lady. She visited city slums and Dust Bowl shacks. She talked to coal miners and California migrant workers. She saw what the Great Depression had done to African-American communities and to Native Americans living on

reservations. Then she went back to Washington and served as their lobbyist as New Deal programs were developed.

Eleanor Roosevelt also got **Molly Dewson** to build a power base in the Democratic Party Committee. She urged her husband to appoint **Frances Perkins** Secretary of Labor and to take racial issues seriously. She supported hiring **Mary McLeod Bethune** for the National Youth Administration, which Eleanor had convinced FDR to set up in 1935. First Lady Eleanor Roosevelt acted on her principles. She resigned from the Daughters of the American Revolution when the group barred **Marian Anderson** from singing at Washington's Constitution Hall in 1939. And she encouraged the President to establish the Fair Employment Practices Committee in 1941 to fight racial prejudice in war industries. The First Lady sometimes came under fire for her liberal ideas and her reform work. Critics often attacked her appearance or her outspokenness as a woman, rather than her ideas or her accomplishments. This was painful, but she didn't let it stop her.

Roosevelt was the first woman to hold a press conference at the White House. She held 350 of them for women reporters only. She broadcast her own radio program, and in 1936 started writing "My Day," which appeared in 60 newspapers across the country and ran for more than 20 years. The First Lady sometimes answered over 100 letters a day from Americans looking for help or hope.

After FDR's death in 1945, President Truman made Roosevelt a delegate to the United Nations. She supported relief work in Europe after World War II, and as chairman of the Commission on Human Rights, helped draft the Universal Declaration of Human Rights in 1948. In 1961, President John Kennedy appointed Roosevelt chair of the Commission on the Status of Women. She always remained an activist and a liberal. "The word *liberal*," she wrote just before she died, "comes from the word *free*. We must cherish and honor the word *free* or it will cease to apply to us."

Augusta Savage

| born 1892 – died 1962 |
| **SCULPTOR** |

Augusta Savage did not let poverty or racism stop her from becoming an artist. When she needed money to study sculpture, she worked as an apartment caretaker and a laundress and applied for scholarships. When she was barred from attending summer school in France because she was African American, she publicized

ROSE SCHNEIDERMAN (1882–1972) immigrated from Poland to New York's Lower East Side in 1890, and there became a mover and shaker in the suffrage and labor reform movements. Named president of the New York Women's Trade Union League in 1918 (and national WTUL president in 1926), Rose (right) became friends with **Eleanor Roosevelt** (left) and was an important source of information about the labor movement for the First Lady, the President, and another friend, Labor Secretary **Frances Perkins**. In 1933, FDR appointed Schneiderman to the National Recovery Administration (NRA). She was the only woman member. As NRA labor adviser, she worked on industry codes to protect women's wages and hours.

1930s – 1940s

her story and her supporters went all the way to the president of the United States to complain.

Augusta was a talented child who began molding the red clay found around her Florida home. She wanted to be an artist, even though her minister father objected. Her talent was recognized at New York's famous Cooper Union college, where in 1921, Savage became one of the first women to study sculpture. The next year, the New York Public Library hired her to sculpt a bust of the famous African-American leader W.E.B. Du Bois. The bust established Savage as one of the finest sculptors of the time. A few years after being denied admission to a Paris program in 1923, Savage won several scholarships that allowed her to study in Rome and Paris. When she returned, she opened the Savage Studio of the Arts and Crafts in Harlem to encourage new young artists. In 1937, she became head of the Harlem Community Arts Center, where she taught students such as Jacob Lawrence, who later became famous themselves. One of Savage's most famous works was the 16-foot-tall statue "Lift Every Voice and Sing." The work was commissioned for the 1939–40 New York World's Fair. Augusta Savage was one of only four women and the only African-American sculptor invited to exhibit.

Gertrude Stein

born 1874 – died 1946

WRITER

She collected paintings, works by Cézanne, Renoir, Gauguin, and her good friend Pablo Picasso. People such as F. Scott Fitzgerald, Ernest Hemingway, Paul Robeson, and hundreds of other writers and artists visited her famous salon in Paris. And she wrote her own collections of experimental poems, plays, and fiction.

Born in Allegheny, Pennsylvania, Gertrude Stein studied philosophy and psychology at Harvard Annex, which became Radcliffe College in Cambridge, Massachusetts. She was influenced by new ideas about "stream of consciousness," or how a person experiences the world as a flow of events. Her writing style clearly shows this influence. Stein spent most of her adult life in Paris, in homes she shared first with her brother

◄ Gertrude Stein (right) and Alice B. Toklas lived in Paris, France. Their home was a salon, or center where artists and intellectuals often met.

and then from 1907, with her lifelong companion Alice B. Toklas. She encouraged the modern writers and abstract painters who visited her and tried to capture the spirit of the modern and the abstract in her own writing. Some people found Stein's work unreadable. Others praised her for creating new styles of writing that involved repetition, like the often-quoted "Rose is a rose is a rose is a rose," or fragmented images such as "Pigeons on the grass alas." In 1933, she published one of her most famous works, *The Autobiography of Alice B. Toklas*. It is really Stein's own autobiography, but written from the point of view of Toklas. That same year, the well-known American composer Virgil Thomson wrote the music for an opera by Stein called *Four Saints in Three Acts*, which helped open up American audiences to Gertrude's work. Thomson and Stein worked together again in 1947, when they staged an opera, *Mother of Us All*, based on the life of **Susan B. Anthony**.

Dr. Helen Brooke Taussig

| born 1898 – died 1986 |
| PEDIATRICIAN |

In 1941, Dr. Helen Brooke Taussig found a way to save hundreds of thousands of lives. She pioneered an operation to save "blue babies," newborns who don't have enough oxygen in their blood. Without this operation, these babies died or suffered brain damage.

Helen Taussig enrolled in Harvard Medical School in Cambridge, Massachusetts, in 1921. Harvard let her attend, but would not give her a degree because she was a woman. That was bad enough, but Taussig had to sit separately in the classroom and in the laboratory. She transferred to Boston University and eventually to Johns Hopkins University in Baltimore, Maryland, where she began to study malformed or abnormal hearts. In 1930, she was named head of the Children's Heart Clinic at Johns Hopkins Hospital.

As a pediatrician or children's doctor, Taussig was familiar with "blue babies," children whose skin was light-blue at birth because they lacked oxygen. Dr. Taussig discovered the problem was with a pulmonary artery, the oxygen-bearing blood vessel that runs between the heart and the lungs. Her idea was to insert an artificial tube to bypass the defective artery. Taussig worked with another doctor, Dr. Alfred Blalock, who performed successful surgery in 1944. Dr. Taussig was the first woman president of the American Heart Association (1965). She was awarded the Presidential Medal of Freedom in 1964 and the National Medal of Science in 1977.

+ + + + + + + + + + + + + + + +

Paris in the 1920s and 1930s was home to several interesting American women.

Using the name Genêt, after a famous French writer, Indiana-born Janet Flanner wrote letters about the art, politics, and people of Paris for a new, sophisticated magazine, *The New Yorker*. She did articles about famous people such as the artist Pablo Picasso, the entertainer Josephine Baker, and the poet **Gertrude Stein**, and infamous people such as Adolf Hitler.

Sylvia Beach ran the Paris bookstore, Shakespeare & Co. The American-born Beach also was responsible for editing and publishing *Ulysses* by the famous Irish writer James Joyce in 1922. *Ulysses* was considered obscene and banned in the United States, although Beach smuggled copies into the country and sold 28,000 copies here and in Europe. When the u.s. Supreme Court said the book was not obscene in 1933, Joyce got a u.s. publisher and got rich. He did not share the money from sales of his book with Sylvia Beach.

1930s – 1940s

 Dorothy Thompson

born 1893 – died 1961

REPORTER

In 1937, there were two women thousands of Americans talked about and listened to: **Eleanor Roosevelt** and Dorothy Thompson.

By the time she was 30, Thompson had already successfully campaigned for women's suffrage in New York state, covered a European political coup, and been named Central European bureau chief for the *Philadelphia Public Ledger* and the *New York Evening Post*. In 1932, she published an interview in *Cosmopolitan* that made her famous. The man she interviewed was Adolf Hitler. From 1933 through America's entry into World War II, Thompson warned about the rise of Nazism and fascism in Europe. She was thrown out of Nazi Germany in 1934 for her views, but hailed as a serious political writer at home. Like Eleanor Roosevelt, Thompson lectured, had a radio show, and had her own column in *Ladies' Home Journal*. Thompson's columns also explored the "woman question," or what women's role in society should be.

Little House in the Big Woods was published in 1932 when **LAURA INGALLS WILDER** (1867–1957) was 65 years old. It was an immediate success. Today, more than 20,000,000 of Wilder's books about American frontier life in the 1870s and 1880s have been sold. Wilder based most of her popular books on her own pioneer childhood in the Midwest and what is now South Dakota. In 1885, she married a farmer, Almanzo James Wilder. Eventually they bought a small farm in Mansfield, Missouri. Laura started writing newspaper columns for the *Missouri Ruralist*. Her daughter encouraged her to write down the stories about her pioneer childhood. After the huge success of her first book, she continued to write – and to work on the farm! Her "Little House" books were made into a hit television series in the mid-1970s.

Gertrude Vanderbilt Whitney

born 1875 – died 1942

SCULPTOR, MUSEUM FOUNDER

When Gertrude Whitney's friends could not find places to show their artwork, she came up with a solution. In 1914, she opened her own gallery, the Whitney Studio. It was next door to her work studio in New York City, where Whitney herself was a successful sculptor.

Gertrude Vanderbilt Whitney had always loved art. After she married Harry Payne Whitney in 1896, she began studying sculpture at the Art Students League in New York City and also in Paris. Whitney often sculpted human beings as heroic or tragic figures. Her work was exhibited at huge events such as the 1901 Pan-American Exposition in Buffalo, New York, and the 1904 World's Fair in St. Louis, Missouri. Because Gertrude was born into one of America's wealthiest families, she was also able to collect art. She started the Whitney Studio Club and the Whitney Studio Gallery in New York's Greenwich Village and showed the work of artists such as Edward Hopper and Frank Stella, who are now famous. By 1929, Whitney had around 500 pieces of art, which she offered to the Metropolitan Museum of Art along with money to build a wing for the art. The Metropolitan wasn't interested, so two years later Gertrude founded the Whitney Museum, now one of the world's most important art museums.

⊜ Babe Didrikson Zaharias MILDRED

born 1914 – died 1956

ATHLETE

Named Woman Athlete of the year six times, and Woman Athlete of the half-century in 1950, Mildred Didrikson was nicknamed Baby, by her Norwegian parents, then Babe (after Babe Ruth) by friends who recognized her outstanding athletic talents.

Didrikson moved from being star player on her Beaumont, Texas, high school basketball team to playing semi-pro basketball. She was named to All-American teams three times. Babe turned from the court to the field in 1932, when she participated in the Amateur Athletic Union's national women's track and field meet. She entered eight out of the 10 events and won half of them. Her personal score was better than the score of the entire 22-member team that placed second at the meet.

At the 1932 summer Olympics in Los Angeles, Didrikson easily shattered world records in the javelin throw (143 feet, 4 inches) and 80-meter hurdles (11.7 seconds), winning two gold medals and a silver one for the high jump. That same year Babe played pro basketball and pitched a pre-season baseball game for the St. Louis Cardinals.

Three years later, this amazing athlete added golf to her winning sports record and moved in and out of playing amateur and professional tournaments. Her golfing was unstoppable. In the mid-1930s, she earned almost $1,000 a week playing in professional golf exhibitions. When she returned to amateur golf competitions, she won the Western Open in 1940, 1944, and 1945. She captured the 1946 National Women's Amateur title and became the first woman from the United States to win the British Women's Amateur Golf Tournament in 1947. That same year, Didrikson won an extraordinary 17 golf tournaments in a row.

Didrikson helped form the Ladies Professional Golf Association around 1948. Several years later, she found out she had cancer. In between operations, she still won the U.S. Open and the All-American Open in 1954.

+ + + + + + + + + + + + + + + + +

During World War II, many male baseball players were in the military. The All American Girls Baseball League (AAGBL) was formed in 1943 to keep people interested in baseball. AAGBL teams such as the Rockford Peaches, the Racine Belles, and the Kenosha Comets played in baseball stadiums in mostly mid-sized cities throughout the Midwest. On the average, AAGBL salaries ranged from $55 to $150 per week, to make playing baseball competitive with women's war production jobs. The "Darlings of the the Diamonds" played tough baseball games, but had to look and dress like ladies, including wearing short skirts. In 1988, the National Baseball Hall of Fame in Cooperstown, New York, opened a women-in-baseball exhibit.

The American Dream

women of color who had to work, the American dream had no connection to their daily reality.

Carrying the Civil Rights Banner

Whether it was about capitalism or racial segregation, protest or political activity that challenged the "American way of life" was dangerous in the 1950s. This was a time when the House of Representatives Un-American Activities Committee (HUAC), led by Senator Joseph McCarthy, was engaged in a campaign to find communists in America. HUAC ruined people's lives and careers by labeling them Communists or radicals.

In the African-American community, people were organizing to fight for their right to be treated equally with white citizens. Laws and social customs kept African-Americans out of "whites-only" stores, restaurants, and neighborhoods. In 1954, the Supreme Court ruled in *Brown v. Board of Education of Topeka, Kansas*, that public education could not be "separate but equal." But many schools in the South were still segregated by race. So were hospitals. And many skilled, high-paying or professional jobs were closed to African Americans. More than one-half of all employed African-American women were domestic workers in homes or businesses. Most of the others

Many Americans found the world after World War II to be a confusing place. There was great economic prosperity. But there was also a great fear of communism and of nuclear weapons. In response to this fear, the media often promoted a very idealized, homey view of life. To achieve the American Dream, women were encouraged to dress and act feminine so they could attract a man. They were expected to marry, raise families, and buy houses, cars, and plenty of consumer goods. Thousands of white families moved into suburbs, the communities that rapidly developed outside major cities. By the 1950s, most Americans were homeowners.

In the suburbs, many women became full-time housewives, mothers, and volunteers for everything from the Girl Scouts to the local Women's Club. Their activities were seen as the natural "domestic" roles that suited women best.

Still, nearly 30 percent of white married women worked outside the home. More women than ever were going to college. But for many

▶ Daisy Bates (left), President of the Arkansas NAACP, pickets outside a store in Little Rock, Arkansas, in 1960. The store did not offer equal service to all people. Boycotts like this were an important strategy in the civil rights movement.

were farm workers. Wages were low in all these jobs.

African-American women were at the forefront of the civil rights movement, the fight to end racial discrimination. They played key roles in the National Association for the Advancement of Colored People (NAACP), the Southern Christian Leadership Conference (SCLC), and the Student Nonviolent Coordinating Committee (SNCC). They stood up to every kind of harassment, and even violence, to help change segregation laws and to register voters. The civil rights struggle inspired many members of what became, in the 1960s, a renewed women's rights movement and the radical student movement.

The Second Wave

In the early 1960s, several things helped produce the "second wave of feminism." (The suffragists who wanted equal rights are considered the "first wave.") African-American and white women who were involved in the civil rights struggle saw how sexual discrimination worked against them. Then in 1961, newly-elected President John F. Kennedy appointed his Commission on the Status of Women to see how the country could make the best use of women's abilities. And two years later, Betty Friedan published *The Feminine Mystique*, a bestseller which said that many middle-class women were bored and frustrated as homemakers.

American women began to examine their social, economic, and personal roles. Like civil rights activists, feminists worked to change laws. When the 1964 Civil Rights Act passed, it outlawed job discrimination based on race, color, religion, national origin – and sex. The Equal Pay Act from the previous year already said men and women doing the same job had to get the same salary.

Women insisted these laws be enforced. Many people did not take them seriously. The Equal Employment Opportunity Commission (EEOC), which was supposed to handle discrimination complaints, treated women's cases very lightly. As a result, the National Organization for Women (NOW) was founded in 1966 to fight for women's equality issues. Some of NOW's early victories included a lawsuit by

flight attendants. NOW helped them win the right to continue working – instead of being forced to quit – if they married or when they hit their mid-30s. NOW also forced newspapers to stop publishing help-wanted ads as "male" or "female," and instead just list them as jobs available to all.

Second-Class Members of the Counterculture

A new kind of youth culture sprang up in the 1960s. Many young people were energized by the civil rights movements. Opposition to American involvement in the Vietnam War in Southeast Asia was on the rise. There were demonstrations and riots on college campuses across the nation. Groups such as the Students for a Democratic Society (SDS) and the Black Panther Party for Self-Defense formed. Their members wanted to revolutionize what they saw as a mainstream culture too caught up in war, racism, and consumerism. Meanwhile, sex, drugs, and rock 'n roll seemed to take over popular culture.

▲ The Woodstock Festival of "peace, love, and music," attracted more than 300,000 people to Bethel, New York in 1969. The concert became a symbol of the 1960s and 1970s revolt against the values of the 1950s.

This new counterculture covered a variety of political opinion and cultural expression. Women, however, usually still had second-class status. In the SDS, they were expected to do cooking and clerical work and leave the political planning to men. Women did not fare much better in the anti-war movement. Their issues were usually not addressed at rallies and their organizing efforts were often overlooked.

More and more women realized they needed their own movement. "Women's liberation" had begun. By the end of the 1960s, the friends and foes of "women libbers," were taking sides – and getting ready to take action.

Hannah Arendt

born 1906 – died 1975

POLITICAL SCIENTIST, PHILOSOPHER

Hannah Arendt, a German-born Jew, fled the Nazis in the 1930s. This experience brought up important questions about human behavior, politics, and moral issues, which she tried to answer in her philosophical work.

Arendt arrived in the United States in 1941. Her first major work, *The Origins of Totalitarianism*, was published in 1951, the same year she became a U.S. citizen. This book explored the rise of totalitarian governments, such as the Nazis, that do not allow any opposing views. It was a big success. In 1958, she followed with *The Human Condition*, an analysis of political action and private life. One observation she made in that book was that "it is in fact far easier to act under conditions of tyranny than it is to think." Arendt later explored this idea in a different way when she wrote a book about the trial of a Nazi war criminal, Adolf Eichmann, saying "so many were like him.... The many were neither perverted nor sadistic,...they were terribly and terrifyingly normal." She called this idea the "banality of evil," meaning that ordinary people could do extraordinarily bad things and still maintain everyday routines. She thought totalitarianism supported the "banality of evil."

In 1959, Arendt became the first woman hired as a full professor at Princeton University. She moved to New York's New School for Social Research in 1967 and began her most ambitious work ever, *The Life of the Mind*, but died before the book was completed. Her close friend **Mary McCarthy** edited the book, which was published in 1978. Arendt is considered one of the keenest political and philosophical thinkers of the 20th century.

Cuban-born **ALICIA ALONSO** (b. 1921) first became famous while dancing in the United States with the American Ballet Theatre (ABT) in the 1940s. Just as her career took off, Alonso was blinded by an eye problem. She was bedridden for a year and spent that time imagining herself learning the movements for the ballet *Giselle*. After her sight returned, the role of *Giselle* became Alonso's ballet signature. She became ABT's principal dancer and starred in ballets like *Fall River Legend* by **Agnes de Mille**. In 1959, Alonso became director of the Ballet Nacional de Cuba. Because she supported Fidel Castro's communist revolution, Alicia and her company were not allowed to perform in the United States until 1971. Alicia Alonso danced at ABT's 50th anniversary in 1990. She was 70 years old.

Joan Baez

born 1941

SINGER, ACTIVIST

Folksinger Joan Baez thrilled audiences at the 1959 Folk Festival in Newport, Rhode Island, with her beautiful ballads. In the 1960s and 1970s, she inspired civil rights marchers and anti-war demonstrators with her stirring protest songs.

After her success at Newport, Baez signed a contract with a record company. Her first solo album, *Joan Baez*, was released in 1960. A collection of traditional folk songs, it became an

◄ Joan Baez, like **Jane Fonda**, was one of the best-known performing artists to protest United States involvement in the Vietnam War.

instant hit. But more and more Joan's music began to reflect her politics. She got involved in the civil rights movement, singing at demonstrations such as the 1963 March on Washington, where 300,000 people heard Baez sing before Martin Luther King, Jr., gave his famous "I Have a Dream" speech. Baez, who was a Quaker and a pacifist, actively opposed the Vietnam war. In 1964, she was arrested for refusing to pay the percentage of her taxes that went for defense spending. Three years later, the Daughters of the American Revolution, who had kept **Marian Anderson** from singing at Washington, D.C.'s Constitution Hall, barred Baez from the same concert hall because of her political beliefs. She gave an outdoor concert for 30,000 people instead. That same year, Joan went to jail for singing anti-war songs outside a California military draft center.

Throughout her career, Joan Baez has used her name and her voice to support activist causes. She founded Humanitas International, a California study center for humans rights and nonviolence in 1979. She was an adviser to Amnesty International from 1979 to 1992. Baez continues to perform at marathon music fundraisers, such as the 1985 Live Aid concert.

Ella Baker

born 1903 – died 1986

CIVIL RIGHTS ACTIVIST

When Ella Baker left New York City for Atlanta, Georgia, to work with Dr. Martin Luther King, Jr.'s Southern Christian Leadership Conference (SCLC), she brought 30 years of civil rights experience with her.

Baker, a graduate of Shaw University in North Carolina, had been New York chapter president of the National Association for the Advancement of Colored People (NAACP). In the 1950s, she helped establish NAACP chapters in the South and worked with **Rosa Parks** to introduce the NAACP to Montgomery, Alabama. Baker was there with advice and strategy during the bus boycott staged by Montgomery African Americans who wanted equal access to public services. She

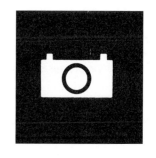

DIANE ARBUS (1923–1971) was a fashion photographer for almost 20 years before she began shooting the haunting photographs that made her famous. Arbus studied with **Berenice Abbott** and other documentary photographers. She began to take pictures of giants, midgets, handicapped people, and others she said "nobody would see if I didn't photograph them." Arbus also shot couples, children, and families in ways that revealed much about their relationships. Her photos were not always flattering, but they were frank. In 1972, Diane Arbus was the first American to exhibit photographs at the famous Venice Biennale art show in Italy.

1950s – 1960s

+ + + + + + + + + + + + + + + +

President Lyndon B. Johnson signed the Civil Rights Act in 1964. The act outlawed racial segregation in public places and discrimination in hiring based on race. Because one section, Title VII, forbid sexual discrimination in the workplace, Senator **Margaret Chase Smith** and others had a special interest in getting the bill passed. The women's movement built on the stuggles and strategies of the civil rights movement.

helped the SCLC start the Crusade for Citizenship voter registration drive in 1959. Baker was the driving force behind many of the SCLC civil rights efforts, but perhaps because she was a woman, she was not named official director of the group.

In 1960, Ella Baker started the Student Nonviolent Coordinating Committee (SNCC) to organize African-American and later white students in the struggle to integrate public places which were segregated by race. The SNCC called many of the boycotts and sit-ins of the 1960s. SNCC members and their supporters picketed stores that discriminated against African Americans. They sat at "whites-only" lunch counters. Baker also fought to integrate politics. She formed the Mississippi Freedom Democratic Party in 1964 to get more political power for African Americans. The party had 60,000 members and made headlines at the Democratic National Convention when it tried to unseat Mississippi's all-white delegation. Baker, along with **Fannie Lou Hamer**, was a leader in the voter drive that registered thousands of Southern African Americans in the 1960s and 1970s.

Gwendolyn Brooks

born 1917

POET

One of Gwendolyn Brooks's often-quoted poems, "The Pool Players. Seven at the Golden Shovel," captures the lives and language of her subjects: "We real cool. We/Left school. We/Lurk late. We/Strike straight...." Brooks, the first African-American poet to win the Pulitzer Prize, was famous for writing about the experiences of African Americans.

Gwendolyn grew up in Kansas and published her first poem when she was 13. As an adult she became active in the National Association for the Advancement of Colored People and eventually moved to Chicago. Her first collection of poems, *A Street in Bronzeville* (1945), dealt with questions of race and poverty. It got great reviews and earned Brooks two Guggenheim writing fellowships. Her second book, *Annie Allen*, included poems about African-American city life and earned Brooks the 1950 Pulitzer. During the 1960s, the African-American arts world explored themes from the civil rights movement. Brooks's writing was influenced by this black arts movement. Her book *In the Mecca* (1968) reflected the growth of African-American political awareness and cultural pride.

In 1968, Brooks was chosen poet laureate, or official poet, of

◄ Gwendolyn Brooks with her poetry book, *A Street in Bronzeville*.

Illinois, succeeding noted poet Carl Sandburg. She was the first African-American woman to serve as the Library of Congress's poetry consultant (1985–86). In 1989, Gwendolyn Brooks received a Lifetime Achievement Award from the National Endowment for the Arts. She was also awarded the 1995 National Medal of Arts.

Maria Callas

born 1923 – died 1977
OPERA SINGER

Maria Callas had such a magnificent voice, such a dramatic style that certain neglected 19th-century operas were staged because she was a soprano who could really sing them!

Born in New York and trained in Athens, Greece, Callas made her opera debut in 1938 in Greece and then toured Italy. In 1954, she debuted in the United States at the Chicago Lyric Opera. When she sang in Bellini's *Norma* in 1956, thousands jammed into New York's Metropolitan Opera house to hear her powerful singing. She was a sensation offstage, too, because of her famous feuds with opera house managers and opera stars. Her performances and recordings were popular. In 1965, Callas returned to the Metropolitan Opera for her farewell operatic appearance in *Tosca*. In 1971, she started teaching at the Juilliard School of Music in New York City.

+ + + + + + + + + + + + + + + + + +

In 1950, about 6 million homes in the United States had television sets. By 1960, almost 60 million homes had TV. But television ignored the lives of many of its viewers, including people of color, people in cities, and working class people. Shows like *Father Knows Best*, *Ozzie and Harriet*, and *Leave It to Beaver* showed a middle-class white suburban lifestyle and portrayed women as housewives and mothers with no interests outside the home.

Rachel Carson

born 1907 – died 1964
BIOLOGIST, ENVIRONMENTALIST

When farmers began using DDT to kill crop-eating bugs in the 1940s, the government and the chemical industries assured everyone that the insecticide was safe. Biologist and science writer Rachel Carson didn't agree. Her research showed that widespread use of toxic chemicals was poisoning the earth. In 1962, she published her observations in *Silent Spring*. The book sold over 100,000 copies in four months and helped launch the modern environmental movement.

Rachel received a master's degree in zoology from Johns Hopkins University in 1932. Three years later, she became an aquatic biologist and then editor-

▶ *The New York Times* called Rachel Carson a "physical scientist with literary genius." She wrote about nature in an easy-to-understand, poetic way that appealed to many readers.

1950s – 1960s

◯ *Pink-collar jobs:* During World War II, many women had "blue-collar" factory jobs. After the war, they were pushed out of these higher-paying jobs to make room for returning soldiers. Many white women moved into lower-paying jobs and became secretaries or sales clerks. Others took "pink-collar" jobs and worked as beauticians or waitresses. A higher percentage of African-American and Hispanic women returned to work as maids and servants. "White collar" professional or management jobs were still mostly held by men.

in-chief at the U.S. Bureau of Fisheries (later called the Fish and Wildlife Service). She devoted what little extra time she had to writing books that would "take the seashore out of the category of scenery and make it come alive." Her 1951 book, *The Sea Around Us*, did just that. It won the National Book Award, stayed on the bestseller list for 86 weeks, and was translated into 32 languages.

Around 1957, a friend in Duxbury, Massachusetts, told Rachel that when the state sprayed DDT nearby to kill mosquitoes, birds and insects in the area also died. Carson investigated, devoting her life and resources to researching the effects of DDT and other chemicals on plants and animals, including people. She reported what she found in *Silent Spring*. The chemical industry attacked Carson's conclusions and tried to discredit her. Rachel publicly defended her ideas, despite the fact that she was battling cancer. She testified before Congress about the harmful effects of pesticides, and President John F. Kennedy ordered a study of the issue. Many of Carson's findings were found to be true. *Silent Spring* inspired a re-examination of government policy toward the environment. In 1963, Rachel Carson received the Conservationist of the Year award of the National Wildlife Federation for her brave and tireless work.

⚖ Shirley Chisholm

born 1924

U.S. REPRESENTATIVE

Shirley Chisholm was a student at Brooklyn College in the 1940s when she heard a white politician say African Americans' lives would improve only under the leadership of white people. Shirley knew she could prove this man wrong.

Chisholm received a master's degree from Columbia University in 1952 and, during the 1950s, worked for the New York City Bureau of Child Welfare. She set up day-care centers for working women in her Brooklyn neighborhood and took an active interest in city politics. In 1964, she became the first African-American woman from Brooklyn to win a seat in the state legislature. Four years later, Chisholm was elected to the United States House of Representatives. When she was sworn in in 1969, she became the first African-

◀ Shirley Chisholm outside a youth agency in Brooklyn, New York, in 1968.

American woman in Congress. Chisholm was a champion of equal rights for people of color and of support for cities. Her slogan was "unbought and unbossed" and she was re-elected five times, holding her seat in Congress for 12 years. Then she set her sights on the White House. Chisholm entered the presidential primaries in 1972, hoping to win the nomination of the Democratic Party. She lost the nomination to George McGovern but paved the way for other African-American politicians, such as Jesse Jackson. Chisholm retired from Congress in 1982 to lecture and teach. A founding member of the National Women's Political Caucus (1971), she founded the National Political Congress of Black Women in 1984.

Septima Clark

born 1898 – died 1987

EDUCATOR

Septima Clark thought African Americans' fight for equality was linked to education. As a teacher and civil rights activist, Clark taught thousands of people to read and write, so that she could "teach them that c-o-n-s-t-i-t-u-t-i-o-n spells constitution." Literacy helped many African Americans gain the rights they were entitled to as citizens.

Clark was born in Charleston, South Carolina, where she became a school principal and teacher when she was eighteen. She worked in the school system for years and continued to study for a master's degree. She also fought for better pay for African-American teachers. In 1956, the Charleston Board of Education fired Clark for this and for being a member of the National Association for the Advancement of Colored People (NAACP). She lost 30 years of retirement pay. No South Carolina school system would hire her, so Clark opened her own schools. At these citizenship schools, as they were called, she taught many African Americans to read and write, especially so that they could pass the literacy tests many Southern states required in order to register to vote. Septima Clark traveled across the South by bus to recruit new

+ + + + + + + + + + + + + + + + +

In 1954, the Supreme Court ruled in the *Brown v. Board of Education of Topeka* case that "separate but equal" schools for white children and children of color were illegal. This meant that public schools could no longer be segregated by race. But changing the law did not change real life immediately. When Daisy Bates, publisher of the *Arkansas State Press*, started a campaign to integrate the Little Rock, Arkansas, high school in 1957, she and the nine African-American teenagers who tried to enter the school were greeted by angry and violent mobs. One of those students was Elizabeth Eckford (below, right). President Dwight D. Eisenhower had to send in federal troops to enforce the law.

PEGGY FLEMING (b. 1948) was the youngest person to win a national women's figure skating championship. Although she was only 15 when she won the title in January 1964, Peggy had skated competitively for almost five years. By the time she was 19, Fleming had won three world figure skating championships and an Olympic gold medal. She then turned professional, touring as the star skater with the Holiday on Ice group in the 1970s.

citizenship schoolteachers. She refused to sit in the "colored" section when she traveled. Everywhere she went, she encouraged people to vote. Once, when employees pretended a voter registration site was closed because they saw African Americans coming to register, Clark sent in a light-skinned woman first. The registrars, thinking the woman was white, opened up again, and all of Clark's group rushed in to register.

During the 1960s, Septima Clark became involved with Martin Luther King's Southern Christian Leadership Conference (SCLC). People now called her schools Freedom Schools. Clark worked hard for the civil rights movement, but saw its one flaw was that men did not treat women well enough. In her autobiography, *Ready From Within* (1986), Clark wrote, "We need women who will get those men by the collar and work with them." She also believed strongly in the power of children. "They need to come forth and stand up for some of the things that are right, " Clark said.

√ Dian Fossey

born 1932 – died 1985

ZOOLOGIST

Dian Fossey was working with disabled children at a hospital in Kentucky when she read a book called *Year of the Gorilla*. It changed her life. Fossey studied, traveled, and became a noted gorilla expert.

In 1966, with a grant from the National Geographic Society, Dian went to Zaire to study mountain gorillas. She later moved to nearby Rwanda and set up the Karisoke Research Centre in the Parc National des Volcans

(Volcano National Park). Fossey's work was hard and slow-going. The 51 gorillas she studied, some of whom were six feet tall and weighed several hundred pounds, were usually her only companions. Dian imitated the gorillas' sounds and movements to get them to trust her and allow her close enough to study their behavior. She discovered that the gorillas were peaceful vegetarians who lived in family groups and used more than 12 different sounds to communicate. She also discovered that the gorilla population was shrinking because hunters and farmers were taking over the primates' habitat. Fossey started an international campaign to save the gorillas.

In 1978, one of Dian's gorillas, Digit, was killed by poachers. Fossey's fight against the poachers made news all over the world. Still, several more gorillas were killed. Dian needed a break from the the stress and came home to teach and write. Her book *Gorillas in the Mist* was published in 1983 and later became a popular movie. But Fossey missed her research work and her gorillas. She went back to Rwanda in 1985. On December 26th, Fossey was murdered in her cabin. Although many people think poachers killed the zoologist, no one was ever charged with her death.

Aretha Franklin

| born 1942 |
| SOUL SINGER |

"R-E-S-P-E-C-T, find out what it means to me!" sang Aretha Franklin in 1967. "Respect" was the song that won Franklin her first Grammy award. And respect is what the Queen of Soul gets for 40 years of jazz, gospel, and pop singing.

Aretha Franklin was born in Memphis, Tennessee. Her father was a minister and at an early age Aretha began singing in his church in Detroit, Michigan. By the time she was a teenager, she was singing with her father's traveling gospel group. Aretha cut her first gospel album when she was 15.

Franklin moved to New York and started singing jazz, rhythm and blues, and pop music. In 1967, she had a big hit single, "I Never Loved a Man The Way I Loved You," and "Respect" hit the rhythm-and-blues and pop charts. Many people thought of that song as an anthem for African Americans, especially during this period, the civil rights era.

People started calling Franklin the Queen of Soul and she sang everywhere from Philharmonic Hall in New York City to the opening of the 1968 Democratic National Convention in Chicago. She also sang at the Democratic National Convention in 1992 and at a major AIDS benefit in 1993. By 1994, Franklin had won 15 Grammys, including a Lifetime Achievement Award.

+ + + + + + + + + + + + + + + + +

The Chicano or Mexican-American civil rights movement, *la causa*, had *Venceremos* as its motto. *Venceremos* was similar to *We Shall Overcome*, the anthem of the African-American civil rights movement. Jesse Lopez de la Cruz, **Dolores Huerta**, and other Chicana women worked in *la causa* to help secure equal economic, political, and social rights and build a strong cultural identity for Mexican Americans. Chicana activists sometimes had to deal with sexism in their own communities as well.

1950s – 1960s

⚖ Betty Friedan

born 1921

FEMINIST WRITER

"The feminine mystique says that the highest value and the only commitment for women is the fulfillment of their own femininity," Betty Friedan wrote in 1963 in her groundbreaking book, *The Feminine Mystique*. She said that "fulfillment had only one definition for American women after 1949 – the housewife-mother." Her book exploded the myth that all women were "happy housewives" and helped launch the second wave of the women's movement.

Friedan grew up in Peoria, Illinois, where her mother had given up a journalism career to be a housewife. After attending Smith College in Massachusetts, and the University of California, Berkeley, Betty herself became a journalist and studied to become a psychologist. But after getting married, she, too, gave up her career, had children, and became a housewife. Friedan still did freelance writing, and in 1957, polled some of her Smith classmates to find out how they felt about their lives. Many of them were bored and frustrated. The social pressure to limit their goals and ambitions and see themselves solely as wives and mothers was intense. The public image of the happy suburban "mom" was not everyone's personal experience. Friedan surveyed and interviewed other psychologists and college-educated housewives. Then she wrote *The Feminine Mystique*.

The success of her book changed Friedan's life personally and politically. She gave up being a housewife and eventually divorced. In 1966, she, Pauli Murray, and several other feminists founded the National Organization for Women (NOW), which became the strongest women's rights group in the country. Friedan served as NOW's president until 1970. The next year, along with other women such as **Shirley Chisholm**, **Fannie Lou Hamer**, and **Gloria Steinem**, Friedan formed the National Women's Political Caucus to bring more women and women's issues into politics. She also helped establish the First Women's Bank and Trust Company in 1973.

Friedan's work in the 1970s became more and more radical as she fought for abortion rights, equal pay for women, government-sponsored child care,

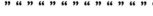

Q *Baby Boom:* the era from roughly 1946 to 1964 when the birthrate shot up. This rise in the number of babies born per family was fueled largely by the end of World War II and the prosperity that followed. For the previous 100 years, the birthrate had been going down. During the Baby Boom, families with two, three, or four children became common.

and the Equal Rights Amendment. Interestingly, her book, *The Second Stage* (1981), was criticized by other feminists for putting too much emphasis on traditional family values. Friedan claimed that the book was a realistic look at the conflicts women faced in balancing personal freedom with a desire for love. In *The Fountain of Age* (1993), Friedan challenged the way society undervalues growing old.

Althea Gibson

born 1927

TENNIS PLAYER

Althea Gibson was born in Silver, South Carolina, but grew up in New York City's Harlem. There she discovered paddle tennis, and a local coach discovered her. He gave Althea her first tennis racket. Within five years, she won the national Negro women's title and was on her way to becoming queen of the tennis courts.

In 1950, Gibson was the first African American to enter the prestigious Forest Hills tennis tournament in New York. The following year, she was the first African American invited to play at Wimbledon, England's world-famous tennis competition. Gibson's experience playing on Harlem's wood courts prepared her for the fast grass courts of Forest Hills and Wimbledon.

When she wasn't on the court, Gibson was in the classroom. She earned a college degree from Florida A&M in 1953 and became an athletic instructor at Lincoln University in Jefferson City, Missouri. Four years later, in 1957, Gibson made history by becoming the first African American to win the singles and doubles tennis championships at Wimbledon, and the singles at Forest Hills. New York City threw a ticker-tape parade for the tennis champ. Althea repeated her victories at Wimbledon and Forest Hills before turning to professional tennis in 1959, and later taking up professional golf. In her 1958 autobiography, *I Always Wanted to Be Somebody*, she described her rise to the top, despite prejudice against African Americans in the world of tennis. Gibson is in the International Tennis Hall of Fame and the Black Athletes Hall of Fame. She has also served on the New Jersey Governor's Council on Physical Fitness and Sports.

◄ "I knew that I was an unusual, talented girl…. I didn't need to prove that to myself. I only wanted to prove it to my opponents, " Althea Gibson said about her tennis skills.

In the 1950s, **BETTE NESMITH GRAHAM** (1924–1980) was a secretary with a big problem – her poor typing. She thought about how artists and sign painters simply paint over their mistakes. Bette mixed up a little bottle of white water-based tempera paint and took it and a watercolor brush to the office. When her co-workers saw Bette successfully painting over typing errors, they wanted her recipe. Graham started selling batches of "Mistake Out." In 1956, she did some research, improved her formula, and patented the product she now called Liquid Paper. Graham turned her garage into a Liquid Paper factory and filled thousands of bottles. By 1968, Liquid Paper, Inc., sold more than 10,000 bottles a day and earned more than $1 million a year. Graham sold the company in 1979 for $47.5 million. After Bette died, her son, Michael Nesmith, a member of the 1970s pop group The Monkees, used part of his inheritance to help pioneer music videos.

1950s – 1960s

⚖ Fannie Lou Hamer

born 1917 – died 1977

CIVIL RIGHTS ACTIVIST

When Fannie Lou Hamer was arrested in 1963 for helping other African Americans register to vote, police officers forced another prisoner to beat her. Fannie was beaten so badly that one of her hands was permanently damaged. She still did not give up her fight for justice and equality.

Born the last of 20 children, Fannie Lou Hamer grew up in Ruleville, Mississippi. Her grandparents had once been enslaved, and her parents were sharecroppers. Fannie Lou started picking cotton when she was six years old to help the family earn money. After she married Perry Hamer in 1942, the couple continued to work as sharecroppers on the Ruleville plantation for almost 20 years – until Fannie registered to vote in 1962. As a result, the Hamers lost their jobs and their house was shot at. They moved, but Hamer was unmovable about claiming her rights as a citizen and helping other African Americans do the same. By the early 1960s, she was active in the Southern Christian Leadership Conference (SCLC) and the Student Nonviolent Coordinating Committee (SNCC), the two major forces behind the civil rights movement. SCLC and SNCC were working to register black voters. Hamer, along with activists such as **Ella Baker**, led a huge voter registration drive that turned into the Mississippi Freedom Democratic Party (MFDP). The MFDP protested the all-white Mississippi delegates at the Democratic National Convention in 1964. Fannie Lou Hamer's speech to the Convention Committee about her prison beating was broadcast on

▲ Fannie Lou Hamer at the 1968 Democratic Convention. Her motto, "I am sick and tired of being sick and tired," is carved on her gravestone.

national television. The Democratic Party banned segregated delegations as a result of her testimony. Hamer also played an important role in getting the 1965 Voting Rights Act passed. This act got rid of unfair tests that kept many African Americans from voting. In the late 1960s and 1970s, Hamer joined the anti-Vietnam war movement and was a key member of the women's rights movement, joining **Betty Friedan**, **Shirley Chisholm**, **Gloria Steinem**, and others to form the National Women's Political Caucus in 1971.

Lorraine Hansberry

born 1930 – died 1965
PLAYWRIGHT

In 1959, Lorraine Hansberry's first play, *A Raisin in the Sun*, opened on Broadway. A drama about the struggles of an African-American family's decision to move into an all-white neighborhood, it challenged many stereotypes about African-American family life. It also drew from Hansberry's real-life experience. In 1938, her family moved into an all-white neighborhood in Chicago. They were welcomed by people throwing bricks through the windows.

Hansberry discovered her love of theater when she attended the University of Wisconsin. She moved to New York City in 1950. There she wrote for *Freedom*, a newspaper owned by noted actor Paul Robeson. Hansberry married and became active in the civil rights movement. She also started working on her own writing. *Raisin* was the first play by an African-American woman produced on Broadway. And it was a smashing success! Hansberry won the New York Drama Critics Circle Award for Best Play. *A Raisin in the Sun* was produced and directed by African Americans and included Ruby Dee in the cast. It ran for 538 performances. In 1961, it was made into a prize-winning film; then in 1974, into a prize-winning musical. Hansberry died of cancer shortly after her second play, *The Sign in Sidney Brustein's Window*, opened on Broadway in 1964.

▲ Lorraine Hansberry receiving the New York Drama Critic's Circle Award.

Lillian Hellman

born 1905 – died 1984
PLAYWRIGHT

"I cannot and will not cut my conscience to fit this year's fashions," Lillian Hellman, one of America's most famous playwrights, wrote in a 1952 letter to the House Un-American Activities Committee (HUAC). Congress's HUAC wanted Hellman to testify against her friends who were suspected of being members of or sympathetic to the Communist Party, a big fear during the "red scare" of the 1950s Cold War era. She was willing to speak to the HUAC, but only about herself. She refused to give information about anyone else.

Hellman's principles were reflected in the highly successful plays she wrote from the 1930s through the 1960s. *The Children's Hour*, which made her an overnight success when she was 29, is about two women whose lives are

+ + + + + + + + + + + + + + + + +

In 1950, women made up 29% of the work force. Half of those women were married and most of them worked in low-paying jobs. In 1955, the Women's Bureau of the United States Department of Labor was part of the White House Conference on Effective Use of Womanpower. The bureau sought to help women get jobs that "give them a feeling of accomplishment" in business, the sciences, or any other field.

1950s – 1960s

destroyed when they are falsely accused of being lesbians. Hellman won the New York Drama Critics Circle Award in 1941 for *Watch on the Rhine* and again in 1960 for *Toys in the Attic*. In 1970, she won the National Book Award for one of her autobiographies, *An Unfinished Woman*.

Lillian Hellman's life was as dramatic as her plays. She accepted an invitation from communist dictator Joseph Stalin to visit the Soviet Union in 1945. Because she refused to identify Communist Party members or sympathizers, the HUAC called her a hostile witness and she was blacklisted, which meant people were reluctant to hire her as a writer. Hellman went from making nearly $150,000 a year to barely having any income. She had public feuds, even court battles, with other writers, such as **Mary McCarthy**. Her tough personality and her writing talent made Lillian Hellman a legend in her time.

+ + + + + + + + + + + + + + + + +

The women who served in the armed forces during World War II weren't eligible for many of the postwar benefits male veterans received. In 1948, the Women's Armed Services Integration Act, with the backing of Representative **Margaret Chase Smith,** passed. It gave women pay and privileges on an equal scale with men, but set limits on the ranks military women could achieve and jobs they could do.

√ Grace Brewster Murray Hopper

born 1906 – died 1992

COMPUTER ENGINEER

▲ "I was born with curiosity," Rear Admiral Grace Brewster Murray Hopper once said about herself. Her peers called her Amazing Grace. She was the first to call programming errors "computer bugs."

When she was seven, Grace took apart all of her family's alarm clocks to see how they worked. This kind of curiosity turned into a career. By the time she retired at 79, Hopper was a Rear Admiral in the U.S. Navy who had revolution-ized computer programming.

When the United States entered World War II in 1941, Grace Murray Hopper, who had a doctoral degree in mathematics from Yale University in New Haven, Connecticut, decid-ed to volunteer for military service. Hopper needed special permission to enlist in the Navy's WAVES, because she was considered over-age and underweight. But by 1944, she had completed officer's training and became Lieutenant Hopper, U.S. Naval Reserve. Hopper's first assignment was at a military computation center at Harvard University. There she helped to develop and program the world's first large-scale digital computer, a 50-foot-long, eight-foot-high computer called the Mark I.

After the war, Hopper remained a reserve officer. She also taught at Harvard and worked for computer companies. In 1952, she invented the first computer compiler, which automatically turns mathematical codes into machine codes that the computer can read. This meant programmers did not have to spend long hours writing the machine codes. They just put in the math codes and let the computer do the calculating. Hopper's work on the compiler led to her development of COBOL, the first user-friendly computer language, in the 1960s. President Ronald Reagan promoted Hopper to Rear Admiral in 1985.

$ Dolores Huerta

| born 1930 |

UNION ORGANIZER

"Walk the street with us into history!" Dolores Huerta, co-founder of the United Farm Workers (UFW) labor union, was urging workers to join UFW demonstrations. "Work for justice!" she told her fellow Mexican Americans. Through her courage and dedication, Huerta helped win justice for thousands of poor farm workers.

As a child in the 1930s, Dolores Fernandez helped her mother run a boarding house in Stockton, California. Many Mexican-American migrant workers rented rooms at the Fernandez house. These farmworkers hired themselves out to pick whatever crops were in season. They worked long hours for very little money and no benefits. As an adult, Dolores Fernandez Huerta has devoted her life to making things better for farm workers.

In 1962, she joined with Cesar Chavez to create the National Farm Workers Association (NFWA) to fight for workers' rights to minimum wages, paid holidays, unemployment insurance, and pensions. By the 1970s, the

▲ Dolores Huerta (right) with Cesar Chavez at a UFW demonstration in 1984.

Janis Joplin (1943–1970) was rock and roll's first female superstar, but her musical sources were blues singers such as **Bessie Smith** and Odetta. Joplin's star rose after she sang "Love is Like a Ball and Chain" at the 1967 Monterey Pop Festival. Her first album, *Cheap Thrills,* quickly sold over a million copies when it was released in 1968. Janis Joplin was a powerful singer who threw her whole body into her wild performances. Her life was just as wild and included many love affairs, along with drug and alcohol abuse, which ended her life at age 27. In her short career, Joplin helped open up the world of rock 'n' roll to women.

1950s – 1960s

NFWA had more than 100,000 members, had joined the AFL-CIO (the country's most powerful union), and had changed its name to United Farm Workers (UFW).

When California grape pickers went on strike for fair pay in 1965, Huerta helped lead a 300-mile march to the state capitol in Sacramento to call attention to their struggle. She also helped organize a successful national boycott, convincing people not to buy grapes until the farm workers' demands were met. When the boycott succeeded, Huerta negotiated the first contract between the farm workers' union and the landowners. Huerta was elected vice-president of the UFW in 1972. She continues to fight for labor, health, and education issues, and in 1993 was given a Woman of Courage award by the National Organization for Women (NOW).

Barbara Jordan

born 1936 – died 1996

U.S. REPRESENTATIVE, LAWYER

"If you're going to play the game properly you'd better know every rule," Barbara Jordan once told an interviewer. In her 30-year career as a lawyer, legislator, teacher, and public speaker, Jordan learned all the rules about how to succeed. Then she fought to change the rules that kept discrimination legal and poverty crippling.

Barbara Jordan grew up in Houston, Texas, in the 1930s, when the South was still segregated. African Americans did not have the same freedom and opportunities as white citizens. Barbara had to ride in the "colored" section of the bus to get to college, where she was the star of Texas Southern University's debate team. But she believed the best way to fight discrimination

Many people call **CORETTA SCOTT KING** (b. 1927) the "keeper of the flame" because she carries on the civil rights efforts of her late husband, Dr. Martin Luther King, Jr. Coretta and Martin were married only a few years when Dr. King became a national figure during the Montgomery, Alabama, bus boycott that stemmed from **Rosa Parks**'s 1955 arrest. Coretta stood by her husband when their home was bombed, their lives and their children's lives threatened, and when he was jailed. She worked for the Women's Strike for Peace effort in 1962. After Dr. King's assassination in 1968, she kept her husband's speaking dates and wrote a book about her life with him. Coretta Scott King directed the effort to create the Martin Luther King, Jr., Center for Non-Violent Social Change. The center opened in Atlanta in 1982. It sponsors educational projects and attracts over 300,000 visitors a year.

▶ Barbara Jordan gave the keynote address at the 1976 and 1992 Democratic National Conventions.

was by forging new laws. In 1956, Jordan enrolled in Boston University's law school. There were 600 students in her class, but only one other woman, who was also African-American.

After graduating from law school in 1959, Jordan returned to Texas to practice law. She campaigned for the John F. Kennedy and Lyndon B. Johnson presidential ticket in 1960 and was "bitten by the political bug" herself. Twice she ran for office unsuccessfully, but in 1966, Jordan won election to the Texas State Senate. She was the first African-American member since 1883, and the first woman member ever. Senator Jordan helped get the first Texas minimum wage law passed. She worked to outlaw racial discrimination in hiring for any jobs funded by the state and she was involved in passing environmental laws. Her powerful public speaking won her many admirers. In 1972, Texas voters sent Barbara Jordan to Washington, D.C., to the U.S. House of Representatives.

During her six years in Congress, Jordan helped create laws that made life better for poor people and people of color. She authored a 1973 bill that outlawed racial discrimination at schools and at companies receiving money from the federal government. Two years later, she introduced a bill that made it easier for Spanish-speaking people to vote. Jordan was also a member of the House's Judiciary Committee and made a famous televised speech during the Watergate hearings in 1974 explaining why President Richard Nixon should be impeached for disregarding the Constitution.

Jordan retired from office in 1978 to concentrate on teaching at the University of Texas. She also wrote her autobiography, *Barbara Jordan: A Self-Portrait* (1979). In 1994, she was awarded the Presidential Medal of Freedom.

Clare Boothe Luce

born 1903 – died 1987
WRITER, POLITICIAN

"These days, ladies do all the things men do. They fly aeroplanes across the ocean, they go into politics and business." Clare Boothe Luce wrote these lines for her 1936 smash hit *The Women*, which featured a cast of 44 women and no men. She herself showed that "ladies" could do just about anything.

Her 1929 divorce from a wealthy man left Clare Boothe a wealthy woman. Although it was uncommon at the time in her social circle, she pursued a career. In the 1930s, she worked as an editor at *Vanity Fair*. She wrote intelligent, witty articles for that magazine and others such as *Vogue*. She also

ESTÉE LAUDER (b. 1908) knew two things would make her cosmetics business a success: perfect products and a personal touch. She started making her own beauty products in her New York City kitchen in the 1940s and demonstrated them herself in local beauty salons. To attract customers, she always gave them a free gift. By the 1960s, Estée Lauder Inc., was an international company with a full line of women's and men's beauty products. By 1993, Lauder was on the *Forbes* 400 list of people whose wealth was worth $300 million or more.

1950s – 1960s

began writing plays, many of which would become hits on Broadway. In 1935, Clare Boothe married millionaire Henry Luce, publisher of *Time* and *Fortune* magazines. She is often credited with giving him the idea for a new photojournalism magazine, *Life*. The first issue came out in 1936 and featured the work of great photographers such as **Margaret Bourke-White**. *Life* was an instant success. Clare Boothe Luce served as one of the magazine's correspondents in Europe before and during World War II.

Her journalism experiences sparked her interest in politics. In 1942, Luce, a Republican, was elected to Congress, even though her Connecticut district was heavily Democratic. The media seemed more interested in Clare's glamour than in her political ideas. Luce began making waves – and enemies – with her attacks on President Franklin D. Roosevelt and her independent political views. *Vogue* called her "the country's most controversial woman." In 1953, President Dwight D. Eisenhower appointed her ambassador to Italy, and she became the first woman to occupy a top-rank diplomatic post. Luce was awarded the Presidential Medal of Freedom in 1983.

⬤ Dr. Maria Goeppert Mayer

born 1906 – died 1972
PHYSICIST

German-born Maria Goeppert had a doctoral degree in physics and had written an important work on quantum mechanics. But when she married an American scientist in 1930 and moved to the United States, she had a hard time getting a job. Most universities would not hire couples. Her husband got the academic jobs. Nevertheless, more than 30 years later, Dr. Maria Goeppert Mayer won the Nobel prize.

While her husband Joseph taught at Johns Hopkins in Baltimore, Maryland, Maria was allowed to lecture as an unpaid volunteer. When Joseph got a job at Columbia University in 1939, the Mayers finished writing a physics textbook together. Meanwhile, Maria Mayer worked with the noted nuclear scientist Enrico Fermi and held a part-time teaching job at Sarah Lawrence College in Bronxville, New York. Then she was offered a research job on the government's top-secret Manhattan Project, where she and many other scientists, such as **Dr. Chien-Shiung Wu**, contributed to the development of the first atomic bomb.

Dr. Mayer's studies in nuclear physics led to her breakthrough theory about the way protons and neutrons are arranged in the nucleus of an atom. Together with a German scientist, Hans Jensen, she wrote *Elementary Theory of Nuclear Shell Structure* in 1955. Four years later, Dr. Mayer was finally offered a full-time professorship at the University of California at San Diego. In 1963, she and Hans Jensen received the Nobel Prize for Physics.

Mary McCarthy

born 1912 – died 1989

WRITER

Mary McCarthy knew the power of the written word, and she wasn't afraid to wield the power of her writing talent on subjects such as Catholicism, college women, or the Vietnam War.

McCarthy was already writing for intellectual magazines such as the *Nation* and the *Partisan Review* when she married well-known critic Edmund Wilson in 1938. He encouraged Mary to write fiction. In the 1940s and 1950s, she published several well-received works, including short stories and novels. Her 1963 novel, *The Group*, which followed the lives and loves of eight women college graduates, became one of her most popular works.

McCarthy remained a master at nonfiction, too. In her autobiography, *Memories of A Catholic Girlhood* (1957), Mary told about the death of her parents and the strict relatives who raised her in an unloving household. McCarthy wrote books and essays about a wide range of subjects including the arts and travel, and was a leader in the country's intellectual circles. Mary did not shy away from politics, either. She was one of the first to write critically about the United States's role in Vietnam and also wrote about Watergate. She bluntly disputed **Lillian Hellman**'s writings about the House Un-American Activities Committee (HUAC) hearings, and Hellman sued her for libel. McCarthy finished **Hannah Arendt**'s memoirs when the great philosopher died, but died before finishing her own *Intellectual Memoirs*.

CARSON McCULLERS (1917–1967), novelist, short story writer, and playwright, once said her work was about "spiritual isolation." In her popular books such as *The Heart Is a Lonely Hunter* (1940) and *The Member of the Wedding* (1946), she created sensitive and sympathetic characters who are cut off from personal happiness and emotional connections with other people. Both books were made into successful films. *The Member of the Wedding,* which is about a lonely young girl who feels abandoned when her brother gets married, was also made into an award-winning Broadway play. McCullers's own life was much like the stories she wrote. She struggled through complicated love relationships and a difficult marriage. She had two strokes in 1947, but kept writing.

1950s – 1960s

Marilyn Monroe NORMA JEAN MORTENSON

born 1926 – died 1962

ACTOR

Marilyn Monroe, whose real name was Norma Jean Mortensen, was born in Los Angeles. She lived in foster homes and orphanages while her divorced mother worked, then moved in with family friends when her mother was institutionalized for mental illness. Norma Jean married when she was 16 and went to work building airplanes. When an army photographer asked her to model for an article on women workers, Norma Jean was on her way to becoming Marilyn. She continued modeling for the next few years, signed a short movie-studio contract, and changed her name.

Monroe's small part in the 1950 movie *The Asphalt Jungle* got people's attention. That same year, she also made a striking appearance in *All About Eve*, starring **Bette Davis**. Twentieth-Century Fox studio signed a contract with Marilyn and started promoting her as a "dumb blonde bombshell." Her movies earned more than $200 million.

But Monroe insisted it was not money or power she was seeking, but love. It proved hard to find. Marilyn married baseball great Joe DiMaggio in 1954. The marriage lasted less than one year. Two years later, she married playwright Arthur Miller. Marilyn continued acting in successful comedies like *Bus Stop* (1956) and *Some Like It Hot* (1959), films where Monroe's acting ability was taken seriously by critics. Monroe and Miller divorced in 1961, the same year she starred in *The Misfits,* a movie Miller had written. It was her last film. In 1962, Fox studios fired Marilyn because she was not showing up on the film set. Monroe, depressed and addicted to drugs, decided to write her autobiography. She never finished it. Marilyn Monroe died of an overdose of sleeping pills in August 1962, at the age of 36. Twenty-five years later, **Gloria Steinem** helped finish the book Monroe had started.

+ + + + + + + + + + + + + + + + +

 Barbie dolls were among the first dolls to look like sex objects and dress like movie stars. The invention of Ruth Handler, co-founder of Mattel, Inc., Barbie was introduced in 1959. More than 775 million Barbie dolls have sold since then.

Grandma Moses ANNA MARY ROBERTSON MOSES

born 1860 – died 1961

PAINTER

Grandma Moses was over 70 years old when she displayed her paintings in a drugstore window in Hoosick Falls, New York. By the time she died at age 101, people throughout the United States and Europe knew her work.

Anna Mary Robertson grew up on a farm in Washington County, New York. After marrying Thomas Moses in 1887, she had little time left for the art she had enjoyed as a child. The Moseses became dairy farmers in Virginia and later New York and raised five children. Anna Mary sometimes still embroidered pictures.

Thomas died in 1927. The Moseses' eldest son took over the farm, and Grandma Moses now had more time for her embroidery. Then she got arthritis and had to give up her thread-and-yarn pictures. She started painting pictures instead, using house paint and old canvas. In 1939, art collector Louis Caldor saw Moses's paintings exhibited at the drugstore, visited her farm, and bought 15 of her paintings. In October 1939, three of those paintings were included in a show at the Museum of Modern Art in New York City. People loved her work.

Grandma Moses had her first one-woman show in 1940, when she was 80 years old, at New York City's Galerie St. Etienne. It was the first of 150 solo shows. Her work was also in 100 national and international group shows. Grandma Moses painted around 2,000 pictures, mostly rural landscapes or scenes from her childhood, such as "Catching the Thanksgiving Turkey" (1943), "In Harvest Time" (1943), "Snowballing" (1946), and "The Quilting Bee" (1950). Her paintings have a simple, colorful, childlike quality that is now known as American primitive.

▲ Grandma Moses (right) presents her painting, "Battle of Bennington," to a member of the Daughters of the American Revolution (DAR).

When Congress met in 1965, there were two women in the Senate and ten women in the House of Representatives. **PATSY MINK (b. 1927)**, the first Asian-American woman elected to Congress, was the Representative for Hawaii. A practicing lawyer, Mink had already served in the Hawaii legislature from 1957 to 1964. As a member of the United States Congress, she worked hard for women's issues. Representative Mink sponsored a women's educational equity act and helped pass legislation to fund the Head Start education program in 1992. She is a strong supporter of women's rights and health care reform.

1950s – 1960s

Louise Nevelson

born 1899 – died 1988

SCULPTOR

Louise Nevelson, one of America's finest modern sculptors, was born Leah Berliawsky in Kiev, Russia. To escape attacks on Jews, the Berliawskys immigrated to Rockland, Maine, when Leah was five. There, Leah felt like an outsider but later found an escape in art class. In 1920, she married Charles Nevelson, a wealthy businessman, and moved to New York City.

In 1928, Nevelson began studying at the Art Students League. Two years later, she left her huband and their son and went to study art in Germany. By 1933, she was exhibiting the abstract sculptures she made from wood, stone, metal, and other materials in New York. Her first one-woman show was held in 1940. Over the next ten years, Nevelson created the large, often one-color sculptures that made her famous. Many of her sculptures are wooden and box-like and include layers of different "found" objects – anything from wheels to bowling pins to chair legs. Louise painted these sculptures one color: black, white, or gold. By the 1960s, Nevelson's work was exhibited in major museums such as New York City's Museum of Modern Art and Whitney Museum. In the 1970s, Nevelson created large sculpture environments, including the room-sized *Mrs. N's Palace* (1977) and Louise Nevelson Plaza (1979) in New York City.

Jacqueline Kennedy Onassis

born 1929 – died 1994

FIRST LADY, EDITOR

President-elect John F. Kennedy's advisers suggested that his wife, Jacqueline, keep a low profile. They thought she was too different from the average American woman and would not be well received by the American public. They were wrong. Jackie Kennedy became one of the most popular First Ladies at home and abroad.

Jacqueline Bouvier was born into a wealthy family in Long Island, New York. After graduating from George Washington University in 1951, she got a job as a newspaper photographer on the *Washington Herald-Tribune*. Shortly afterward, she met Massachusetts State Senator John F. Kennedy, who became her husband in 1953.

As First Lady, Jacqueline Kennedy set new standards of style. Women's fashions were influenced by her clothes, her hair-dos, and her famous pillbox hats. Kennedy brought a new glamour to presidential entertaining and public appearances. She declared she wanted "to make the White House the most perfect house in the United States" and started a restoration project at the Executive Mansion. In 1962, nearly 56 million people tuned in to watch Jackie Kennedy give the first televised tour of the White House.

Kennedy served as First Lady for 1,000 days. Following her husband's assassination in 1963, she retired into private life with her two children. In 1968, she married Aristotle Onassis, a Greek millionaire, but was widowed again when Onassis died in 1975. Jacqueline Kennedy Onassis moved to New York City, where she worked as a book editor for Viking Press and Doubleday. She was an important supporter of various charities and the arts until her death from cancer in 1994.

Rosa Parks

born 1913

CIVIL RIGHTS ACTIVIST

"People always say I didn't give up my seat because I was tired, but that isn't true," Rosa Parks once said. "No, the only tired I was, was tired of giving in." She was talking about the day in 1955 when she refused to give her seat on a Montgomery, Alabama, bus to a white passenger. The 42-year-old seamstress was arrested on the spot. Her arrest sparked a bus boycott that was one of the earliest mass actions of the civil rights struggle.

Rosa Parks, the granddaughter of slaves, joined the Montgomery chapter of the National Association for the Advancement of Colored People (NAACP) in 1943 and served as its secretary. She also had attended workshops given by **Septima Clark** in 1955, which strengthened Parks's willingness to "face whatever came" in the struggle for civil rights. After her arrest on December 1, 1955, Parks and other activists staged a boycott, urging

+ + + + + + + + + + + + + + + + +

President Kennedy appointed a Commission on the Status of Women in 1961. **Eleanor Roosevelt** was its chairperson. The commission was charged with finding out what prevented "the full partnership of women in our democracy." They found plenty: unequal wages, lack of child care, no maternity leave. The commission was important because it focused national attention on women's economic and social problems. It also paved the way for the Equal Pay Act of 1963, which said men and women doing the same job had to be paid the same amount.

1950s – 1960s

> *Divas:* female star singers. They were always highly prized in the opera world. But female directors and conductors were another story. Sarah Caldwell was one of the first. She founded the Opera Group of Boston in 1957 and built up the company over the next ten years. In 1976, she became the first woman conductor at New York's Metropolitan Opera house. Met star **Beverly Sills** had refused to sing unless Caldwell was given the podium.

African Americans not to ride the segregated city buses. A new young pastor, Martin Luther King Jr., helped lead the boycott. For 381 days, thousands of African Americans walked, rode bicycles, or car-pooled across Montgomery. The bus company lost money. Rosa Parks and her husband lost their jobs for participating in the boycott. But the whole country heard about the boycott and the woman who was later called "the mother of the civil rights movement." In 1956, Parks's case went to the Supreme Court, which ruled that segregation in public places was unconstitutional.

Rosa Parks, however, no longer felt safe in Montgomery and moved with her family to Detroit, Michigan, in 1957. She got a job with Congressman John Conyers in 1965, and when she retired in 1988, opened the Parks Institute for Self-Development to offer career training to young African Americans. Rosa Parks has received many awards, including the Martin Luther King, Jr., Nonviolent Peace Prize in 1980.

Leontyne Price

born 1927

OPERA SINGER

Leontyne Price sang her last note of *Il Travatore*. The audience at New York's Metropolitan Opera House applauded – for 42 minutes! The seventh African American to debut at the Metropolitan, Leontyne was born in Laurel, Mississippi, where she first sang in church choirs. When her mother took her to hear **Marian Anderson** sing, Leontyne found her musical path: opera. She graduated from college in 1948 and got a scholarship to the famous Juilliard School of Music in New York. In 1952, Price debuted on Broadway as a singer in **Gertrude Stein** and Virgil Thomson's *Four Saints and Three Acts.* A starring role in George Gershwin's opera *Porgy and Bess* followed. Price made her debut in a classical opera in 1957 when she sang in *The Dialogues of the Carmelites* at the San Francisco Opera. Her brilliant performances were enormously popular with European audiences in the great opera centers of Vienna, Austria, and Milan, Italy. After her 1961 triumph at the Metropolitan Opera, Leontyne Price became one of the Met's leading sopranos. In 1966, she sang in the first opera at its brand-new home at Lincoln Center. Price has received the Presidential Medal of Freedom (1964), the National Medal of the Arts (1985), and more than 20 Grammys for her recordings.

◄ Leontyne Price in *Il Travatore.*

⚖ Ethel Rosenberg

born 1915 – died 1953
POLITICAL ACTIVIST

"Always remember that we were innocent and could not wrong our conscience." Ethel Rosenberg wrote these words in June 1953, in her last letter to her two sons. She was then executed for espionage.

In 1936, Ethel Greenglass, a labor organizer, met Julius Rosenberg, a member of the Communist Party, at a union rally. Three years later, they married. Julius got an engineering job with the United States Signal Corps. Ethel worked at various places as a typist before she became a full-time mother.

In 1950, Ethel's brother was accused of passing atomic bomb secrets to the Soviet Union. He quickly said that Julius Rosenberg had hired him. That July, Julius Rosenberg was arrested and accused of being a spy. By August, Ethel Rosenberg was also arrested. She was jailed for eight months before she was charged with any crime. The U.S. government wanted to punish Ethel to pressure Julius to confess. And it was a time when political and public opinion about communists and suspected communists was highly charged. Both Rosenbergs were convicted and sentenced to death in 1951. After two years in solitary confinement in Sing Sing prison, Ethel Rosenberg died in the electric chair on June 19, 1953, one day after the Rosenbergs' 14th wedding anniversary. On July 12, 1995, the National Security Agency (NSA) released decoded cable messages that showed the Rosenbergs were part of a Soviet spy ring. Although they had this evidence at the time, NSA did not allow it to be used in the Rosenbergs' trials for security reasons. However, as late as 1989, some Soviet officials denied getting information from the Rosenbergs.

▲ Many people, such as **Mary Church Terrell**, thought the trial of Julius and Ethel Rosenberg was unfair. They organized legal appeals and published the loving letters Julius and Ethel wrote to each other from their jail cells. The appeals failed.

⊖ Wilma Rudolph

born 1940 – died 1994
ATHLETE

In 1944, Wilma Rudolph couldn't move her left leg because of polio and scarlet fever. In 1960, Wilma, nicknamed "La Gazelle," was the fastest woman runner in the world and the first American woman to win three gold medals at a single Olympics.

Rudolph's family devoted themselves to helping her walk again, giving her massages four times a day and encouraging Wilma's efforts. Their determination – and hers – paid off. Not only did Wilma walk

+ + + + + + + + + + + + + + + + + +

 Popular sports competitions like the famous Boston Marathon were often not open to women. In 1967, a female runner enrolled in the Boston Marathon under the name K. Switzer. When a race official discovered that "K" was a Katherine, he tried to block her path and rip her race number off her chest. Other runners blocked the official and Switzer finished running the marathon. The Boston Marathon was not officially open to women runners until 1972.

1950s – 1960s

again, she became a star athlete at her Clarksville, Tennessee, high school. And before she even graduated, Rudolph ran on the United States Olympic relay team in 1956 and won a bronze medal in the 400-meter relay.

Rudolph enrolled at Tennessee State University in Nashville and in 1960 made record-breaking sports headlines. She set a world record for the 200-meter dash and then won three Olympic medals for the 100-meter sprint, the 200-meter dash, and the 400-meter relay race. The Associated Press and United Press International named Wilma Athlete of the Year. Her hometown wanted to throw her a parade. At the time, public events in the South were often segregated because of race. As an African American, Rudolph insisted the parade be integrated or she wasn't coming. She got what she wanted.

Rudolph set records at indoor and outdoor track events before retiring in 1962. She continued to be a major presence in amateur sports, working with Olympic committees, writing her autobiography, and setting up the Wilma Rudolph Foundation to encourage young disadvantaged children to enter athletics. In 1993, Wilma Rudolph became the first woman to win the National Sports Award.

+ + + + + + + + + + + + + + + + +

 Not all women believed in a military build-up. In 1961, 50,000 women, mostly young housewives, walked out of their homes or off their jobs as part of Women Strike for Peace. They protested the nuclear arms race, the attention given to building bomb-shelters, and the military focus of the Cold War. Six years later, nearly 2,500 women stormed the Pentagon in Washington, D.C., to protest the war in Vietnam. Women were an important part of the influential peace movement in the 1960s.

⚖ Margaret Chase Smith

born 1897 – died 1995

U.S. REPRESENTATIVE, SENATOR

Margaret Chase Smith switched from being a politician's wife to being a politician when her husband died in 1940. She served the last few months of Maine Congressman Clyde H. Smith's term and then got re-elected herself. Smith went on to serve eight years in the House of Representatives and 24 years in the Senate, becoming the only woman to be elected to both houses of Congress.

Born and raised in Maine, Smith represented that state in the House from 1941 to 1949 and then in the Senate from 1949 through 1975. Smith was a Republican, but voted as she thought best, not just along party lines. Her peers called her the "conscience of the Senate." She supported a strong national defense and played a major role in passage of the Woman's Armed Services Integration Act of 1948, which gave military women equal pay and privileges. Smith also supported Democratic President Franklin Delano Roosevelt's New Deal policies and led the battle against fellow Republican Senator Joseph McCarthy's anti-communist campaign, which had ruined many lives and careers. She was the senior Republican on the Armed Services and the Aeronautical and Space Sciences Committees and also served on the Appropriations, Government Operations, and Rules Committees. Senator Smith was famous for her faithful attendance at all Senate debates and votes. She answered present at 2,941 consecutive roll-calls. Smith ran for the Republican presidential nomination in 1964 but lost to Senator Barry Goldwater from Arizona. In 1975, she lost her Senate seat to a Democrat, but remained an important elder stateswoman. Smith published two books, *Gallant Women* (1968) and *Declaration of Conscience* (1972).

Maria Tallchief

born 1925

BALLERINA

As a teenager on the Osage Reservation in Oklahoma, Maria Tallchief studied to become a concert pianist. Then she discovered ballet. Maria went on to become one of the most technically accomplished ballerinas in the United States.

Tallchief, the daughter of an Osage Indian father and a Scottish-Irish mother, began her professional ballet career after high school. In 1942, while she was in Europe as a member of the Ballet Russes de Monte Carlo, she met the famous choreographer George Balanchine. Tallchief quit Ballet Russes and joined Balanchine's new company, the Grand Ballet de Monte Carlo. Soon after, the ballerina and the choreographer married. Although the marriage lasted only six years, their professional relationship provided some of Tallchief's greatest roles. Her dancing in Balanchine-arranged ballets such as *The Firebird*, *Symphonie Concertante*, *Swan Lake*, *Allegro Brillante*, and *The Nutcracker* was widely praised.

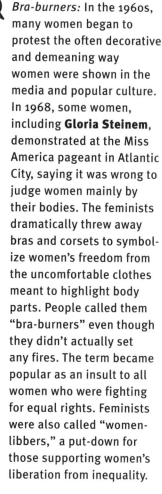

" " " " " " " " " " " "

Bra-burners: In the 1960s, many women began to protest the often decorative and demeaning way women were shown in the media and popular culture. In 1968, some women, including **Gloria Steinem**, demonstrated at the Miss America pageant in Atlantic City, saying it was wrong to judge women mainly by their bodies. The feminists dramatically threw away bras and corsets to symbolize women's freedom from the uncomfortable clothes meant to highlight body parts. People called them "bra-burners" even though they didn't actually set any fires. The term became popular as an insult to all women who were fighting for equal rights. Feminists were also called "women-libbers," a put-down for those supporting women's liberation from inequality.

1950s – 1960s

In 1947, Tallchief went with Balanchine's company to Paris. She was the first American to dance at the famed Paris Opéra in more than 100 years. The couple then joined the New York City Ballet. Tallchief danced with the New York City Ballet as well as other companies for the next 18 years. The recipient of the *Dance* magazine award in 1960, Tallchief also won the Capezio Award for distinguished service to dance in 1965. She retired from dancing soon after, but served as artistic director of the Lyric Opera Ballet and in 1981 founded the Chicago City ballet company.

Lila Acheson Wallace

The 1950s economy heavily depended upon women's purchases. Advertisements – which always featured successful middle-class white families – encouraged women to buy automobiles, appliances, and other items for their homes, if not bigger and better homes, too. Many women worked part-time so that they and their families would have enough money for consumer goods or for improving their economic status. By the 1960s, 30 percent of married women worked outside the home. In the 1960s, many young people from this same white middle class rejected the attention devoted to material goods.

born 1889 – died 1984

PUBLISHER, PHILANTHROPIST

In 1922, Lila Acheson Wallace helped her husband start a magazine in a basement in New York's Greenwich Village. They borrowed $5,000 to mail out the first 5,000 copies of their *Reader's Digest*. Today *Reader's Digest* has the largest circulation of any magazine in the world. It's published in 17 languages and reaches 100 million people every month.

A Canadian-born graduate of the University of Oregon, Lila Acheson taught school and worked on women's issues for the Department of Labor before she married De Witt Wallace in 1921. Along with her husband, Wallace dedicated her life to *Reader's Digest*, which grew into a publishing empire that includes other magazines, books, and computer software. The Wallaces became very rich. They were also very generous, donating hundreds of millions of dollars to charities, hospitals, museums, and the arts. In 1956, Wallace created the Lila Wallace-Reader's Digest Fund, the largest private funder of arts and culture in the United States. Wallace also began the Reader's Digest Art Collection, which is displayed in the company's Pleasantville, New York, office. When Wallace died in 1984, she was the richest woman in the United States with more than $250 million.

Mary Georgene Wells

born 1928

ADVERTISING EXECUTIVE

All the major advertising agencies were headed by men until Mary Wells opened Wells, Rich, Greene, Inc. in 1966. Wells said she didn't think it made any difference to clients if she was a man or woman. All that interested people was her strong track record. Wells had more than 16 years of advertising experience, and a vice-presidency and senior partnership at two of the country's biggest agencies. By 1972, Wells was the highest paid woman executive in the United States, and Wells, Rich, Greene, Inc. was a top ad agency.

One of her agency's first accounts, Braniff Airlines, took off. Wells hired the famous sculptor Alexander Calder to design the bright color scheme of Braniff's airplanes. She brought in the top fashion designer Emilio Pucci to design the flight attendants' uniforms. The advertising campaign for Braniff got a lot of media attention. So did Mary when she married the president of the airline in 1967. Wells, Rich, Greene, Inc. became a leader in the use of humor in advertising. It was well-known for its cigarette advertising aimed at a female audience. Mary Wells was named advertising woman of the year in 1971 by the American Advertising Federation.

√ Dr. Chien-Shiung Wu

born 1912

PHYSICIST

Dr. Chien-Shiung Wu became famous by helping revise an accepted law-of-science. From around 1925, scientists believed that particles and anti-particles should behave the same way. In 1956, following the theory of two of her peers, Dr. Wu performed a very long, complicated experiment. Her results showed that particles did not behave identically. Dr. Wu's findings revolutionized ways of thinking about physics.

Born and raised in China, Dr. Wu earned her doctorate in physics from the University of California at Berkeley. She joined the scientific staff of the Division of War Research at Columbia University in New York City in the 1940s and, like **Dr. Maria Goeppert Mayer**, worked on the Manhattan Project, which developed the first atomic bomb. In 1957, Wu became a full professor of physics at Columbia. She was the first woman to receive the Comstock Award from the National Academy of Sciences (1964) and the first to win the Research Corporation Award (1958). Dr. Wu was named Woman of the Year by the American Association of University Women in 1962 and elected president of the American Physical Society in 1975. She won the National Medal of Science that same year.

+ + + + + + + + + + + + + + + + +

In 1950, two scientists working for the government made an important discovery: nystatin, an antibody that works against diseases caused by fungi. Elizabeth Hazen, an authority on fungi, and Rachel Brown, a chemist with the U.S. Department of Agriculture, separated the substance nystatin from soil samples they got from a Virginia farm. They patented their discovery with a non-profit corporation, and nystatin was used in cures for everything from human intestinal diseases to Dutch elm tree disease. Nystatin sales earned almost $13 million. Hazen and Brown decided not to profit by this. Through their corporation, most of the money went back into scientific research. Hazen and Brown retired on civil service pensions.

1950s – 1960s

Woman Power!

The women's liberation movement was one of the powerful forces shaping the nation in the 1970s. Feminists challenged society's ideas about work, family, love, and sexuality. Consciouness-raising (c-r) groups of primarily middle-class women met to discuss what it meant to be female in the United States. These groups raised the participants' consciousness, or awareness, of how their lives might be limited by their gender and offered members support in their struggle for personal and public equality. C-r groups were an important way that feminist values spread.

Women staged hundreds of rallies across the country to publicize their demands for equality. They started labor and community groups, health clinics, rape crisis centers, and battered women's shelters. Feminist lawyers filed anti-discriminaton lawsuits. Feminist scholars helped create women's studies programs. Feminist politicians lobbied for government sponsored day care and fought to get the Democratic and Republican parties to back women candidates. And there was a renewed interest in the Equal Rights Amendment (ERA).

ERA - Not Quite All the Way

The ERA, a proposed constitutional amendment, says "Equality of rights under the law shall not be denied or abridged by the United States or by any State on account of sex." It was originally written by **Alice Paul** in 1923. Over the next decades, feminists argued for and against the amendment. Some thought it was the most important way to guarantee equality. Others thought the ERA would end legal protection of women in the workplace. In 1943, the ERA was rewritten by the Senate Judiciary Committee. But it wasn't until 1972 that the Senate, responding to the growing women's movement, voted 84 to 8 to send the ERA to the state legislatures for ratification. Approval of three-quarters of the states was needed. Like the efforts to pass the suffrage amendment, the campaign to pass the ERA was difficult. Conservative forces mobilized to oppose its ratification. When the June 30, 1982, deadline came, the ERA still needed three more states for ratification. The amendment failed. So did a 1993 Congressional bill to bring it up again.

Many Women, Many Voices

Sisterhood, the idea that all women share in the struggle for equality, was an important idea in the 1970s and 1980s. It was also a complicated one. Women of color did not always feel that their issues

▲ Selba Walker, Director of the Columbus, Ohio, Native American Indian Center, leads a 1990 march to protect tribal burial grounds.

were being addressed by the white, middle-class leaders of the women's liberation movement. New groups such as the National Black Feminist Organization, the Mexican-American Women's National Association, and the Organization of Pan Asian American Women emerged. Some Native American women joined the American Indian Movement (AIM).

Many women, for religious or cultural reasons, did not embrace a feminist agenda that included issues such as abortion rights and civil rights for homosexuals. While the Supreme Court's decision on *Roe v. Wade* (1973) legalized abortion, the issue remains highly charged. "Right-to-life" groups who oppose abortion on religious or moral grounds, work at state and federal levels to ban or restrict abortions, while "pro-choice" groups work to keep abortions legal and available.

The civil rights and women's movements spurred a similar struggle for homosexual rights. The role of lesbians within the women's movement was hotly debated. Some feminists thought the fight for equality should include all women. Others worried that conservatives would use homosexual rights as yet one more example of what made the feminist movement anti-family, anti-religion, and wrong.

Backlash

By the late 1970s, there were signs that feminists' liberal ideas about gender roles were threatening to many Americans. Though liberals were in the majority, there was a strong – and very visible – showing of conservatives at a government-funded women's conference held in Houston, Texas, in 1977. When Republican Ronald Reagan became president in 1981, it signaled a new era of conservatism,

which had a big impact on the women's movement.

In keeping with the 1980s emphasis on success and material goods, "superwomen" or "yuppies," (young, upwardly-mobile professionals) were encouraged to "go for it all." To do so, they had to balance jobs in a highly competitive, male business world with homemaking, and childrearing. Meanwhile, there was an increase in the number of households headed by women, partly because of a rising divorce rate. Many of these women had little chance of earning a good salary to provide for their families, especially during economic hard times.

Feminists found themselves under attack. Many people blamed them for the complex changes that were occurring in American society. As a result, there was a countermove to cut social welfare benefits to the poor and limit access to abortion.

Heading Toward a New Century

As this century closes, women in the United States face many challenges. More than 70 percent of the adults living in poverty are women. AIDS among women is on the rise. According to the Labor Department's Women's Bureau, there are more than 58 million women in the labor force – but they outnumber men in low-paying jobs, and still earn roughly 77¢ for every $1 men earn. And unresolved policies toward child care, health insurance, and welfare have a serious effect on many women's lives.

But women are also seizing new opportunities. They hold 48 percent of all managerial and professional speciality jobs. In 1995, 86 women were elected to state-wide offices, including 19 women lieutenant governors. There are 47 women now seated in the House of Representatives and eight in the Senate.

From the kitchen to the Cabinet, American women are making their marks on American society and helping the nation move forward into the 21st century.

And women's history, like all histories, is a never-ending story.

◀ Republican Governor Christine Todd Whitman of New Jersey

Maya Angelou

born 1928

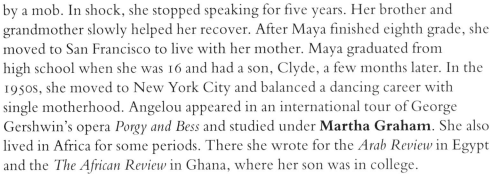

WRITER, POET

In 1993, President-elect Bill Clinton invited Maya Angelou to read at his inauguration. It was the first time a poet had been asked to do so in more than 30 years.

Maya was born in St. Louis, Missouri, but raised by her grandmother in Stamps, Arkansas, after her parents divorced in 1932. Her first and one of her most famous autobiographies, *I Know Why the Caged Bird Sings*, is about those early years in the South during the Great Depression. The book deals with the hardships and racism Maya faced and with her painful childhood. When she was seven years old, Maya was raped by her mother's boyfriend. He was later convicted and killed by a mob. In shock, she stopped speaking for five years. Her brother and grandmother slowly helped her recover. After Maya finished eighth grade, she moved to San Francisco to live with her mother. Maya graduated from high school when she was 16 and had a son, Clyde, a few months later. In the 1950s, she moved to New York City and balanced a dancing career with single motherhood. Angelou appeared in an international tour of George Gershwin's opera *Porgy and Bess* and studied under **Martha Graham**. She also lived in Africa for some periods. There she wrote for the *Arab Review* in Egypt and the *The African Review* in Ghana, where her son was in college.

Angelou returned to the United States in 1966 and started working on stage, in film, and in television. She also started writing her autobiographies and poetry. *I Know Why the Caged Bird Sings* (1970) was nominated for the National Book Award, and was made into a television movie. Her collection of poems, *Just Give Me a Cool Drink of Water 'fore I Diiie* (1971), was nominated for a Pulitzer Prize. She received an Emmy Award nomination for her acting in the TV series *Roots* (1977), and a Tony Award nomination in 1978 for her role in the Broadway play *Look Away*. By 1993, Angelou's list of published works included several more collections of poetry and autobiographies, the bestselling book of essays, *Wouldn't Take Nothing for My Journey Now* (1993), and a poetry book for children called *Life Doesn't Frighten Me* (1993). She has been the Reynolds Professor of American Studies at Wake Forest University in North Carolina since 1981 and has received more than 50 honorary degrees from colleges and universities across the country.

On her first day in Congress in 1971, New York Representative **BELLA ABZUG** (1920–1998) called for a resolution for complete withdrawal of all United States troops from the Vietnam War going on in Southeast Asia. She was not one to waste time or words. Abzug, the first Jewish woman in Congress, already had a long history of activism in civil rights, peace, and the women's and environmental movements. Abzug got her degree from Columbia University Law School in New York in 1945. She did free legal work for many of her causes. Abzug was a key player in many of the important women's events and organizations of the 1970s and 1980s, such as the National Women's Political Caucus and the National Women's Conference. She was a member of Congress from 1971 to 1976 and was often on the frontlines of political demonstrations, wearing her big hats. In 1995, she participated in the United Nations Fourth Global Conference on Women.

Romana Acosta Bañuelos

Romana Acosta Bañuelos was born in Miami, Arizona, but during the 1930s, she and her family were sent to Mexico, her parents' native country. Because of the Great Depression, the United States government forced many Mexicans and some Mexican Americans to leave because there were no jobs. Bañuelos returned to the United States when she was 19. By the time she was 24, she owned a successful company. Her sharp business sense eventually got her a top government job – secretary of the treasury.

Bañuelos opened a tortilla factory with her aunt in Los Angeles, California, in 1949. They made $36 on their first day of business. Ramona's Mexican Food Products grew into a multimillion dollar business over the next 30 years. Bañuelos also helped found the Pan-American National Bank in 1965 to increase Hispanic economic and political influence in Los Angeles.

President Richard Nixon asked Bañuelos, a fellow Republican, to join his cabinet. Before she was confirmed as secretary of the treasury, her Mexican Food Products business was raided by u.s. immigration agents looking for illegal workers. The raid seemed to have been provoked by some Democrats seeking to embarrass the president through Bañuelos. A Senate Committee said she had been treated unfairly and confirmed her nomination. On December 17, 1971, Romana Bañuelos became treasurer of the United States, the first Mexican American to hold such a high office. She remained there until February 1974, when she resigned to return to her family and business in California.

◄ Before becoming United States Treasurer, business owner Romana Acosta Bañuelos founded the Ramona's Mexican Food Products, Inc., Scholarship Foundation for young Hispanic students.

+ + + + + + + + + + + + + + + + +

Opportunities for Hispanic women in the 1970s were limited. Carmen Rosa Maymi, the first Hispanic director of the u.s. Department of Labor's Women's Bureau (1973–1977), wrote that many were "hampered by a language barrier and discriminated against because of their sex and their ethnic background." By the 1990s, Hispanic women earned a median weekly salary of $283 while African-American women earned $313 and white women earned $361.

1970s – 1990s

French-born sculptor **LOUISE BOURGEOIS** (b. 1911) moved to the United States in 1938. Her early paintings and drawings were influenced by Surrealism and Cubism, both modern art movements, and by geometry. In the 1940s, she turned to sculpture and is now best known for imaginative works made from wood, bronze, marble, glass, or plastic. Some of her startling abstract shapes seem to have human qualities to them. Bourgeois' sculptures often suggest parts of the human body charged with sexuality or raging emotion, such as *The Destruction of the Father* (1974), which looks like a set of jaws. Bourgeois has said that some of her art is a response to the anger she felt when her father brought his mistress to live in the family home. Bourgeois was in her 70s before her art work became widely exhibited. In 1993, her work represented the United States at the famous Venice Biennale art show, in Italy. In 1995, the Museum of Modern Art in Paris exhibited a collection of 50 sculptures and installations, including Bourgeois's long-legged metal sculpture *Spiders* (1995).

Shirley Temple Black

born 1928

ACTOR, DIPLOMAT

Shirley Temple received a special Academy Award for being "the outstanding personality of 1934." She was six years old and earning $2,500 a week starring in films such as *Stand Up and Cheer* and *Little Miss Marker*. Her curly hair and famous dimpled smile made Temple Hollywood's biggest box-office hit from 1935 through 1938. Her winning personality also helped her become an outstanding public servant as an adult.

Shirley Temple retired from the movies when she was 22 and married Charles Black. During the 1960s, she became involved in politics and ran unsuccessfully for Congress in 1967. But she did win the attention of Republican leaders, and in 1969, President Richard Nixon named her a United States delegate to the United Nations General Assembly. Black served as U.S. ambassador to the African nation of Ghana from 1974 until 1976, when President Gerald Ford named her chief of protocol in the State Department. As chief of protocol, Black was responsible for making sure White House events for political and international leaders ran smoothly. She also spoke at many diplomatic events. Black continued her work in international affairs, winning the Gandhi Memorial International Foundation Award in 1988. She was ambassador to the former Czechoslovakia from 1989 to 1992.

Connie Chung

born 1946

TELEVISION JOURNALIST

Connie Chung, the first woman after **Barbara Walters** to anchor a nightly network television evening news program, has been called both a serious and a sensationalist television journalist. She reported on presidents and presidential campaigns as well as health issues, AIDS, and violence. But she's also known for her controversial celebrity interviews.

Chung was born in Washington, D.C., where her father was a Chinese diplomat. After graduating from the University of Maryland in 1969, she got her first job in journalism, working

◄ When Connie Chung went to work for CBS in 1971, she became the first Asian-American reporter on network television.

as a secretary at a Washington television station. There she quickly rose to reporter. In 1971, she moved to CBS, and in five years was its highest paid local news anchor, hosting three newscasts a day for CBS's Los Angeles station. In 1983, Chung moved to NBC to cover national news.

In the 1980s, Chung co-hosted several television news-magazine shows and produced several documentaries for NBC, including a 1987 report from China, where Chung's bilingualism gave her a journalistic advantage. In 1989, she moved to the CBS network for what was reported to be a $1.5 million annual salary. There, Chung hosted several of her own shows and became the main fill-in for Dan Rather, the anchor of the *CBS Evening News*. In 1993 Chung joined Rather as co-anchor. She also hosted a primetime news magazine program, *Eye to Eye with Connie Chung*.

In 1995, Connie Chung was a leading news story herself, when CBS removed her as co-anchor of its *Evening News*. Chung and Rather had had an uneasy working relationship. The newscasters had different styles and there was competition over assignments. Chung, however, claimed she was being blamed for the show's low viewer ratings and that her firing "would be a very significant setback for women in television."

Sandra Cisneros

born 1954

WRITER

In 1986, Sandra Cisneros, the first Chicana, or Mexican-American, writer to get a major publishing contract, was worried about how she was going to pay her bills. Less than ten years later, she received a 1995 MacArthur Foundation grant, often called a "genius award." The award gave Cisneros a large annual amount of money in recognition of her powerful body of writing.

Sandra grew up in poverty in a Chicago *barrio*, or poor Hispanic neighborhood, and used her experiences as a rich source of inspiration. She was accepted by the Iowa Writers' Workshop, where she wrote and studied poetry in the 1970s. There she also got the idea for her first book of fiction, *The House on Mango Street*. A collection of narrations by a

++++++++++++++++++

At a time when jobs for women in real newsrooms were few, Mary Tyler Moore portrayed a plucky young producer in CBS's popular *The Mary Tyler Moore* show. The show, which ran from 1970 to 1977, featured Moore as a single, 30ish assistant producer who's trying to make it in a Minneapolis TV station. In real life, Moore was such a success that she formed a leading Hollywood production company, MTM Enterprises. By the time CBS premiered another sitcom about TV, *Murphy Brown,* in 1988, women had been promoted. Candice Bergen played Murphy Brown, star reporter of a newsmagazine show.

young Chicana, it won the Before Columbus American Book Award in 1985.

Cisneros received a master's degree from the University of Iowa, then a fellowship. She moved to Texas in 1986, where she published her first book of poems the following year. The book got good reviews, but that didn't help Cisneros earn a living. Her luck changed when she received a grant from the National Endowment of the Arts. Next she published *Woman Hollering Creek and Other Stories*, a book about the lives of Chicana women in Texas and Mexico. This book brought Cisneros enormous attention from readers and critics. In 1994, her book of poems, *Loose Woman*, was published.

⚖ Hillary Rodham Clinton

born 1947

FIRST LADY, LAWYER

+ + + + + + + + + + + + + + + +

In 1993, President Bill Clinton appointed more women to his cabinet than any other president had. They included **Janet Reno**, United States Attorney General, Donna E. Shalala, Secretary of Health and Human Services, Hazel O'Leary, Secretary of Energy, Alice Rivlin, Deputy Director of the Office of Management and Budget, Carol Browner, the Administrator of the Environmental Protection Agency, and Madeleine K. Albright, u.s. Ambassador to the United Nations.

Like **Eleanor Roosevelt**, First Lady Hillary Rodham Clinton has been criticized for the way she looks and acts, and for having too much influence with the President of the United States. Though she often changed her image in response, she made the role of First Lady a powerful political job.

Hillary Rodham was born into a conservative Republican family and became involved with civil rights and poverty programs through her Methodist church. She graduated from Wellesley College in Massachusetts, and from Yale Law School in New Haven, Connecticut. In 1973, she took a job as a lawyer with **Marian Wright Edelman**'s Children's Defense Fund before serving as legal counsel on the House of Representatives's Judiciary Committee investigating President Richard Nixon and the Watergate scandal in 1974.

In 1975, Hillary married Bill Clinton, whom she met at Yale. Three years later, he was first elected governor of Arkansas. Hillary Rodham joined Rose Law Firm, a well-known legal office in the state's capital. The Clintons were a strong political team. As governor, Bill appointed Hillary head of the Rural Health Advisory Committe and later the Education Standards

Committee. The Arkansas State Legislature passed an education improvement bill based on her committee's findings.

After her husband became president in 1993, he appointed Hillary Rodham Clinton to head the National Health Care Task Force. When the national health care plan it proposed was rejected, much of the blame was put on the First Lady. She was held responsible for the committee's secretiveness and for the complexity of its plan. She also came under fire for her role in some real estate deals and investments in which the Clintons had been involved in Arkansas. What came to be known as the Whitewater Scandal was investigated. Despite her controversial image, Hillary Rodham Clinton remains an active and determined health-care and women's and children's rights supporter.

Celia Cruz

born c. 1929

SINGER

"My message is always *felicidad*, happiness" says Celia Cruz, Grammy-Award winning Queen of Salsa. Her music backs up her message.

Born in Havana, Cuba, Cruz was lead singer for La Sonora Matancera, a popular orchestra. In the 1950s, she played on radio shows, in films, and in Havana's famous nightclubs.

When Fidel Castro came to power in 1959, Cruz and the other musicians defected, or moved, to the United States. She starting touring in the late 1960s, with the legendary musician Tito Puente. Cruz and Puente helped build a new young audience for salsa, a popular form of Latin-American dance music that combines jazz, blues, and other music forms with a lively Afro-Caribbean beat.

Cruz is a powerful singer who, with her elaborate costumes and animated choreography, is also a popular performer. She has recorded more than 70 albums and has influenced many younger musicians, including **Gloria Estefan**.

"Poetry is actually a witness for life," RITA DOVE (b. 1952) once said. She used her own talents to create verses about such topics as the lives of slaves and the lives of her grandparents. In 1993, Dove became Poet Laureate of the United States, appointed by the Library of Congress as the nation's official poet. She was the youngest person and the first African American to receive this honor. By that time, she had already won several grants and fellowships as well as the 1987 Pulitzer Prize for *Thomas and Beulah,* a book of 44 poems about her grandparents. Dove grew up in Akron, Ohio. She was a Presidential Scholar, one of the top 100 high school students in the country so honored. After graduating from Miami University in Oxford, Ohio, in 1973, Dove received a Fulbright Fellowship and went to study in Germany. She started publishing her poetry in 1974 and has since also written short stories and a novel, taught college, and edited several poetry journals.

1970s – 1990s

🎓 Angela Davis

born 1944

ACTIVIST, EDUCATOR

Angela Davis has been unemployed and even imprisoned because of her radical activism and outspoken political views.

The daughter of civil rights activists, Angela grew up in Birmingham, Alabama, in a middle-class African-American community called "dynamite hill." It was nicknamed that because so many of its homes were bombed by the Ku Klux Klan.

Davis became a civil rights activist and then worked with the Black Panthers. In 1968, while completing a master's degree at the University of California at San Diego, she joined the Communist Party because she believed communism was the best way to eliminate racism, sexism, poverty, and injustice. As a result, she was unable to get a teaching job.

Part of Davis's political activism included work on behalf of African-American prisoners. In 1970, authorities suspected she was involved in the Soledad Brothers shoot-out in a California courtroom, where four people were killed when two prisoners tried to escape. Davis was accused of supplying the weapons they used and charged with conspiracy, murder, and kidnapping. Her name was placed on the FBI's Most Wanted list. After spending a few months on the run, Davis was captured and held in jail without bail. Some people were angered by the government's treatment of her. Thousands of supporters joined the "Free Angela" campaign. In 1972, after a 13-month trial and 16 months in prison, Davis was acquitted of all charges and set free. Although she was banned from many teaching positions, she did find work at several U.S. colleges, as well as at Moscow University in the Soviet Union, and Havana University in Cuba. Davis is co-founder of the National Alliance Against Racist and Political Repression, and is active in the Black Women's Health Project and the National Political Caucus of Black Women.

▲ Angela Davis in the 1970s. She is now a professor of philosophy at the University of California at Santa Cruz.

Marian Wright Edelman

born 1939

Marian Wright Edelman sees children as "God's presence, promise, and hope for humankind." As founder of the Children's Defense Fund (CDF), and author of the bestseller, *The Measure of Our Success* (1992), Edelman has led a passionate crusade to improve the lives of the country's children.

CHILDREN'S RIGHTS ADVOCATE, LAWYER

Marian grew up in Bennettsville, South Carolina, at a time when the South was still segregated and many African Americans faced poverty and discrimination. From her father, a Baptist minister, she learned the importance of serving others. "Working for the community was as much a part of our existence as eating and sleeping and church," she said. Both her parents also emphasized hard work and education.

In 1963, after graduating from Yale Law School, Edelman moved to Mississippi. She became the first African-American woman to pass the state's bar exam, which meant she could practice law there. She trained with the National Association for the Advancement of Colored People (NAACP), then set up a private practice. As a lawyer, Edelman fought against school segregation and helped get civil-rights protesters out of jail. She herself was jailed and threatened by attack dogs for her civil rights activities.

Edelman soon decided that the best way to make things better for poor people in places like Mississippi was to change federal government policies. In 1968, she moved to Washington, D.C., and started an organization called the Washington Research Project, which represented the rights of poor people and people of color. She also married and had three children. "The children — my own and other people's — became the passion of my personal and professional life," she later wrote. In 1973, Edelman founded the CDF. Under her leadership, CDF has developed into a powerful advocacy group for better child care, health care, education, and employment opportunities for young people.

Sesame Street: the long-running public television show, developed by Joan Ganz Cooney and her Children's Television Workshop (CTW). In 1966, Cooney researched for the Carnegie Corporation the possibilities of using television to teach preschoolers. She then raised almost $8 million to put *Sesame Street* on the air in 1969. Cooney and CTW designed the program to teach the alphabet, numbers, thinking, and respect for others. The characters are not stereotyped by gender, race, ethnicity, age, or physical ability. The show, aimed at all young children, particularly disadvantaged preschoolers, was a huge success. *Sesame Street* is set in a city-style neighborhood, and features songs, comedy, famous Muppets such as Big Bird, Bert and Ernie, Oscar the Grouch, and Cookie Monster, along with actors and celebrities. It has won television awards such as the 1970 Emmy and the Peabody.

1970s – 1990s

√ Dr. Gertrude Belle Elion

born 1918
BIOCHEMIST

When she was 15 years old, Gertrude Elion witnessed her grandfather's painful death from cancer and hoped that one day "maybe I could do something about it." She did. During her 50-year career as a scientist, Elion developed drugs that helped save the lives of thousands of people. In 1988, when she was 70 years old, she was one of three scientists who shared the Nobel Prize in Medicine.

Elion studied biochemistry and graduated from New York University in 1941. It was difficult for women scientists to find jobs then. During World War II, with so many men away in the military, more jobs became available to women, and in 1944, Elion was hired as a research chemist by Burroughs Wellcome, a pharmaceutical company. There she began as an assistant to scientist George Hitchings, but soon they were working as a team. Together they studied the chemical makeup of the body's cells to see how healthy cells differed from cancer cells, bacteria, and viruses. They developed many drugs to combat leukemia, a cancer of the blood cells, and malaria, an attack on the blood cells by parasites, as well as other diseases. Elion's and Hitchings's research also made the first successful organ transplants possible and led to the development of AZT, a drug used in the treatment of AIDS.

+++++++++++++++++

In 1848, **Elizabeth Cady Stanton, Lucretia Mott,** and several hundred other people held the first Women's Rights Convention in Seneca Falls, New York. In 1969, the women of Seneca Falls started the National Women's Hall of Fame to honor women's achievements. The Hall of Fame opened in a former bank building and features exhibits and artifacts about women's history in the United States. Every year women who have made significant contributions in a wide range of fields are inducted into the Hall of Fame.

Gloria Estefan

born 1958
SINGER

Cuban-born Gloria Estefan was one of the first Spanish-speaking pop artists to cross over into English-speaking markets.

Gloria Fajardo and her family moved from Cuba to the United States in 1959, eventually settling in Miami, Florida. There she cared for her father, who suffered from multiple sclerosis, while her mother worked.

"Music was the only way I had to let go," she later said. In 1975, she met Emilio Estefan and became the singer for his band, the Miami Latin Kings, later called the Miami Sound Machine. Gloria and Emilio were married three years later. By that time the band had a strong reputation for its ballads, disco, and pop songs – and its talented lead singer. They signed with the Hispanic Division of CBS Records in 1980 and were a success in Spanish-speaking countries, but did not break into the United States market. But in 1985, "Conga," a song from *Primitive Love,* changed all that. It became the first single in recording history to make the dance, pop, Latin, and black music charts in *Billboard,* the magazine of the music industry. The album sold more than 2 million copies. Gloria Estefan's popularity in the U.S. grew as she toured, cut more albums, and made music videos. While on tour in 1990, Estefan was seriously injured in a bus crash and needed extensive surgery on her spine. After a long, painful period, Estefan astonished fans with not only a new album, *Into the Light,* but also with a comeback tour. On August 30, 1995, she gave a concert for 10,000 refugees at the U.S. Naval Base at Guantanamo Bay, Cuba. It was her first singing appearance in her homeland.

◄ Gloria Estefan is sometimes called the Latin **Madonna**.

Geraldine Ferraro

born 1935
POLITICIAN

When Democratic presidential candidate Walter Mondale nominated Geraldine Ferraro as his vice-presidential running mate in 1984, she became the first woman on the highest election ticket of a major political party. The Democrats lost to Republicans Ronald Reagan and George Bush, but Ferraro won a major victory for women in politics.

Born in Newburgh, New York, to Italian parents, Geraldine was raised by her mother after her father died when she was eight years old. She graduated from Marymount College in New York in 1956, and worked as a public school English teacher while she went to Fordham University Law School at

+ + + + + + + + + + + + + + + +

 As a result of the 1994 elections, 47 women were seated in the United States House of Representatives and eight women in the U.S. Senate. Many had received campaign contributions from a group called Emily's List. This political action group, founded in 1985 by IBM heiress Emily Ellen Malcolm, has more than 24,000 members who raise money to help elect women Democratic candidates.

1970s – 1990s

night. She passed the bar exam in 1960, married, raised children, and worked as a private-practice lawyer until 1974. That year she became an assistant district attorney in Queens, New York, and helped set up a bureau to help women who were abused at home or raped. She quit when she found out she wasn't getting paid as well as male co-workers.

Ferraro became involved in local politics, and in 1978 was elected to the United States House of Representatives from New York's ninth district. In Congress, Ferraro worked for passage of the Equal Rights Amendment and for bills benefiting working women. In 1984, she became the first woman to chair the Democratic platform committee, where the party states its position on important issues. Ferraro's 1984 run for vice-president was hurt when her husband's company was charged with tax fraud. Ferraro was also investigated for the funding of her earlier congressional campaign. After the Democrats lost the presidential election, Geraldine published *Ferraro: My Story* (1985). In 1992, she made an unsuccessful run for the U.S. Senate and then returned to work as an attorney and supporter of other women politicians.

Jane Fonda

born 1937

ACTOR, ACTIVIST

Jane Fonda's career has taken many different directions. She's appeared in plays, Hollywood movies, and her own exercise videos. She's been an activist in the anti-Vietnam War movement and in the feminist movement, which she discovered after reading **Betty Friedan**'s *The Feminine Mystique*. Now married to media head Ted Turner, Fonda produced an important television documentary, "A Century of Women," in 1994.

Born in New York City, Jane Fonda appeared in a few plays with her father, Henry, a distinguished actor. Her career took off in the mid-'60s when she starred in films such as *Barefoot in the Park* (1967) and won a New York Film Critics Award for her role in *They Shoot Horses, Don't They?* (1969). During this time, Jane married French director Roger Vadim, who cast her as a futuristic sex symbol in his science-fiction film *Barbarella* (1968).

◄ Jane Fonda demonstrated against the U.S. war in Vietnam and visited North Vietnam in 1972, where she interviewed people about the conflict. Some Americans thought this was a disloyal act and called her Hanoi Jane, after North Vietnam's capital.

Fonda's fame as an actor and activist spread. She won an Academy Award for her 1971 film *Klute*. In 1973, Fonda married Tom Hayden, one of the founders of Students for a Democratic Society (SDS), a left-wing political action group. After spending time and money on Hayden's unsuccessful race for the California state senate, Fonda returned to her film work. In 1977 she played **Lillian Hellman** in *Julia* and formed her own production company, Indochina Peace Campaign (IPC). IPC produced films meant to increase public awareness about war and injustice. Fonda won her second acting Oscar in 1978 for the IPC film *Coming Home*, which dealt with issues facing Vietnam veterans. Through IPC, she also produced and acted in *9 to 5* (1980), a film about women's rights in the workplace. She also appeared with **Katharine Hepburn** and Henry Fonda in his last film, *On Golden Pond*, in 1981.

In the late 1970s, Jane Fonda turned her attention to women's health issues. Her bestselling workout books and videotapes helped make aerobic exercise popular.

⚖ Ruth Bader Ginsburg

born 1933

SUPREME COURT JUSTICE

When Ruth Bader Ginsburg was appointed to the United States Supreme Court in August 1993, she became only the second woman, after **Sandra Day O'Connor**, to serve in this position. She was also the first Supreme Court justice, appointed by a Democratic president since 1967, and the first Jewish Supreme Court justice since 1969.

Having few women colleagues wasn't new to Ginsburg. When she enrolled in Harvard Law School in Cambridge, Massachusetts, in 1956, there were only eight other women in a class of more than 500 students. Ruth found being female, Jewish, a mother, and a lawyer was even harder. Though she had been editor of the *Harvard*

" " " " " " " " " " " "

🔍 *Roe v. Wade:* the name of the 1973 legal case that resulted in the landmark Supreme Court ruling about abortion, the termination of pregnancy. At that time, most states had anti-abortion laws, although abortion had been legal up until the mid-1800s. Norma McGorvey, a young pregnant woman using the name Jane Roe to protect her identity, sued in a Texas state court for the right to legally have an abortion. The case went to the Supreme Court, which ruled 7–2 that women had an unrestricted right to an abortion in the first three months of pregnancy.

1970s – 1990s

Law Review and had completed her law degree at New York's Columbia University Law School in New York City in 1959, no law firm would hire her. Ginsburg finally found a job as a clerk for a federal district judge in New York. Four years later she became the second woman to join the faculty at the Rutgers University Law School in New Brunswick, New Jersey. While there, Ginsburg had to hide the fact she was pregnant with her second child. She might have lost her position if the school had found out. Because of her experiences, Ginsburg was the perfect lawyer to represent the American Civil Liberties Union (ACLU) in sex discrimination cases. In three years, 1973–76, Ginsburg argued six women's rights cases before the Supreme Court and won five of them. One of her most famous cases was about the rights of pregnant schoolteachers to keep their jobs.

President Jimmy Carter appointed Ginsburg to the United States Court of Appeals for the District of Columbia in 1980. There she did work on abortion rights, gay and lesbian rights, and affirmative action. She held this judgeship for 13 years until President Bill Clinton nominated her for the U.S. Supreme Court in 1993. Ginsburg's nomination was approved by a Senate vote of 96–3. Supreme Court Justice Ginsburg has said that she and Justice Sandra Day O'Connor want to help the male justices "look at life a bit differently."

" " " " " " " " " " " "

Q **Ms.:** a non-sexist formal title used with women's names. Like Mr., it does not indicate marital status, as Miss (single) and Mrs. (married) do. The use of Ms. became widespread with the rise of the women's movement in the 1970s. **Gloria Steinem** made it even more popular when she started *Ms.* magazine in 1972. That year, the United States Government Printing Office authorized its use in federal publications. The influential *New York Times* did not allow the use of Ms. until the 1980s. Today, many women use the title, and it is usually a choice on most applications and official forms.

◈ Katharine Graham

born 1917

NEWSPAPER PUBLISHER

Katharine Graham has been called "America's most powerful woman executive" with good reason. When she chaired the board of the Washington Post Company, Graham headed a media empire that included the *Washington Post* newspaper, *Newsweek* magazine, and several radio, cable, and television stations.

Katharine's father bought the *Post* in a bankruptcy sale in 1933. Meanwhile, she graduated from the University of Chicago in 1938 and hit the beat as a reporter for the *San Francisco News*. In 1939, she joined the *Washington Post* staff and worked in both the editorial and circulation departments before marrying Philip Graham and raising a family. Katharine and her husband bought the *Post* from her father for $1 million in 1948.

◀ In 1973, *Washington Post* executive Katharine Graham was the first woman to win the Peter Zenger publishing award for contributions to freedom of the press. In 1974, she was the first woman named to the board of the Associated Press, a major news service.

Philip committed suicide in 1963, and Katharine became president of the Washington Post Company. By 1969, she was also publisher and chief executive officer (CEO). In 1973, she became chairperson of the board. Graham's goal was to make the *Washington Post* one of the nation's most important newspapers. She increased its editorial budget, hired more reporters and editors, and built the paper's reputation for hard-hitting investigative reporting. In the early 1970s, *Post* reporters Carl Bernstein and Robert Woodward uncovered the Watergate scandal, which eventually led to President Richard Nixon's resignation. The *Post* won a Pulitzer Prize for this coverage.

Katharine Graham stepped aside as publisher of the *Post* in 1979, handing the position over to her son. However, she still chaired the Washington Post Company and continued to expand *Newsweek* and purchase television and cable stations. Graham resigned as chairperson in 1993 to serve as head of the board's executive committee.

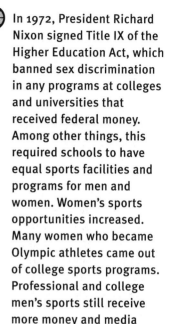

+ + + + + + + + + + + + + + + +

In 1972, President Richard Nixon signed Title IX of the Higher Education Act, which banned sex discrimination in any programs at colleges and universities that received federal money. Among other things, this required schools to have equal sports facilities and programs for men and women. Women's sports opportunities increased. Many women who became Olympic athletes came out of college sports programs. Professional and college men's sports still receive more money and media coverage, however.

Florence Griffith-Joyner

born 1959 – died 1998

OLYMPIC ATHLETE

Florence Griffith-Joyner was one of the most dazzling sights at the 1988 summer Olympics in Seoul, South Korea. She captured three gold medals and one silver medal in track events. But her athletic talent wasn't the only thing that impressed Flo-Jo's audiences. They were also bowled over by her polished six-inch fingernails and her bright one-of-a-kind running outfits.

Joyner grew up in a Los Angeles housing project, where she spent most of her time doing homework, writing, designing clothing, and styling her friends' hair. But when she visited her father who lived near the Mojave Desert, Florence loved to race jackrabbits. It was her earliest sprint training.

During her college years at California State and the University of California, Los Angeles, Joyner set championship records in the 200- and 400-meter races. She joined the Olympic team in 1984 and took home a silver Olympic medal for the 200-meter dash. At the next Olympics in Seoul, she became a three-time gold medal winner for the 100-and 200-meter races and the relay, and a silver medalist for the 1,600-meter relay. Joyner, who was co-chair of the President's Council on Physical Fitness and Sports, was married to world-class jumper Al Joyner, and her sister-in-law is fellow track-and-field gold medalist **Jackie Joyner-Kersee**.

1970s – 1990s

Mother Hale CLARA MCBRIDE HALE

born 1905 – died 1992

SOCIAL WORKER

"I'm not an American hero," Clara McBride Hale once said. "I'm a person who loves children." Through her New York City-based program, Hale House, Mother Hale, as she came to be called, cared for nearly 1,000 babies of drug-addicted mothers over the course of 20 years.

Hale's work with children began long before 1969, the year she started what eventually became Hale House in Harlem. Hale's husband died when she was 27, leaving her with three small children. Hale didn't like leaving her children while she worked outside her home, so she began taking in other people's children for $2 a week. Eventually, Hale began caring for foster children. The 40 foster children she raised all finished high school and many went to college.

Mother Hale decided to retire from child care when she was 63. But soon after, her daughter Lorraine spotted a drug-addicted mother with her two-month-old baby passing out on a Harlem street. Lorraine sent the woman to see Clara, who took the baby in while its mother sought treatment for her addiction. Word spread, and soon Mother Hale's three-bedroom apartment was filled with babies. Many slept in cribs right next to her bed.

Using government grants and public and private donations, Mother Hale was able to buy a five-story Harlem brownstone building. She offered programs to help babies recover from the effects of their parents' drug and alcohol addictions and to care for babies born with the AIDS virus. Mother Hale actively cared for the children of Hale House right up until her death at age 87 from a stroke. Lorraine Hale has continued the work of Hale House, expanding its programs to include housing and education for mothers after they recover from their addictions, job training for young people, and a home for mothers and children with AIDS.

+ + + + + + + + + + + + + + + + +

In the early 1990s, nearly 35% of the families that lived in poverty were headed by women and one out of every four children in the United States was poor. African-American and Hispanic-American women and children were increasingly among the poor and homeless. They often have to struggle against race or ethnic and sex discrimination.

▶ In 1985, President Ronald Reagan called Mother Hale (center) an "American hero" in his State of the Union address. Hale is shown here with First Lady Nancy Reagan (right).

⚖ Patricia Roberts Harris

In May 1965, Patricia Roberts Harris became the first African-American woman ambassador in United States history. That was just the beginning. In 1976, she became the first African-American woman appointed to a presidential cabinet .

Patricia graduated from Howard University in Washington, D.C., where she was vice-president of the student chapter of the National Association for the Advancement of Colored People (NAACP), in 1945. After working for the Chicago Young Women's Christian Association (YWCA) and the American Council on Human Rights, Harris returned to Washington to attend George Washington University law school, graduating in 1960. She was co-chairperson of President John Kennedy's National Women's Committee for Civil Rights and taught at Howard. In 1965, President Lyndon Johnson sent Harris to Luxembourg as the U.S. ambassador. Over the next decade, she also served on many important committees, including the National Commission on the Causes and Prevention of Violence.

In 1976, Harris was named secretary of housing and urban development by President Jimmy Carter. She served for three years before Carter made her secretary of the department of health, education, and welfare. After Carter left the White House, Harris became a professor at the George Washington National Law Center in Washington, D.C., a post she held until her death in 1985.

√ Dr. Mae C. Jemison

born 1956

ASTRONAUT

When astronaut Mae Jemison boarded the space shuttle *Endeavor*, she carried an Alvin Ailey Dance Company poster and a flag from the Organization of African Unity. The first African-American woman in space was taking symbols of her heritage with her.

Mae attended Stanford University in Palo Alto, California, where she majored in engineering and in African Studies. During her senior year, she heard that the National Aeronautics and Space Administration (NASA) was hiring specialists for its space flights. Jemison entered Cornell Medical School in New York in the fall of 1977. Her goal was to become a biomedical engineer – and then work for NASA. After graduating from Cornell in 1981,

 In the 1960s, **LADONNA HARRIS** (b. 1931), a Comanche, organized Oklahoma's first meeting of representatives from all the state's 60 Native American tribes so they could work together to improve the status of tribal members. In 1967, President Lyndon Johnson made her chairperson of the National Women's Advisory Council of the War on Poverty. Harris's reputation as a strong advocate for equal rights and equal opportunity for all grew. In 1970, she helped found the National Women's Political Caucus with other leaders such as **Gloria Steinem** and **Shirley Chisholm**. Harris received appointments in the Johnson, Nixon, and Carter administrations. Harris (above, right) is shown with Shirley Chisholm. Both were honored as "Women of the Year" in 1973, at the John F. Kennedy Center for the Performing Arts in Washington, D.C.

1970s – 1990s

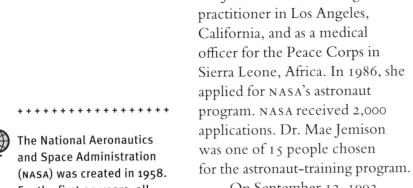

Dr. Jemison worked as a general practitioner in Los Angeles, California, and as a medical officer for the Peace Corps in Sierra Leone, Africa. In 1986, she applied for NASA's astronaut program. NASA received 2,000 applications. Dr. Mae Jemison was one of 15 people chosen for the astronaut-training program.

On September 12, 1992, Jemison and six other crew members boarded the space shuttle *Endeavor*. During the *Endeavor*'s eight-day space orbit, Jemison studied how the absence of gravity affects the development of frogs' eggs. Six months after the *Endeavor* returned to Earth, Jemison left NASA and joined the faculty of Dartmouth College in New Hampshire, where her science courses focus on the health care of women and people of color. She also founded a company that researches space-age technology.

+ + + + + + + + + + + + + + + +

 The National Aeronautics and Space Administration (NASA) was created in 1958. For the first 20 years, all NASA astronauts were men. In 1978, **Dr. Sally Ride** was one of six women who broke the gender barrier. Since then, other notable women in space have included Ellen Ochoa, the first Hispanic woman astronaut; Kathryn Thornton, a member of the *Endeavor* space shuttle team who went up to repair the Hubble Telescope; Lieutenant Colonel Eileen Collins, the first woman astronaut to pilot a space shuttle, the *Discovery* (February 1995), and Drs. Ellen Baker and Bonnie Dunbar, who were on board the *Atlantis* space shuttle that linked up with the Russian spaceship *Mir* in June 1995.

☺ Jackie Joyner-Kersee

born 1962

OLYMPIC ATHLETE

It was a family affair at the 1984 Olympics. Jackie Joyner-Kersee and her sister-in-law, **Florence Griffith-Joyner**, both were Olympic medal winners. Jackie, whose grandmother named her after **Jacqueline Kennedy (Onassis)** so that someday she would be "first lady" in some field, is considered by many to be one of the greatest athletes of all time.

Joyner-Kersee won a 1984 silver medal for the heptathlon, a grueling seven-event Olympic competition that includes the long jump, the high jump, the shotput, the javelin, the 200-meter dash, the 100-meter hurdles, and the 800-meter run. It was the start of a headline-making, record-breaking Olympic career. In 1986, Joyner-Kersee set a world record for the heptathlon, winning more points than anyone in history. Two years later, she won a 1988 Olympic gold medal for the heptathlon, breaking her own world record. She also became the first American woman to win a gold medal for the long jump, after soaring 24 feet and 3½ inches. She scored the heptathlon gold medal at the 1992 Olympics.

Joyner-Kersee was born in East St. Louis, Missouri. Having grown up in poverty, she later opened the Jackie Joyner-Kersee Community Foundation in Los Angeles in 1988. The foundation organizes special trips and events and offers scholarships for inner-city children interested in sports.

◉ Billie Jean King

born 1943

TENNIS PLAYER

More than 30,000 people filled the Houston Astrodome to watch Billie Jean King take on former champion Bobby Riggs in a "Battle of the Sexes" tennis match in 1973. Another 60 million people watched the match on television. King beat Riggs to win $100,000, the largest sum ever paid for a single tennis match. She also won an important symbolic victory for women, especially those who were professional tennis players.

King grew up in Long Beach, California, and was a natural athlete from an early age. When she was 18, Billie Jean and her tennis partner, Karen Hantze, also 18, became the youngest pair to win the women's doubles title at England's famous Wimbledon tennis tournament. The team repeated its Wimbledon victory two years in a row. By 1967, King had won six major titles, including the Wimbledon singles, doubles, and mixed doubles, and the United States doubles and mixed doubles. In 1971, she became the first woman to win over $100,000 in one season, when she won 19 singles tournaments and 21 doubles. Billie Jean scored a total of 20 Wimbledon titles in her career, winning her 20th match in 1979 with doubles partner **Martina Navratilova**.

Male chauvinist pig: a phrase that became popular during the 1970s. It describes men who believe that women's roles should be limited to what is traditionally considered "feminine," and that men should have more authority than women. There were men who could be called chauvinist pigs among both conservative and liberal groups. Women in civil rights, anti-war, and radical groups such as the Black Panthers or the Students for a Democratic Society (SDS), often found that male leaders ignored their contributions and capabilities.

1970s – 1990s

King was an outspoken leader in women's tennis on and off the courts. She helped create what was originally called the Virginia Slims women's tennis circuit. She founded the Women's Tennis Association in 1973 to promote professional women's tennis and fight for prize money equal to men's tournament awards. King's last major appearance on court was in 1983 when, at the age of 39, she reached the singles semifinals at Wimbledon. She later became Navratilova's coach and adviser, as well as the first woman commissioner in professional sports at the World Team Tennis League.

Maxine Hong Kingston

born 1940

WRITER

Maxine Hong Kingston's book *Woman Warrior: Memoirs of a Girlhood among Ghosts* opens with a warning from her mother: "You must not tell anyone…what I am about to tell you." But Kingston did use the stories her mother told her about life in China and with her own experiences as a Chinese American they helped her build an award-winning career as a writer.

Woman Warrior won the 1976 National Book Critics Award for nonfiction and was named one of the top 10 books of the decade by *Time* magazine. In it Kingston uses female narrators to tell the story of her family's immigration from China; her childhood in Stockton, California; the family laundry business; and the rich heritage of Chinese culture, language, and myths that were part of her upbringing. She also explores the difficulties women face in Chinese and American societies. Her second book, *China Men* (1980), won the American Book Award. Its all-male characters include Maxine's grandfathers, father, and brother. It is a very human look at the history of the Chinese laborers who built the railroads and worked the mines in the West during the 19th century.

Kingston says that in her writing, she is "trying to find an American language that would translate the speech of the people who are living their lives with the Chinese language." Maxine herself spent her early years surrounded by Chinese-speaking people. Her first language is Cantonese, and she did not learn English until she went to school. It was a difficult experience. She felt like a "foreigner" and spoke very little in class. But by the time she was nine, Maxine was writing poems in

English. She later majored in English at the University of California, Berkeley. She graduated in 1962 and married another Berkeley student, Earll Kingston.

Maxine taught in California, and then in Hawaii when the Kingstons moved there in 1967. After the success of *Woman Warrior*, she was able to do what she truly wanted, which was to write full-time. Her third book, *Tripmaster Monkey: His Fake Book*, created a sensation when it was published in 1989. Some critics favorably compared its main character to Mark Twain's Huck Finn. Kingston has won several honors and awards, including a Guggenhiem fellowship in 1981. Kingston has also written short stories, poetry, and articles for publications such as the *New Yorker* magazine and the *New York Times Magazine*.

⚖ Jeanne Kirkpatrick

born 1926

DIPLOMAT

In 1981, Jeanne Kirkpatrick was the highest-ranking woman in the history of United States foreign policy. Although she was a Democrat, she became ambassador to the United Nations, a cabinet-level job, during President Ronald Reagan's Republican administration and was a member of his National Security team.

Kirkpatrick, who has a doctoral degree in political science from Columbia University in New York City, has had a long and often controversial career. She wrote *Political Woman*, an analysis of 50 women state legislators elected in 1972, and was a leading figure in the world of international diplomacy, a world where men are generally the majority. She is famous for her strong anti-Communist views and has been criticized by some feminists for her conservative political views. While Ambassador to the United Nations, Kirkpatrick opposed economic bans against South Africa, whose apartheid system denied nonwhite citizens their rights, and she supported the military government in El Salvador. She resigned as ambassador in 1985.

Dr. Kirkpatrick is a professor at Georgetown University, a senior researcher at the American Enterprise Institute in Washington, D.C., and a columnist for *The Los Angeles Times*.

 DR. MATHILDE KRIM (b. 1926), the founder of the American Foundation for AIDS Research (AmFAR), is a powerful health advocate.

Born in Italy, Krim received a Ph.D. from the University of Geneva, Switzerland, in 1953. She conducted biomedical research projects at several medical centers in Israel and the United States, and in 1980 directed the interferon laboratory at New York's Memorial Sloan-Kettering Cancer Center. Interferon is a cell protein that fights cell viruses. During this time, Krim became aware of AIDS, (acquired immune deficiency syndrome) which was not widely recognized or researched at the time. As a scientist and health advocate, Dr. Krim became increasingly alarmed by the destructive potential of the disease. She co-founded AmFAR, the AIDS research and advocacy group, with family money. And since her husband was chairman of Orion Pictures movie studio, Krim was able to enlist Hollywood celebrities, such as **Elizabeth Taylor**, to help her.

1970s – 1990s

Maggie Kuhn

born 1905 – died 1995

FOUNDER OF THE GRAY PANTHERS

"Out of the rocking chair, into the street!" was one of Maggie Kuhn's mottos. When Kuhn was forced to retire from her job in 1970 because she had turned 65, she quickly organized the Gray Panthers, a powerful group that fights against age discrimination.

Kuhn was an activist long before 1970. She started a League of Women Voters chapter when she attended Case Western Reserve University in Cleveland, Ohio, in the 1920s. In the 1930s, she worked at the Young Women's Christian Association (YWCA) in Cleveland and in New York City, and helped unionize women workers. Then for the next 25 years, Kuhn worked for the United Presbyterian Office of Church and Society in New York. She wrote and edited the church paper, *Social Progress*, and was a strong supporter of civil rights, women's rights, and seniors' rights. After her retirement, Kuhn formed the Consultation of Older and Younger Adults for Social Change to look at issues that affected old and young people. Because of the group's social activism for seniors, the media called it the Gray Panthers, after another activist group, the Black Panthers. Within a few years, there were nearly 70 Gray Panther chapters across the country. Under Maggie Kuhn's leadership, the Gray Panthers lobbied for laws to improve nursing homes and marched in anti-Vietnam War demonstrations. They fought for better portrayals of seniors on television and opposed any cuts in Social Security. They rallied for national health care, housing for the elderly, and for environmental awareness. Kuhn was a tireless writer and speaker and won many awards for her work.

Even as a girl, NANCY LOPEZ (b. 1957) showed such extraordinary talent at golf that she was excused from family chores such as washing dishes because the water softened the calluses on her hands. Lopez needed strong, callused hands for the hours of practice and the golf competitions she was winning by age 12. Lopez became a professional golfer in 1978, immediately broke several records, and became the first woman to win five Ladies Professional Golf Association tournaments in a row. She also earned nearly $200,000, more than any other male or female rookie pro golfer. Lopez maintained this winning streak throughout the 1980s. She was the champion in 40 tournaments and became a multimillionaire. In 1987, she passed the strict qualifications and was elected to the Ladies Professional Golf Association Hall of Fame.

Maya Lin

born 1959

ARCHITECT

In 1981, a committee of architects, sculptors, and designers chose the winning design for a national Vietnam veterans memorial from 1,421 entries. Committee members praised the planned memorial, writing "All who come here can find it a place of healing." They were shocked to find out the designer was Maya Lin, a 21-year-old graduate student at Yale University in New Haven, Connecticut.

The competition had three design requirements. The memorial had to include the names of all 58,175 armed services men and women killed or missing in action in Vietnam. It could not make a political statement, and it had to fit in with the landscape of the Washington Mall. Lin designed a V-shaped sculpture of polished black granite, inscribed with all the names. The V was built right into the ground. Lin's idea was startling, powerful, and controversial. The merits of her memorial continued to be debated even after it was finished and dedicated in 1982. But people came in droves, and most were struck by its emotional power. One of her next major projects was to create a monument honoring those who had died in the struggle for civil rights. Lin used black granite and falling water in her design for the Civil Rights Memorial dedicated in Montgomery, Alabama, in 1989. Lin also designed the Museum for African Art in New York City.

Audre Lorde

born 1934 – died 1992

FEMINIST POET AND ESSAYIST

When Audre Lorde was a child, she liked to answer people's questions with one of many poems she had memorized. At the age of 12, she was writing her own poems, and by the time Lorde died of cancer in 1992, she had published several books, been poet laureate, or first poet, of New York, and founded a publishing company, Kitchen Table: Women of Color Press. Lorde grew up in Harlem, New York. After

+ + + + + + + + + + + + + + + + +

More than 11,500 women served in the Vietnam War in noncombat roles. Their work went largely unrecognized. It took former army nurse Diane Carlson Evans nearly 10 years to raise enough interest and money to get the Vietnam Women's Memorial built. The bronze sculpture, designed by Glenna Goodacre, was dedicated in Washington, D.C., in 1993. By that time, 40,000 military women in crucial combat support jobs had had a very visible role in the 1990 Persian Gulf War.

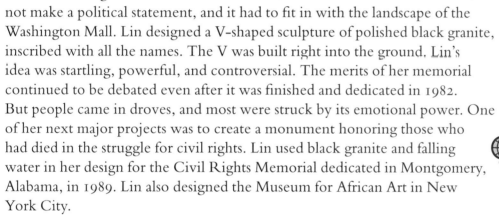

1970s – 1990s

 In the documentary movie *Madonna Truth or Dare*, **MADONNA** (b. 1958) boasts that she likes to "push people's buttons." That's what makes her one of the most successful – and controversial – contemporary pop artists. Madonna Louise Veronica Ciccone grew up in Detroit, Michigan, and first appeared on the pop music scene in 1983. Her hit songs, such as "Borderline," "Holiday," and "Material Girl," brought her national fame. Madonna became even more famous as her next recordings and music videos broke all kinds of religious and sexual taboos. During her 1990 Blond Ambition tour, some people criticized her erotic performance of her hit "Like a Virgin." That same year, MTV would not run her "Justify My Love" video because of its sexual content. Madonna heads her own multi-million dollar company and is known as a shrewd businessperson.

getting her master's degree in library science from Columbia University in 1961, she worked as a school librarian and wrote poetry. She published her first book of poetry, *The First Cities*, in 1968, and published poems in the new feminist magazine *Ms*. When Lorde's third book, *From a Land Where Other People Live*, was nominated for a National Book Award in 1974, she gained an even wider audience.

In the 1970s and 1980s, Lorde lectured, taught, and produced poetry and essay collections, one of which, *Sister Outsider* (1984), is included in many college women's studies and political science courses. Her first book of nonfiction, *The Cancer Journals* (1980), told of her struggle with breast cancer and the poor treatment she received from medical professionals. One of her poems, "The American Cancer Society Or There Is More Than One Way to Skin a Coon," also shows Lorde's anger about how women with breast cancer are treated. Her second collection of essays about cancer, *Burst of Light*, won the 1989 American Book Award. "There are so many roots to the/tree of anger/that sometimes the branches shatter/before they bear," Lorde wrote in *From a Land*. In her poetry, Lorde explored the anger – and joy – of her experiences as an African American, a feminist, and a lesbian.

Wilma Mankiller

born 1945

CHIEF OF THE CHEROKEE NATION

"The issues are our programs, the breaking of the circle of poverty, not me," Wilma Mankiller, the first woman chief of a major Native American tribe, said in her 1985 inaugural speech. Mankiller, who had been deputy principal chief of the Cherokee Nation, was promoted when the previous chief took a job in Washington, D.C. In 1987, she was elected to the position and then re-elected in 1991.

Mankiller, who has dedicated herself to encouraging economic growth while preserving Cherokee culture, grew up on the family farm in Mankiller Flats, Oklahoma. The farm did not have electricity or running water and it was difficult to eke out a living. Wilma and her family were encouraged by the government to move to San Francisco, California. But the government did not deliver on its promises of help, and life was still hard for the Mankillers. In California, Wilma became part of the American Native Rights Movement in the 1960s. By the mid-1970s, she had moved back to Mankiller Flats.

In 1977, Mankiller worked as an economic coordinator for the Cherokee, creating projects to improve housing and social services. She had studied social science and community planning and was skilled at drawing political and media attention to the issues facing the Cherokee Nation.

◄ Chief Wilma Mankiller met with President Ronald Reagan and others at the White House in 1988. She represented the Cherokee Nation, which has more than 100,000 members and is the second largest Native American tribe, after the Navajos.

Mankiller had a near-fatal car accident and suffered from kidney and muscle diseases, but continued to work as an activist. As chief, she developed programs such as the Institute for Cherokee Literacy, where young tribal members learn to read and write Cherokee. She also successfully lobbied for health, education, and job training programs. Mankiller was named Woman of the Year by *Ms.* magazine in 1987.

◐ Dr. Barbara McClintock

born 1902 – died 1992

GENETICIST

Dr. Barbara McClintock was 81 years old when she received the Nobel Prize for medicine in 1983, only the third woman so honored. The prize was especially important to her as a scientist because many in the scientific community had labeled her work crazy.

In 1924, her first year of graduate school at Cornell University in Ithaca, New York, McClintock identified the individual chromosomes of maize, or wild corn. Chromosomes contain the genes which determine the distinctive characteristics of living things. McClintock devoted her life to studying chromosomes and genetic traits, focusing on corn. She received her doctoral degree from Cornell in 1927 and, over the next few years, published several important papers about chromosomes. Like other women scientists at the time, she found it difficult to find work as a full-time professor or a full-salaried researcher. McClintock spent the next years shuttling among projects at Cornell, the University of Missouri in Columbia, and the California Institute of Technology in Pasadena.

In 1941, the Carnegie Institution of Washington made McClintock an ideal job offer: a cornfield, a laboratory, a home, and a salary. She moved to

Carnegie's Cold Spring Harbor laboratory on Long Island, New York, to continue her maize experiments. Three years later, she was invited to join the National Academy of Sciences and was elected president of the Genetics Society of America. That same year, Dr. McClintock began to study what she called "transposition." Most scientists at the time believed genes were stable or fixed in place. McClintock suspected this was not true, based on her observations of color mutations in some corn kernels in her fields. She found that there were moving or "controlling" genetic elements on the chromosomes that affected development cycles. When McClintock delivered a paper on her radical theory to 100 scientists in 1951, there was complete silence.

Though no one took her "jumping genes" theories seriously, McClintock continued her research. However, she gradually withdrew from much involvement with other scientists. In the 1970s, research into DNA, the basic element of genes, suggested that some of McClintock's theories might be correct. She was showered with attention and awards, including the MacArthur Foundation Award, a "genius" grant that gave Dr. McClintock $60,000 a year for life.

+ + + + + + + + + + + + + + + + + +

Today, more than one-half of all college students are women. They receive about 36 percent of the doctoral degrees given. Less than 30 percent of college faculty are female.

Toni Morrison CHLOE ANTHONY WOFFORD

born 1931

WRITER

"Writing," says Toni Morrison, "is discovery; it's talking deep within myself." The winner of the 1993 Nobel Prize for literature, Morrison has always looked within herself, her family, and her community to gather material for her powerful novels and essays about racism, sexism, and elitism in the United States.

Born Chloe Anthony Wofford in Lorain, Ohio, Morrison grew up during the Great Depression surrounded by poverty. As a child, she heard about the racial violence her grandparents had faced as sharecroppers in the South. She heard her relatives' ongoing discussions about whether racial equality and integration were really possible. And she heard the stories and

▶ After Toni Morrison won the Nobel Prize in 1993, more than 500,000 copies of her books sold in three months. Her Nobel acceptance speech was also published as a book.

folktales about her heritage that gave her a strong sense of the injustices African Americans had endured and the spirit through which they survived. All of these were important influences on Morrison as a writer.

Chloe began calling herself Toni when she enrolled at Howard University in Washington, D.C., in 1949 to study English literature. She got her master's degree at Cornell University in Ithaca, New York, in 1955. After teaching and working as a textbook editor, Morrison moved to New York City and became a senior editor at Random House in 1968. There she focused on getting more books by African Americans such as **Angela Davis** and Toni Cade Bambara into print. She also published her first novel, *The Bluest Eye* (1970), a story about three young girls searching for their African-American identities in a world that values blonde hair and blue eyes. Another novel, *Sula* (1973), followed. During this time, Morrison also produced *The Black Book,* an African-American history. Toni was inspired by the photographs and other artifacts she saw while working on this book. As a result, her next book, *Song of Solomon*, was the first of her novels to incorporate a more historic look at racism and oppression in the United States. It won the 1977 National Book Critics Circle Award and was such a success that Morrison could devote herself to writing full-time. When Morrison's *Tar Baby* came out in 1981, it made the *New York Times* bestseller list and Toni made the cover of *Newsweek*. She was the first African-American woman featured on the front of the magazine.

While researching *The Black Book*, Morrison had found a newspaper clipping from 1851 about an escaped slave who killed her daughter rather than see her returned to slavery. Morrison turned the true story into one of her most powerful works, *Beloved* (1987). She won the 1988 Pulitzer Prize for Literature for this book, which is one of three books about African-American history. The second book, *Jazz*, was published in 1992, and Morrison began work on the third book, *Paradise*. In 1993, Toni Morrison became the first African-American woman to win the Nobel Prize for Literature. She has been a professor at Princeton University in New Jersey since 1989.

+ + + + + + + + + + + + + + + + +

Many women writers have used their own lives to explore what it means to be a woman outside the white mainstream culture in the United States. Louise Erdrich (b. 1954) has written poetry, stories, and novels about Chippewa life in North Dakota. *Love Medicine*, a collection of her stories set on a reservation, won the 1984 National Books Critics Circle Award. Nicholasa Mohr (b. 1935) celebrates her Puerto Rican heritage by writing children's books such as *The Song of El Coqui: and Other Tales of Puerto Rico* (1995) and the award-winning *Nilda* (1973), the story of a young girl's life in Spanish Harlem during the 1940s and 1950s. Her other books include *El Bronx Remembered* (1975) and two books, *Felita* (1979) and *Going Home* (1986), which also feature a young Puerto Rican girl as the main character. Chinese-American writer Amy Tan (b. 1952) started with her relationship with her mother and wrote a bestseller, *The Joy Luck Club* (1989), which later became a movie. Her second novel, *The Kitchen God's Wife* (1991), was based on stories of her mother's life in China. Tan's children's book, *The Moon Lady* (1992), is based on a Chinese folktale.

Martina Navratilova

born 1956

TENNIS PLAYER

Before Martina Navratilova stepped off the tennis court at Wimbledon, England, in the summer of 1994, she bent down and pulled up a small clump of grass. The crowd cheered. It was the tennis champ's last singles appearance on the famous court and this was her souvenir. Though she lost her last match at Wimbledon, 38-year-old Navratilova was leaving the singles tennis circuit with the best record of wins by any man or woman in the history of tennis.

Navratilova was born and raised outside of Prague, in what was then Czechoslovakia. When she was four years old, she was given her grandmother's old wooden racket. Martina knew immediately that tennis was the sport for her and she was heavily involved in it by the time she was nine years old. In 1973, when she was 17, Martina traveled to the United States for her first tournament. She returned the following year and won the famous Virginia Slims tournament. *Tennis* magazine named her rookie of the year. Martina defected, or refused to return to Czechoslovakia, in 1975, and settled in the United States.

Navratilova won the first of a record-breaking nine Wimbledon singles victories in 1978 and played on a winning doubles team with **Billie Jean King** in 1979. King later became Navratilova's coach, and in the 1980s, Martina added power-lifting and excellent nutrition to her tennis training and redefined what it meant to be an aggressive woman athlete. Her hard work led to 18 Grand Slam singles titles and 37 Grand Slam doubles titles. In her 20-year career, Navratilova played more than 1,600 tennis matches, earned more than $19 million, and was often named top athlete by various sports organizations. She also made headlines when she came out as a lesbian, saying, "How can you be happy if you can't be honest about who you are? It is so liberating." Navratilova is a national spokesperson for gay and lesbian rights.

▲ Martina Navratilova with the 1978 Wimbledon Women's Singles trophy.

+ + + + + + + + + + + + + + + +

Tennis, now one of the more popular sports in the United States, may have been introduced to this country by Mary Ewing Outerbridge in 1874. Outerbridge was a member of New York's exclusive Ladies Club for Outdoor Sports. She may have seen lawn tennis played in Bermuda. There sportsman Walter Wingfield had organized and presented the rules of tennis, which had been played as an indoor game for centuries.

The famous Wimbledon, England, tennis tournaments began in 1877, but only men could compete at the time. Seven years later, the first Wimbledon women's singles competition took place in 1884.

Jessye Norman

born 1945

OPERA SINGER

As a young child growing up in Augusta, Georgia, Jessye Norman loved to listen to the radio on Sunday afternoons. That's how she discovered her great love, the opera.

Norman's own singing began in Mt. Calvary Baptist Church, where her father was a singer. She started entering vocal competitions when she was 16 and her talent won her a scholarship to Howard University in Washington, D.C. She continued her studies, first at the Peabody Conservatory in Baltimore, Maryland, and then at the University of Michigan.

In 1968, Norman won first prize at the International Music Competition in Munich, Germany. One year later, she signed a three-year contract with the Deutsche Oper in Berlin. She eventually left the company, and in the 1970s spent time recording and touring the United States, Europe, South America, the Middle East, and Australia. By the 1980s, opera fans loved Norman for the passion she put into her performances. Like other great African-American divas, such as **Marian Anderson** and **Leontyne Price**, Norman eventually sang at New York's famous Metropolitan Opera House. Her 1983 debut, singing in Berlioz's *Les Troyens*, was of special note because it was opening night of the Met's 100th season.

Eleanor Holmes Norton

born 1938

LAWYER

In 1968, a group of white supremacists was refused permission to hold a political rally in Maryland. They took their case to the Supreme Court, where they were represented by Eleanor Holmes Norton, an African-American American Civil Liberties Union (ACLU) lawyer. She won the case. Eleanor didn't agree with the group's racist ideas, but she did believe that the First Amendment guarantees freedom of speech for everyone.

Born in Washington, D.C., Holmes graduated from Antioch College in Yellow Springs, Ohio, in 1960. She earned her master's degree in American Studies in 1963, and a doctor of jurisprudence degree in 1964 from

+ + + + + + + + + + + + + + + + +

The Women's Bureau of the Unites States Department of Labor estimates that women will make up 47 percent of the nonmilitary labor force by the year 2005.

1970s – 1990s

Yale University in New Haven, Connecticut. Norton went to work as assistant legal director of the ACLU, and in 1970, became the first woman to chair the New York City Commission on Human Rights. She also co-founded the Black Feminist Organization in 1973.

In 1977, President Jimmy Carter asked Norton to head the Equal Employment Opportunities Commission (EEOC), another first for a woman. The EEOC investigated charges of racial or sexual discrimination, and Norton was a leader in women's battle for equal pay for equal work. She held the job until 1981 and then taught at the George Washington University Law Center in Washington, D.C. In 1990, she successfully ran for the nonvoting representative for the District of Columbia in the U.S. House of Representatives. Today she continues to fight for equal rights because "One ought to be against racism and sexism because they are wrong, not because one is black or one is female."

+ + + + + + + + + + + + + + + + +

In 1994, children and women made up more than two-thirds of the 37 million Americans who did not have health insurance.

Dr. Antonia Novello

born 1944

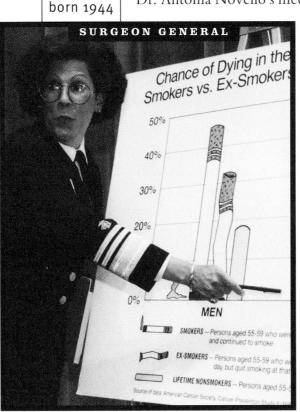

Dr. Antonia Novello's medical career and her dedication to public service so impressed President George Bush that he nominated her as Surgeon General of the United States, the nation's highest medical officer. Congress approved, and on March 9, 1990, Antonia Novello became the first woman and first Hispanic Surgeon General. She was sworn in by Supreme Court Justice **Sandra Day O'Connor**.

Novello, who earned her medical degree from the University of Puerto Rico in San Juan in 1970, completed her training at the University of Michigan Medical Center in Ann Arbor, where she specialized in pediatrics. While working at the university hospital, Novello "learned how many people slipped through the cracks" of the medical system. She wanted to improve health care services for all people, especially women and children.

Dr. Novello moved to Washington, D.C. in 1974 and joined the staff of Georgetown University Hospital. Then she worked for the National Institutes of Health, the government agency responsible for health and medical programs and research. In 1987, she moved to the National Institute of Child Health and Human Development to coordinate its AIDS research, especially in ways the disease affected women and babies. She later became Deputy Director of the Institute.

As Surgeon General, Dr. Novello traveled across the country promoting health awareness. She warned against the dangers of smoking, teenage drinking, and of mixing drinking and driving. She often confronted the companies that produce tobacco and alcohol. She also addressed the issue of domestic violence and gave special attention to caring for children with AIDS, and to treating breast cancer and other women's diseases.

Sandra Day O'Connor

born 1930

SUPREME COURT JUSTICE

"I happily share the honor with millions of American women of yesterday and today," Sandra Day O'Connor said in 1981, when she became the first woman ever appointed to the United States Supreme Court. A little over 100 years earlier, **Belva Lockwood** had had to lobby Congress for a bill to allow women lawyers to even practice before the highest court in the nation, which O'Connor was now joining.

O'Connor was a 1952 graduate of Stanford Law School in Palo Alto, California. Men outnumbered women 30 to one in her class. Despite the fact that she had graduated third in a class of 102, O'Connor did not find legal firms were eager to hire a woman lawyer, though one did offer her a job – as a legal secretary. She went into government work instead, and was hired as a county attorney in San Mateo, California, and later assistant attorney general for the state of Arizona in 1965. By 1979, O'Connor had held a seat in the Arizona State Senate, risen to the top of the state Republican party, served as a county judge, and been appointed by the

◄ Sandra Day O'Connor, the first woman Supreme Court Justice, said of her historic appointment, "**Abigail Adams** would be pleased."

Congress and the courts felt the effects of the rebirth of the women's movement in the 1970s. *The New York Times, Reader's Digest, Time,* and *Newsweek* magazines were sued for sexual discrimination. The Department of Labor created new rules to make sure women were employed by companies getting government contracts. Congress passed the Equal Opportunity Act in 1972, which detailed anti-sex discrimination guidelines for employers. The National Organization for Women (NOW) pressured the Equal Employment Opportunity Commission (EEOC) to investigate charges of sexual discrimination. The EEOC took the American Telephone and Telegraph (AT&T) corporation to court, calling it "the largest oppressor of women workers in the United States" for having a gender-segregated work force and for failing to pay and promote women the same way as men.

1970s – 1990s

governor to the higher Arizona Court of Appeals. She and her husband had had three children. She thought she was at the height of her career.

But on September 22, 1981, the United States Senate voted 99–0 in favor of Sandra Day O'Connor becoming the first woman appointee in the 191-year history of the Supreme Court. Justice O'Connor votes, along with eight other judges, on the most important legal cases in the nation. As a member of the Supreme Court, O'Connor has participated in cases that involve issues such as abortion rights, affirmative action, and censorship. O'Connor frequently votes with her more conservative colleagues, but she is also known as an independent thinker and tireless worker. Even in 1988, when she underwent surgery for breast cancer, O'Connor quickly returned to work for the rest of the Court's session. O'Connor became one of two women on the Supreme Court when **Ruth Bader Ginsburg** was appointed in 1993.

✓ Dixy Lee Ray DR. MARGARET RAY

born 1914 – died 1994
SCIENTIST, POLITICIAN

Dixy Lee Ray was the first woman to head the Atomic Energy Commission and the second woman to be elected a governor without being married to a man leaving that office.

Margaret "Dixy Lee" Ray was born in Tacoma, Washington. Her interest in sea and animal life took her to Mills College in Oakland, California, where she earned a degree in zoology in 1937, and to Stanford University in Palo Alto, California, where she earned her Ph.D. in 1945. Ray taught zoology before she became director of the Pacific Science Center in Seattle, Washington, in 1963. While director, she worked to increase public interest in science and supported environmental research.

Dixy Lee Ray was in favor of research and development of nuclear power plants. Some environmentalists ridiculed her as Ms. Plutonium when she joined and later chaired the Atomic Energy Commission in 1973. Ray served on the commission until 1975 when she returned to Washington. There Ray was elected governor in 1976, becoming the second woman, after Ella Grasso of Connecticut, to be elected to the office in her own right, without connections to a gubernatorial husband. In 1990, Ray published a book about the environment, *Trashing the Planet: How Science can Help Us Deal with Acid Rain, Depletion of the Ozone and Nuclear Waste* .

++++++++++++++++++

 On April 21, 1970, thousands of people gathered, marched, protested, and even committed civil disobedience to protest pollution, nuclear development, ecology problems, and wasteful misuse of the earth's resources. Mother Nature was a popular image in this call to environmental action.

⚖ Janet Reno

born 1938
ATTORNEY GENERAL

Janet Reno was confirmed as the first woman attorney general of the United States on March 12, 1993. The next month, she had to explain to Congress and the nation what happened in the FBI's conflict with the Branch Davidians, a religious cult in Waco, Texas. Eighty-six people, including some children, were dead. "I made the decision. The buck stops with me," Reno said. Though Reno might not be fully to blame for the fiery tragedy, as attorney general, she felt responsible for it.

▲ In 1963, Janet Reno was refused an internship at a law firm because she was a woman. Thirty years later, Reno became the first woman attorney general of the United States.

Reno, who also has a degree in chemistry from Cornell University in Ithaca, New York, attended Harvard Law School in Cambridge, Massachusetts, as one of 16 women in a class of 500 students. She graduated in 1963 and returned to Dade County, Florida, where she had grown up. There Reno spent 15 years as the state prosecutor. She was a powerful advocate for children's rights and reform of the criminal justice system. As a result of the summer riots and many arrests in Miami in 1986, Reno helped create special courts where nonviolent drug offenders were sentenced to treatment for their drug addiction instead of long jail terms. Reno's program was praised by community leaders and imitated in other cities. Reno was President Bill Clinton's third choice as attorney general. He withdrew his first two nominees, Zoë Baird and Kimba Wood, because of the controversy over their hiring of immigrant household workers. As head of the U.S. Justice Department, Reno had to investigate not only the Waco crisis but also terrorist bombings of the World Trade Center in New York City and the federal building in Oklahoma City.

✓ Dr. Sally Ride

born 1951
ASTRONAUT

Nearly 250,000 people jammed into the areas surrounding Cape Kennedy Space Center on June 18, 1983. They were there to see Sally Ride lift off into space – and history. The 32-year-old astronaut on board the space shuttle *Challenger* was the first American woman in space and the youngest American astronaut to ever circle the earth.

In 1977, Dr. Ride, who has a Ph.D. in astrophysics from Stanford University in Palo Alto, California, saw a help-wanted ad in the university

1970s – 1990s

 ++++++++++++++++++

The space shuttle *Challenger* exploded approximately 73 seconds after it took off from Cape Canaveral, Florida, on January 28, 1986. All seven astronauts were immediately killed in what NASA at the time called "obviously a major malfunction." Among them were Christa McAuliffe (second from left), a New Hampshire schoolteacher who had beat out 11,000 applicants to become the first civilian in space, and Dr. Judith Resnick (right), a NASA astronaut who became the second woman in space when she traveled on the *Discovery* in 1984.

newspaper. The National Aeronautics and Space Administration (NASA) was looking for space mission specialists. Ride and 8,079 other people applied to NASA's astronaut training program. NASA selected 35 applicants, including Ride. At NASA's training school she learned about computer systems and how to launch and fly a spacecraft. She also spent two years developing a 50-foot robot arm that would be tested on the *Challenger*.

The *Challenger* mission lasted six days. On board, Dr. Ride monitored science experiments while dealing with zero gravity. She also operated the robotic arm, designed to retrieve and launch space satellites. When the *Challenger* landed, Ride and the other four astronauts in the shuttle crew had traveled 2.5 million miles.

Dr. Ride went into space a second time in 1984 and was scheduled for a third space trip when the *Challenger* exploded on January 28, 1986. She was appointed to the commission that investigated and reported on the causes of the disaster. The following year she issued what came to be called the Ride Report, her analysis of how NASA's space exploration program should be redesigned. In 1987, Dr. Ride retired from NASA and went to work at Stanford University.

🎨 Faith Ringgold

born 1930

ARTIST, WRITER

In her art, Faith Ringgold uses painting, writing, and the traditional women's art form of quilt-making to create her unique "story quilts." Ringgold's quilts and other "soft sculptures" and children's books use art to tell important stories about African-American history. They feature people such as **Harriet Tubman** and Dr. Martin Luther King, as well as members of Faith's family.

Faith was born in Harlem, New York. As a child, she often missed school because of asthma. She amused herself by creating things with paper, crayons, and fabric. She tried to build on this early interest in art in college, but in the 1950s women weren't allowed to enroll in the liberal arts program of New York's City College. Ringgold had to attend the School of Education.

Ringgold taught art in New York City public schools and painted landscapes. But she also was interested in the black arts and black power movements of the 1960s and 1970s. She read works by African-American writers and studied African art. She produced political works about the struggle for equality, such as her *American People Series*, and started to make story quilts that reflected the social and cultural heritage of African Americans, especially women. In the 1970s, Ringgold painted a mural at the New York City Women's House of Detention at Riker's Island. It shows women of all races in many different occupations – basketball players, doctors, bus drivers, even a woman president. Ringgold's reputation grew, and in 1984, there was a major show of her work in what is now the Studio Museum of Harlem. Her work is also exhibited in the Metropolitan and Guggenheim Museums and the Museum of Modern Art in New York City. *Tar Beach*, a book inspired by a story quilt about Ringgold's childhood, won the Caldecott Honor Award for children's literature in 1992.

⚖️ Phyllis Schlafly

born 1924

POLITICAL ORGANIZER

Author, lawyer, and three-time political candidate, Phyllis Schlafly is a well-known public figure in the United States.

She received her master's degree in political science from Radcliffe College in Cambridge, Massachusetts, in 1945, and then became an active member of the Republican party in Illinois, her home state. Between 1952 and 1970, Schlafly ran for a seat in the United State House of Representatives three times but was never elected. She was, however, elected vice-president of

Soprano **BEVERLY SILLS** (b. 1929) had a long, distinguished opera career that included working with conductor Sarah Caldwell in 20 operas. Sills joined the New York City Opera company in 1955. By the time she sang her last note with the Company in 1980, Bubbles, as Sills was lovingly called, was also director of the City Opera. In 1991, she became managing director of New York's Metropolitan Opera House and, in 1994, became the first woman to chair the famous Lincoln Center for the Performing Arts in New York City.

1970s – 1990s

▲ Phyllis Schlafly is credited with preventing the Equal Rights Amendment from reaching its 1982 deadline for state ratification.

the National Federation of Republican Women in 1964. That year she also published her bestseller, *A Choice Not an Echo*, about Senator Barry Goldwater, the conservative presidential candidate she supported.

In 1972, Schlafly began concentrating her energy on preventing the Equal Rights Amendment (ERA) from becoming law. She started an activist group called the Eagle Forum in 1975. Schlafly's STOP-ERA groups spread throughout the country. Her newsletter, the *Phyllis Schlafly Report*, warned that women would lose the right to be supported by their husbands and protective labor laws if the ERA passed. Through her efforts, issues such as whether or not women would be drafted into combat or have to use the same public toilets as men became connected to ERA discussions. Although not all of what Schlafly claimed about the ERA was accurate, she appealed to a large audience of people who worried that the liberal social movements of the 1960s and 1970s would have bad effects on family values and gender differences they considered important. In 1977, Schlafly organized a group of nearly 15,000 people, mainly women, and held a counter-demonstration in Houston, Texas, where feminists such as **Bella Abzug**, **Gloria Steinem**, First Lady Rosalynn Carter, and more than 20,000 other women had gathered for the National Women's Conference. Schlafly, who holds a law degree from Washington University Law School in St. Louis, has received numerous awards, written several political books, and served on President Ronald Reagan's Defense Policy Advisory Group.

$ Muriel F. Siebert

born 1932

STOCKBROKER

The New York Stock Exchange (NYSE) was a man's world – until 1967. That's when Muriel Siebert paid $445,000 and became the first woman to own a seat on the NYSE. Now she could do business on Wall Street, one of the country's key financial centers. Today Muriel Siebert and Company is a thriving brokerage business.

Siebert received her degree from Western Reserve University in Cleveland, Ohio, in 1952. Moving to New York, she worked as a researcher on Wall Street and as an airlines stock analyst for several years before founding her own company in 1967 and joining the 1,365 men who owned NYSE seats. In 1974, Siebert became superintendent of banks for the state of New York, in charge of regulating all of the banks in the state. She was the first woman in this position.

Siebert is an active supporter of women in politics and business. In 1987, she helped found the National Women's Forum, a professional network for businesswomen. Today it is part of the International Women's Forum, which includes groups from many countries. Siebert also created the Siebert Entrepreneurial Philanthropic Plan in 1990, which gives part of her company's earnings to charity. The plan has raised more than $2 million.

+ + + + + + + + + + + + + + + + +

 The United States Labor Department set up a commission in 1991 to investigate "glass ceilings," or unofficial limits on who gets promoted in corporations. It reported that white men held nearly 95 percent of the top executive jobs in top companies around the country. In 1993, women earned roughly 77¢ for every $1 men earned.

⚖ Gloria Steinem

born 1934

FEMINIST

Gloria Steinem is one of America's most famous women's rights activists. A founder of *Ms.* magazine and the National Women's Political Caucus, she is a veteran of many feminist demonstrations and political campaigns.

Steinem, a graduate of Smith College in Northampton, Massachusetts, moved to New York City in 1960 and became a writer. One of her first magazine articles to get attention was "I Was a Playboy Bunny," published in *Show* magazine in 1963. It described work in a Playboy Club, where waitresses were supposed to wear skimpy "bunny" outfits and act sexy. By 1968, Steinem was a contributing editor of *New York Magazine* and had covered the Democratic and Republican national conventions. She was also committed to the struggle for equal rights for women and became one of the movement's most visible speakers. The media liked "glamorous" Gloria.

In 1971, Steinem and five other women organized *Ms.*, a magazine devoted to exploring all kinds of women's issues, including sexual stereotyping. When *Ms.* first appeared as a special December insert in *New York Magazine*, it sold over 250,000 copies. In January 1972, *Ms.* appeared as an independent issue with Steinem as editor-in-chief. It featured an ad calling for legalized abortion, signed by more than 50 prominent women who had had abortions, including Steinem, **Lillian Hellman**, and **Billie Jean King**. By 1973, *Ms.* had a circulation of 350,000, and those copies reached a readership of 1.4 million.

Gloria Steinem served on President Jimmy Carter's committee on the Observance of International Women's Year in 1977. She has published autobiographical essay collections and a biography of **Marilyn Monroe**, and is a consulting editor at *Ms.* She also helped the *Ms.* Foundation create an annual event to encourage young women to explore different business opportunities. *Ms.*'s first "Take Our Daughters to Work Day" took place on April 28, 1993.

+ + + + + + + + + + + + + + + + +

In 1971, **Gloria Steinem** founded the National Women's Political Caucus with feminists such as **Betty Friedan, Fannie Lou Hamer, Bella Abzug, Shirley Chisholm**, and **LaDonna Harris** to help get more women into political office – both elected and appointed. Shown below, from left to right, are Steinem, Abzug, Chisholm, and Friedan holding a news conference in 1972.

▲ Elizabeth Taylor, like **Marilyn Monroe**, was one of the sex symbols of the 1950s and 1960s. Liz Taylor is co-founder of the American Foundation for AIDS Research (AmFAR), for which she has raised millions of dollars.

🚀 Elizabeth Taylor

born 1932
ACTOR

The year she turned 60, Elizabeth Taylor said she had lived such a full life she didn't know how she could have crammed more into it. The winner of two Academy Awards, the subject of endless media coverage because of her many marriages and illnesses, and a famous advocate for people with AIDS, Taylor still leads a very full life.

Elizabeth was born in London, England, to an American family who moved to Los Angeles, California. There her English accent helped her get a small role in the 1943 film *Lassie Come Home*. She signed a contract with MGM movie studio and spent the rest of her childhood and teenage years starring in films such as *National Velvet* and *Little Women*, based on **Louisa May Alcott**'s novel. By the 1950s, she was a major Hollywood star. She won her first Best Actress Academy Award for *Butterfield 8* in 1961 and her second in 1967 for *Who's Afraid of Virginia Woolf?*, which she starred in with Richard Burton. The two made 10 films together, were married and divorced from each other twice, and had one of Hollywood's more dramatic relationships. Taylor received the American Film Institute's Lifetime Achievement Award and the Jean Hersholt Humanitarian Award in 1993.

🚀 Twyla Tharp

born 1941
DANCER, CHOREOGRAPHER

Twyla Tharp is one of today's most innovative choreographers. She uses movements from modern dance and classical ballet to create dances to classical, jazz, pop, and rock 'n' roll music. And she inserts bits of humor into her pieces.

Tharp trained with **Martha Graham**, among others, before joining the Paul Taylor Dance Company in 1963. She quickly established herself as a very creative dancer, and two years later formed her own dance company. Tharp's group presented a number of new pieces in the 1960s that excited dance audiences open to innovative styles. In 1971, her *Eight Jelly Rolls*, set to jazz music, began to attract a broader audience. In the 1970s, Tharp choreographed works for the Joffrey Ballet, and in 1976 began her association with the American Ballet Theatre (ABT) in New York City. A series of acclaimed dance pieces followed.

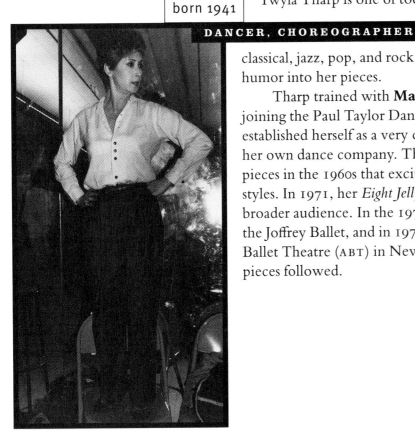

Tharp has also created the dance sequences for films such as *Hair* (1979) and *Amadeus* (1984). In 1995, she presented three new works at ABT's 30th anniversary at the Metropolitan Opera House in New York City. One of the pieces, *Jump Start*, featured jazz by Wynton Marsalis.

Alice Walker

born 1944
WRITER

Alice Walker's 1982 award-winning novel, *The Color Purple*, inspired by stories of her great-grand-mother, shows that, in Walker's words, we "have to cherish everyone." She has devoted many of her poems, novels, and essays to promoting this idea.

Walker was born in Eatonton, Georgia, the eighth child of African-American sharecroppers. As a child, Walker often wrote stories on the type-writer her mother gave her after Alice was accidentally blinded in one eye. Alice later enrolled at Spelman College in Atlanta, where she became a civil rights activist. She continued her involvement in this movement when she transferred to Sarah Lawrence College in Bronxville, New York. After graduating in 1965, Walker went to Mississippi to do civil rights work. While there she discovered the work of **Zora Neale Hurston**. Walker almost single-handedly brought this neglected African-American writer to the attention of American readers. Meanwhile, Walker's own writing career began with a book of poems called *Once* (1968).

In the 1970s, Walker published several more books of poetry and some short stories and novels. But it was *The Color Purple* that brought Walker national attention. The book is written as a series of letters. It tells the story of a Southern African-American woman trying to cope with poverty, isolation, sexual abuse, and racism. *The Color Purple* won the Pulitzer Prize and the American Book Award. Whoopi Goldberg and **Oprah Winfrey** starred in the popular film version of the book made by Steven Spielberg in 1985.

Alice Walker's other works include novels, poetry, and essays celebrating the customs and traditions of African-American women. Her nonfiction book, *Warrior Marks* (1993), looks at ritualistic sexual mistreatment of women in several countries.

+ + + + + + + + + + + + + + + + +

In 1991, law professor Anita F. Hill accused Supreme Court nominee Clarence Thomas of sexual harassment. The Senate Judiciary Committee did not give Hill a full hearing until female reporters discovered that she had given committee staff members damaging information about Thomas. There was a public outcry from women across the country. The all-male Senate committee grilled Anita Hill, and some even suggested she was a liar. The Senate voted 52–48 to approve Thomas's appointment. That same year, a report by the National Council for Research on Women stated that one out of every two women will experience sexual harassment during her working or academic life.

Record numbers of women ran for office in 1992. Feminists made sexual harassment a hot issue and helped women such as Dianne Feinstein (California) and Carol Moseley Braun (Illinois) win Senate races. Braun was the first African-American woman elected to the U.S. Senate. She and Feinstein joined the Senate Judiciary Committee.

1970s – 1990s

🏴 Barbara Walters

born 1931

TELEVISION JOURNALIST

In the 1960s, the popular morning television program *The Today Show* featured a "Today Girl" who had to look good, but did not get much of an on-air role. When Barbara Walters took over the job in 1964, that changed.

Walters was already a writer for the NBC show and as the "Today Girl" she refused to be just a pretty sidekick to her male colleagues. She was a hard-working journalist whose personable interviewing style made her popular. By 1974, Barbara was co-hosting the *Today Show*.

Walters became a news item herself in 1976, when ABC offered her $1 million a year to co-host, or anchor, its evening news program. This was the highest salary ever paid a journalist at the time, and Walters became the first woman in this kind of high-profile position. When the anchor team did not raise the viewer ratings of *ABC Evening News*, Walters was reassigned and produced her own *Barbara Walters Specials*. Her interviews with famous people such as **Katharine Hepburn**, Fidel Castro, **Coretta Scott King**, and six former United States presidents made her famous and won her two Emmy Awards. In 1979, Walters became host of ABC's *20/20*, a weekly news progam.

++++++++++++++++++++

Women who are between 18 and 24 years old watch approximately 25 hours and 42 minutes of television every week. As women grow older, they watch even more. Women between 25 and 54 watch 30 hours and 35 minutes every week; women 55 and over watch 44 hours and 11 minutes every week.

🏴 Oprah Winfrey

born 1954

TALK-SHOW HOST, ENTREPRENEUR

Nineteen eighty-five was a big year for Oprah Winfrey. She was nominated for an Academy Award for her role in the film adaptation of **Alice Walker**'s *The Color Purple*, and the Chicago television talk show she hosted became a 60-minute program called *The Oprah Winfrey Show*. The next year was even better. *Oprah* went national, debuting on more stations than any other syndicated program. Oprah started her own TV production company. And she won the National Organization for Women (NOW)'s Woman of Achievement Award. It all proved her point, that "being able to communicate with people is power."

Oprah grew up with her grandmother on a farm in Kosciusko, Mississippi, and then with her mother in a ghetto in Milwaukee, Wisconsin, where she was sexually abused. When she was 12, she went to Nashville, Tennessee, to live with her father who insisted Oprah get a good education. She was still a sophomore at Tennessee State University when she became the first African-American woman in Nashville to anchor the local evening news.

▲ In 1993, Oprah Winfrey became the first woman to head the *Forbes* Top 40 Entertainers List. The financial magazine listed her combined 1993–1994 income as $105 million.

Winfrey eventually moved to Chicago, where she became host of WLS-TV's *A.M. Chicago* in 1984. Her outgoing personality helped the show's ratings skyrocket. Within a year, it was renamed *The Oprah Winfrey Show*. By 1994, 17 million people were watching. The show won several Emmy television awards, and Oprah became one of the highest-paid entertainers in the country. She also received the National Association for the Advancement of Colored People (NAACP)'s Image Award four years in a row, from 1989 to 1992.

The Oprah Winfrey Show continues to be one of the top television talk shows because of its bold range of topics and Oprah's direct, but warm interviewing style. She works off-camera as well. Winfrey lobbied for passage of the 1994 National Child Protection Act to help prevent child abuse. She has also founded a program for young girls in Chicago's housing projects and another to train people of color for jobs in film and television.

 Dr. Rosalyn Yalow

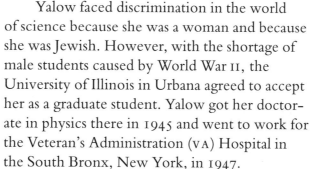

born 1921

PHYSICIST

When Dr. Rosalyn Yalow accepted the Nobel Prize for Physiology or Medicine in 1977, she spoke out on behalf of equal opportunities for women. She had found it necessary to do that throughout her career.

Yalow faced discrimination in the world of science because she was a woman and because she was Jewish. However, with the shortage of male students caused by World War II, the University of Illinois in Urbana agreed to accept her as a graduate student. Yalow got her doctorate in physics there in 1945 and went to work for the Veteran's Administration (VA) Hospital in the South Bronx, New York, in 1947.

Dr. Yalow began research into the use of radioactive materials in medicine. This was a new field and Yalow sometimes had to design her own radiation detection instruments. At the VA Hospital, she met Dr. Solomon Berson, and the two worked as a research team for 22 years until Berson's death in 1972. Their work led to the invention of radioimmunoassay (RAI) in 1959. RAI uses radioactive particles to help measure levels of various substances in the blood. RAI helped doctors diagnose such problems as diabetes and hepatitis. In 1976, Yalow became the first woman to win the prestigious Albert Lasker Medical Research Award. After winning the 1977 Nobel Prize, Dr. Yalow continued her work at the VA medical center.

In 1978, FAY WATTLETON (b. 1943) became the first woman, the first African American, and the youngest person ever to head the Planned Parenthood Federation (PPF), an international reproductive rights organization started by **Margaret Sanger**.

Wattleton faced several big challenges. On the political front, federal funds for abortions for poor women had already been cut off by the Hyde Amendment in 1977. President Reagan's administration was trying to cut funds for family planning centers. And some Right to Life groups were bombing abortion clinics. Wattleton, who has a degree in mother and infant health care from Columbia University in New York, and has held public health jobs in Ohio and Massachusetts, fought back. As PPF president, she was a savvy, articulate spokesperson for reproductive and health-care rights, appearing on radio and television shows and at lectures throughout the country. She created a PPF advertising campaign to educate people about teen pregnancy and wrote *How to Talk to Your Child About Sex*, which sold more than 30,000 copies. Wattleton retired from PPF in 1992.

1970s – 1990s

Topical Index

Index includes biographical entries and Cameos.

Alphabetical Index

* = see Topical Index